The Walker Boys in the Great Northumberland Fusiliers.
By Helen Charlesworth ©

This book is a memorial to the me........ .. ..
Newcastle upon Tyne, who played their part in the Great War. The
men from various backgrounds, who were drawn together to fight in
what at the time was assumed to be the war to end all wars. They
included miners, riveters, barber's, boilermakers, clerks, engineers
and labourers.

When the call for mobilisation was made on 5th August 1914,
Territorial Army reservists gathered at various drill halls across the
city. Many men chose to enlist at the first opportunity and await
their call up, whilst others held off and waited to be conscripted.
Walker being a heavily industrial area at that time needed the men
in the coal mines and the shipbuilding industries to keep the war
machine moving. Heavy losses on the various battlefronts meant
that although conscripts were coming through, more men were
needed. The Government introduced the 'Military Service Act' in
January 1916, which specified that men from the ages of 18 to 41
were liable to be called-up for service unless they were married (or
widowed with children), or else served in one of a number of reserved
professions (usually industrial but also included clergymen). Within
four months a revised version of the Act was passed - All men -
regardless of marital status - from the ages of 18 to 41 were liable to
be called up to serve their country. The government also gained the
right to re-examine men previously declared medically unfit for
service. The act was modified again a number of times during the
war, finally extending the age of eligibility to all men aged 17 to 51
and applied to men in Ireland, the Channel Islands and the Isle of
Man. Between August 1914 and the introduction of the first
Military Service Act as many as three million men volunteered for
military service. From January 1916 until the close of the war a
further 2.3 million men were formally conscripted.

This book isn't just a list of names, dates and regiments. It tells the stories of many of the men who served their country; their military records, commendations, disciplinary actions. In some cases descriptive details of a man's physical appearance, his eye and hair colour. Possibly some defining feature such as a tattoo or scar. News items local to Walker and not about the war, but the daily life for those on the home front.

There are tales of men who travelled from as far as Canada, Australia and New Zealand, to fight for the land of their birth. Officers and men who joined the locally raised 1/5th 'Fighting Fifth' Northumberland Fusiliers battalion, as well as those who joined the many other local and county raised battalions across Britain. The men of the Royal Navy, the Royal Marines, Mercantile Marine, Royal Naval Reserve. Those who worked in the shipyards, not just locally but sent as far away as the Clyde in Scotland and Devonport Dockyard in Plymouth.

The Tyneside Scottish and Tyneside Irish battalion's infamous involvement in the 1st July 1916 battle of the Somme, when over 20,000 men were killed on that day alone? What about the men who returned and of families left behind? Again, many of their tales are told here.

Though from the same small community at birth, in death they were scattered far and wide. France, Belgium, Turkey, Iraq, Egypt, Israel England Wales.

Those who survived the war returned home – but it was never quite the same. The men who were still fit and healthy returned to work, many choosing the route of immigration and a new life in a new country. Their descendants now spread far and wide across the globe. Others meanwhile chose to stay close to the bosom of their family.

The list of names is endless; Robson, Elliott, Heathcote, Goodwin, Edwards, Taylor, Whitehead, Tait, Maddison, Bell, McMurdo, North, Patterson, Phillips, McGee, Bilton, Calvert, Foley, Carmichael, Joicey, Turnbull, English, Snowball, McKee, Dodds, Hardy, Hellens, Lamb, McGinn, Fallon, Millican, Rooney, Henzel, Graham, Moffat, Proctor, Nicholson.......

Royal Navy /Reservists and Mercantile Marine men born in Walker and awarded Campaign medals for their service during the Great War.

The Church Street boys.

The call of the pipes.

The Tyneside Scottish and Tyneside Irish on the 1st July 1916.

The men of Walker known to have lost their lives on 1st July 1916.

Other Walker men who served with the Tyneside Sottish/Irish and survived the 1st July 1916.

The last picture of John and Archie.

Men of Walker whose Military records survived the WWII raids of 1940 on London (also information from other sources).

Families at war.

The Visit (long awaited).

The Young Subaltern.

The Geordie Antipodeans.

Articles reported in the Newcastle Journal 1914-1917 and relating to Walker.

Walker War Memorials.

The Walker Boys.

Prior to the outbreak of war on the 4th August 1914, Walker had been well known for its heavy industrialization. Newly built 'Tyneside flats' had been constructed in the 1890's and 1900's to fulfill the demand for housing made by the vast numbers of families who had migrated south from ship building towns in Scotland, and transient workers who had come to lodge with local families or in boarding houses; whilst in employment at one of the local coal pits or shipyards. Many would travel across the Tyne by ferry daily from Hebburn, to work. Others would travel by tram, by train, or on foot from surrounding areas.

In the 'Parish notes of Northumberland' the population of Walker in 1911 was 14,798 including 200 patients at the Hospital for infectious diseases at Walkergate. Nearby St Anthony's was the 'border' region between Walker and Byker and was a rather grey area - classed by many as being in Newcastle rather than Walker.

The main employers in the area were Swan Hunter & Wigham Richardson shipbuilders, Armstrong Whitworth engineering works and the Walker Colliery. There were also chemical works, the railways, smaller engineering companies and a whole host of other industrial employers as well as the usual forms of occupation you would find in any town across Great Britain at that time.

As you will see as you read on, the majority of the men who went to fight, were employed in the heavy industries and their absence left a huge void in the workforce. Men were often drafted in from other shipbuilding areas to do 'war work' in the shipyards. Often those who signed up to do their bit for King and Country were sent to work in the industries on 'home' territory where they were needed, rather than to the battlefields. Shipbuilders would be called up at short notice to be sent to other yards which were lacking on manpower – the Clyde in Scotland, Devonport in the south west.

Others, having been wounded and deemed fit for war work but not the trenches, would be allotted a job on home soil doing 'war work'. Often this job would be there pre-war occupation. Women, who had likely never seen inside the shipyard gates, were now being employed in a number of occupations only ever filled by men previously.

It was estimated that during the war years of 1914-1918 over three million tonnes of shipping was built on the 12 mile stretch of the river Tyne. The air would have been thick with the sound of riveters hammering, cranes moving, sheet metal being hoisted in to place. Boilermakers, labourers, platers, machinist, stoker, joiners all doing their work – 24 hours a day.

It wasn't just the building of ships that took place in the yards, but also repair work to damaged vessels.

When the call for mobilisation was made on 5th August 1914, Territorial Army reservists gathered at various drill halls across the city.

1/5th Northumberland Fusiliers (Territorial Battalion).

The battalion was first raised in August 1914 at the outbreak of war. The 'HQ' based at the Drill Hall on Church Street, Walker. There is no definitive number of men that joined the battalion, but a 'full' battalion, at any one time during the Great War consisted of approximately 800 to 1000 men. According to the Commonwealth War Graves Commission, 1,051 men and officers of the 5th battalion Northumberland Fusiliers lost their live; either being killed in action or died of wounds or illness during the Great War, very many more were injured.

The Northumberland Fusiliers as whole lost 16,159 men and 846 officers.

The growing battlefield demand for men outstripped the number of conscripts coming through and in 1915 the 'Derby Scheme' was introduced, to encourage men to voluntarily register their name on the principle that once registered they would be called up for service only when necessary. As an added incentive, married men were advised that they would only be called up once the supply of single men was exhausted. However, the scheme proved unsuccessful and was abandoned in December the same year. Just 350,000 men had volunteered under the Derby Scheme.

The Military Service Act of January 1916 specified that men from the ages of 18 to 41 were liable to be called-up for service unless they were married (or widowed with children), or else served in one of a number of reserved professions (usually industrial but which also included clergymen).

Within four months a revised version of the Act was passed - All men - regardless of marital status - from the ages of 18 to 41 were liable to be called up to serve their country. The government also gained the right to re-examine men previously declared medically unfit for service.

In April 1917, the Act was again modified. 'Home Service' Territorials were to be examined with a view to drafting them into service abroad. Men who had left the military on account of wounds or ill-health were to be re-examined as to determine whether they were fit to resume service; and a revised list of reserved occupations was published.

In January 1918, exemptions from military service on occupational grounds were quashed and each case would be looked at on its own merit.

Three months later, in April 1918 - at the height of the great German Spring offensive on the Western Front - a fifth version of the Act came in to force, extending the age of eligibility to men aged 17 to 51 for call up. In addition, the act was, for the first time, to be applied to men in Ireland, the Channel Islands and the Isle of Man (although the policy was never actually implemented in Ireland).

Between August 1914 and the introduction of the first Military Service Act as many as three million men volunteered for military service. From January 1916 until the close of the war a further 2.3 million men were formally conscripted.

The recruitment process during WW1

In 1914 the British Army had a strength of approximately 710,000 men including reserves, of which around 80,000 were regular troops. By the end of the Great War, 1 in 4 of the total male population of Great Britain had joined or been called up to serve his King and Country - over five million men. Of these; 2.67 million joined as volunteers and 2.77 million as conscripts.

At the start of the war the British Army consisted of six Divisions based within the United Kingdom aided by one cavalry Division. There were also four Divisions based overseas. Fourteen Territorial Divisions existed and there were 300,000 in the Army Reserve.

Lord Kitchener, who was the then Secretary of State for War, believed the Territorial Army to be untrained and not of much use in a state of war. He believed that the regular Army must not be wasted in immediate battle, but instead used to help train a new Army with 70 Divisions – the same size as the French and German Armies. This was so that Britain would have enough strength in their forces should the war last many years.

It was still possible to enlist into the regular Army on standard terms, usually twelve years, but, on Lord Kitchener's instructions in August 1914 a new form of "short service" was introduced, under which a man could serve for *"three years or the duration of the war, whichever the longer"*. Men joining on this basis, including all of "Kitchener's Army" and the "Pals" units were technically of the regular army but on a shorter service basis. The volunteer Army of 1914-15 brought an initial rush of volunteering at the outbreak of war. At the beginning of August 1914 Parliament called for an extra 100,000 soldiers. Recruitment in the first few weeks of war was good, but the real 'recruiting boom' began in the last week of August, with news of the British retreat following the Battle of Mons.

The wartime 'short service' volunteers continued to have a certain amount of choice over which regiment they joined. They had to meet the same physical criteria as the peace time regulars, but men who had previously served in the Army would now be accepted up to the age of 45. *(It was not necessary to produce evidence of age or even of one's name in order to enlist.)* Enlistment into the Special Reserve and the Territorial Force remained open and the men were mobilised as soon as war was declared. Men joining the Territorial Force after 5th August 1914 were expected to sign the "Imperial Service Obligation" which gave the Army powers to send them overseas or transfer them to a different Territorial unit if required.

By the spring of 1915 it had become clear that voluntary recruitment was in no way going to provide the numbers of men required. The Government passed the *'National Registration Act'* on 15 July 1915 as a step towards boosting recruitment and to discover how many men between the ages of 15 and 65 were engaged in each trade of profession. The results of this census became available in September 1915. On 11 October 1915, Lord Derby was appointed Director-General of Recruiting and five days later he brought in the' Derby Scheme'. Officially it was the 'Group Scheme', for raising the numbers of troops. It was half-way towards conscription.

In 1916, after seeing poor results from the Derby Scheme, the Government introduced the 'Military Service Act' on 27 January 1916 and voluntary enlistment was stopped. All British males were now deemed to have enlisted on 2 March 1916 - that is, they were *conscripted* - if they were aged between 19 and 41 and resided in Great Britain (excluding Ireland) and were unmarried or a widower on 2 November 1915. Conscripted men were no longer given a choice of which service, regiment or unit they joined, although if a man preferred the Navy, it got priority to take him. This act was extended to married men, and the lower age dropped to 18, on 25 May 1916.

A system of appeals tribunals was established, to hear cases of men who believed they were disqualified on the grounds of ill-health, occupation or conscientious objection. Some trades were deemed to be vital to the war economy; 'reserved occupations' as they were known, these included; police officers, medical practitioner, some mining occupations as well as certain railway, engineering and ship building jobs. Jobs that were seen of National importance. Though saying that, many of these men did enlist as they were needed on the war front as well as the home front. A number of men would be released from Military Service abroad to come back to the UK and finish the war in their former occupations, whilst still under Military rules.

The Act initially failed to deliver: only 43,000 of the men called up qualified for general service in the Army. Another 93,000 failed to report when called up. 748,587 men claimed some form of exemption. In addition, were the 1,433,827 already in 'reserved occupations' or those who were ill or who had already been discharged on medical/unfit for service grounds.

From September 1916, men called up were first assigned to a unit of the *Training Reserve*. It had been found that the traditional regimental means of training was not keeping up with the flood of men coming through, and the Training Reserve was established as a means of doing so.

A further extension of the Military Service Act on 10 April 1918, which followed a political crisis concerning the lack of manpower; it was said to be the prime cause of the defeat of the Fifth Army in March 1918 and at the time when the British army were heavily involved in the great German Spring offensive on the Western Front. This act increased the eligibility of male civilians even further. It lowered the minimum age of obligation to 17 and increased the maximum age to 55. The law was extended to include Ireland, the Channel Islands and the Isle of Man. It also called for the abolition of the tribunal system. Released or exchanged prisoners of war were no longer exempt and provision was made for the recall of time-expired soldiers.

Conscription ended on 11 November 1918 and all conscripts were discharged, if they had not already been so, on 31 March 1920. Many of the men attached to the Labour Corps helped with the Battlefield Clearances in 1919; recovering and then reinterring the bodies of dead soldiers; also helping with the repatriation of Military equipment.

Men who could demonstrate genuine conscientious objection to wartime participation, could feasibly escape front-line service. These men though were expected to serve in non-combatant positions, i.e. in other than a combat capacity, either at home (in an avenue such as farming or shipbuilding) or in non-combatant or army medical corps as cooks, medical orderlies, stretcher-bearers, etc. 3,400 conscientious objectors accepted call-up into the Non-Combatant Corps (NCC) or the Royal Army Medical Corps (RAMC) as non-combatants. The NCC was set up in March 1916, part of the army and run by its regular officers. The CO's assigned to it were army privates who wore army uniforms and were subject to army discipline; but didn't carry weapons or take part in battle. Their duties were mainly to provide physical labour (building, cleaning, loading and unloading anything - except munitions) in support of the military.

Many Walker men joined the RAMC – possibly some of them were conscientious objectors? Conscientious objection was usually on religious ground i.e. Jehovah's Witnesses or Quakers or moral convictions - a disinclination to harm one's fellow man. Men who could not satisfactorily demonstrate a conscientious objection, and who persisted in their refusal to serve, suffered financial penalties and many were sent to prison. Although many were granted full exemption from military service, most were expected to serve non-directly. 16,000 men were officially recorded in Britain as 'conscientious objectors' during the First World War.

Fifty conscientious objectors were shipped to France 1916, and when they continued to refuse to obey orders "in a theatre of war" 35 of them were formally sentenced to death by court martial. The sentences were immediately commuted to 10 years penal servitude, and the men returned to British prisons. In 1919, they were released. Eighty-one conscientious objectors died as a result of their treatment in the army, prisons, or work centres.

The Conscientious Objector:

(This is written with help from an article by the Peace Pledge Project.)

One local objector was John George Sadler (Jack) a Before the First World War had never been compulsory military service in Britain. The first Military Service Bill was passed into law in January 1916 following the failure of recruitment schemes to gain sufficient volunteers in 1914 and 1915. From March 1916, military service was compulsory for all single men in England, Scotland and Wales aged 18 to 41, except those who were in jobs essential to the war effort, the sole support of dependents, medically unfit, or 'those who could show a conscientious objection'. This later clause was a significant British response that defused opposition to conscription. Further military service laws included married men, tightened occupational exemptions and raised the age limit to 50., who was 28 when he was called up in in 1916. He was a self-employed jobbing builder/ joiner living in Kirk Street, Byker, Newcastle upon Tyne. His belief was that if there were no armies or navies there would be no war, and the way to stop war would be for everyone to refuse to join the armed forces. When conscription came, he along with his two brothers, James and Mark, refused their call-up. Jack applied to his local Tribunal committee in Newcastle for recognition as a conscientious objector. Their application was brusquely refused and they were shouted down by members of the tribunal. Jack then appealed to the Northumberland Appeal Tribunal, which recognised him as a conscientious objector, but granted him exemption only on condition of undertaking, within one month, civilian work deemed to be of national importance. Jack felt that by complying with this request it would make him a cog in the machinery of the warfare state. He was willing to play his part in the community, and saw his job as a builder a contribution towards that; but he was not willing to accept the authority of the state to order him what to do. Having no further right of appeal, Jack carried on with his normal daily life and job.

The period of a month passed and as Jack had not found himself an occupation deemed to be of 'national importance' he now became liable to full military service. A letter arrived ordering him to report to barracks. He ignored this, and was eventually arrested by the civilian police and taken before the Magistrates' Court. Here he was fined, and handed over to the military authorities. He was charged with the military offence of disobedience, and held in the Guard Room until a Court-Martial sentenced him to two years imprisonment with Hard Labour (meaning that he would have no mattress for the first 28 days) – this was because he had refused to put on a soldier's uniform, saying he' was a conscientious objector and would never be a soldier.' His sentence was commuted to six months, which he served in Newcastle Prison, Wandsworth Prison and Wormwood Scrubs, in London.

Whilst imprisoned at Wormwood Scrubs Prison, Jack was interviewed by the Central Tribunal, who agreed that he was a genuine conscientious objector. They offered to suspend his sentence if he would join the Army Reserve and on condition of his accepting work under a scheme specially organised by the Home Office for objectors in his position. Jack refused; for the same reason, he had refused the Appeal Tribunal's offer of conditional exemption – he was not willing to be a cog in the machinery of a warfare state.

When he left prison, Jack was returned to the Army and again refused to put on a soldier's uniform. He again was sentenced to two years Hard Labour, which was once more commuted to six months. The cycle began a third time, in which Jack tried without success to get a fresh hearing of his case for absolute exemption, and the military authorities did not commute his sentence, requiring him to serve the full two years.

Jack and some of his fellow objectors began a hunger strike in Newcastle Prison, announcing that they would refuse food until they were given the absolute exemption they claimed. They were forcibly fed through a tube. Eventually being granted temporary release from prison under the same provision as that made for suffragette hunger strikers, whereby such prisoners could be released until their health recovered. By this time, however, it was March 1919, the war was over; arrangements were being made for release of conscientious objectors alongside the demobilisation of soldiers. Jack's temporary release became permanent, and in June 1919 he was finally discharged from the Army on grounds of 'misconduct': one way of describing a waste of two and a half years of both his time and the Army's.

Jack died in 1961

Names of the men who were enlisted into the 1/5th Northumberland Fusiliers Battalion at Walker, and whose life was sacrificed during the Great War.

(These lists are as complete as possible but unfortunately some names may be missing, due to extenuating circumstances).

Key: K.I.A Killed in action.

D.O.W Died of wounds.

Pte John W. Abbot : Service number 2712 K.I.A on 27 Apr 1915

Pte Daniel Allan: Service Number 1677 K.I.A 13 Mar 1916

CSM James Allan : Service number 2258 K.I.A 23 May 1915

L/Cpl Nicholas Anderson : Service number 2177 K.I.A 10 Jul 1915

Pte James Allan : Service number 3069.D.O.W 5 Jun 1916

L/Cpl William Allan : Service number 1397 Died 24 May 1918

Pte John Arkle : Service number 240327 K.I.A 26 Oct 1917

Pte James Arnold : Service number.1544 D.O.W 26 May 1915

Pte Henry R. Arthur : Service number 2024 K.I.A 25 May 1916

Pte Edward Atkinson : Service number 240334 K.I.A 12 Apr 1918

Pte George Atkinson : Service number 240731 K.I.A. 14 Nov 1916

Pte Thomas Atkinson : MM Service number 2596.K.I.A. 15 Nov 1916

Pte John Baistow : Service number 3881.K.I.A 11 Mar 1916

Pte Thomas W. Baggaley : Service number 242556 Died 26 Nov 1917

Pte George H. Barber : Service number 4043 K.I.A 2 Jun 1916

Pte James Bain : Service number 2539 K.I.A 2 May 1915

Pte William Baxter : Service number 2833 Died.2 Apr 1915

Pte Charles Beadnell : Service number 4229 K.I.A 15 Sept 1916

Pte John Baistow : Service number 3881.K.I.A.11 Mar 1916

Pte John Bennett : Service number 240335 Died 1 Oct 1916

Pte Robert Blackett : Service number.240880 D.O.W 14 Nov 1916

Pte William Boyle : Service number 241020 K.I.A 14 Nov 1916

Pte James R. Bradley : Service number 1651 K.I.A 11 Sept 1916

Pte David Bruce Service number 3089/478071 Died 7 Apr 1919

L/Cpl Robert Brown : Service number 240164 D.OW 28 Oct 1917

L/Sgt Archibald Buchanan : Service number 2469.K.I.A.14 Nov 1916

Pte Stephen Burnipp : Service number.2352.K.I.A 22 Apr 1916

Pte James Burton : Service number 3643 D.O.W 2 Aug 1916

L/Cpl John Campbell : Service number 334 K.I.A 24 May 1916

Pte Isaac Cardwell : Service number 3380 Died 4 Jul 1915

Pte Robert Carson : Service number 3583 K.I.A 18 Feb 1916

Pte William Christie : Service number 2187 K.I.A 21 Feb 1916

Pte William Coates : Service number 2589 K.I.A 27 Apr 1915

Pte Thomas Cowan : Service number 2508 K.I.A 2 May 1915

Pte George Craig : Service number 241004 K.I.A 26 Oct 1917

Pte William Croft : Service number 3190 K.I.A 3 Oct 1916

Pte Thomas Cuskern : Service number 2534 K.I.A 2 May 1915

Pte Alexander Darby : Service number 1760 D.O.W 1 Jul 1915

Pte Benjamin Davis : Service number 1829 D.O.W 14 Mar 1916

Sgt Philip Deagle : Service number 240093 Died 14 Nov 1916

Pte Henry Dearden : Service number 2566 K.I.A 29 Jul 1916

Pte Thomas Dickinson : Service number 2482 K.I.A 28 Jan 1916

Pte Thomas C. Dodds : Service number 2537 D.O.W 2 May 1915

Pte David Douglass : Service number 340360 K.I.A 27 May 1918

Sgt Robert Dryden : Service number 263040 K.I.A 27 Mar 1918

Pte John Duffy : Service number 2044 D.O.W 24 May 1915

Pte James Dunleavy : Service number 3124 K.I.A 29 Jan 1916

L/Cpl Thomas Dunn : Service number 220 K.I.A 22 Apr 1916

Sgt Robert Elliott : Service number 2498 D.O.W 14May 1915

Pte John W. English : Service number 2124 D.O.W 15 Sept 1916

L/Cpl George Fairclough : Service number 240495 K.I.A 24 Oct 1918

Pte Joseph Fee : Service number 240986 Died 4 Nov 1916

Pte James Ferguson : Service number 2521 D.O.W 28 May 1915

Pte Robert Ferguson : Service number 1728 K.I.A 27 Apr 1915

Pte Frederick Featherstone : Service number 8058 K.I.A 15 Set 1916

Pte William Gibbins : Service number 3692 K.I.A 24 May 1916

Pte Alfred S. Gibson : Service number 4421 K.I.A 15 Sept 1916

Pte George Gilbert : Service number 240102 Died 14 Nov 1916

Pte Ralph B. Goldsworth : Service number 4175 K.I.A 1 Nov 1916

L/Cpl Levison Goodwin : Service number 692 K.I.A 31 Dec 1915

Pte Robert Goring : Service number 4440 K.I.A 28 July 1916

Pte Samuel J. Gorman : Service number 240688 K.I.A 27 Oct 1917

Pte James H. Graham : Service number 3214 Died 20 Mar 1916

Drummer Stephen Gray : Service number 3253 Died 8 April 1916

Cpl William Gray : Service number 2926 D.O.W 27 May 1916

Pte Alfred Green : Service number 3929 K.I.A 13 July 1918

Pte Douglas F. Griffin : Service number 37056 D.O.W 22 Jan 1916

Cpl John W. Hadaway : Service number 240979 K.I.A 26 Oct 1917

Pte George Hardy : Service number 240963 Died 14 Nov 1916

Cpl Henry Hardy : Service number 1902 D.O.W 15 No 1916

L/Cpl Thomas Bell Hardy : Service number 1363 K.I.A 2 May 1915

Pte Robert Hellens : Service number 1284 K.I.A 24 May 1915

Pte William Heron : Service number 2565 K.I.A 27 Apr 1915

Pte Joseph Heslop : Service number 3163 K.I.A 3 Mar 1916

Pte Robert Heslop : Service number 1229   K.I.A 2 May 1915

Pte Samuel A. Hood : Service number 240707 K.I.A 15 Sept 1916

Pte James Hume   : Service number 1972 K.I.A 11 Mar 1916

Pte James Hutchinson : Service number 2870 Died 20 Apr 1916

Pte Robert Inglis : Service number 4079 Died 1 Oct 1915

Pte Thomas Ireland : Service number 3702 K.I.A 9 Apr 1916

Cpl Gibson Irwin : Service number 2217 D.O.W 6 Jun 1916

Pte John D. Jenkins : Service number 2568.K.I.A 9 Apr 1916

Pte George Jobe : Service number 1436 K.I.A 24 May 1915

Pte John R. Johnson : Service number.2553.Died 8 Dec 1916

Pte Thomas Knox : Service number 240798 D.O.W 3 Jun 1918

L/Cpl Robert Lemin : Service number 240787 K.I.A 20 Apr 1917

Pte Henry Lewis : Service number 2880 Died 29 Dec 1915

Pte Hutchinson Lindsay : Service number 240119 K.I.A 11 Apr 1918

Pte George Logan : Service number 240885 K.I.A 10 Apr 1918

L/Cpl William Logan : Service number 240004 K.I.A 10 Apr 1918

Pte William Longworth : Service number 1764 D.O.W 15 Nov 1916

Pte James Lough : Service number 2570.D.O.W.27 May 1915

Pte Thomas Lough : Service number 240348 Died 12 Apr 1918

Pte Samuel Lowden : Service number 240349 K.I.A 26 Oct 1917

Pte John Lowery : Service number 240708 K.I.A 14 Nov 1916

Pte David Mair : Service number 2223 D.O.W 31 Jan 1916

Pte George Marshall : Service number 3133 Died 17 Jan 1915

Pte Samuel Mason : Service number 1381 K.I.A 22 Apr 1916

Pte Andrew Maughan : Service number 3604 K.I.A 4 Apr 1916

Pte Archibald Maughan : Service number 1351 K.I.A 11 Mar 1916

Pte Joe Maughan : Service number 2013 K.I.A 29 Jan 1916

Pte William Maughan : Service number 2263 Died 25 May 1916

Pte Lacey Mayles : Service number 241060 Died 26 Oct 1917

Pte Joseph McFarlane : Service number 240659 K.I.A 14 Dec 1917

Pte Robert McLachlan: Service number 1165   Died 18 Nov 1918

Pte Bernard McKevitt : Service number 242116 K.I.A 26 Oct 1917

Pte John Miller : Service number 1421 K.I.A 1 Oct 1916

L/Cpl William Mitchell : Service number 240353 K.I.A 14 Nov 1916

Pte William Morr : Service number 2573   K.I.A 1 Oct 1916

Cpl Harry Moss : Service number 2546 D.O.W 26 May 1916

Pte B'nard Mulholland : Service number 3494 D.O.W 26 May 1916

Pte Martin Murray : Service number 1898 K.I.A 18 Jun 1915

Pte Frank Napier : Service number 1269 D.O.W 25 Jul 1915

Pte Conelius Noble : Service number 1856 K.I.A 24 May 1915

L/Cpl Joseph M North : Service number 4257 Died 20 May 1916

Pte John H. Norton : Service number 3336 K.I.A 9 Mar 1916

Pte Alfred O'Dell : Service number 2547 K.I.A 28 Jun 1915

Pte Samuel V Oliver : Service number 1590 K.I.A 9 Mar 1916

Pte Frank Orr : Service number 3212 Died 24 May 1915

Pte Walter Pattison : Service number 1804 K.I.A 24 May 1915

Pte Thomas Paxton : Service number 2967 K.I.A 4 Mar 1916

L/Cpl James Pearson : Service number 240964 K.I.A 31 Dec 1916

Pte William Pearson : Service number 240964 D.O.W 10 Jul 1918

Pte Peter Pirnie : Service number 3676 K.I.A 23 Sept 1916

Pte Thomas Quinn : Service number 2974 K.I.A 25 May 1916

Pte Thomas Ramsay : Service number 1726 K.I.A 29 Jan 1916

Pte Robert Ramshaw : Service number 241034 K.I.A 14 Nov 1916

Pte John Raniggan : Service number 4131 K.I.A 16 Nov 1916

Pte Benjamin T. Ratcliffe : Service number 2091 K.I.A 11 Apr 1916

Pte Sidney Redgrave : Service number36 K.I.A 16 Nov 1916

Pte Lawrence Reed : Service number 8117 K.I.A 15 May 1916

Pte James Richardson : Service number 3591 D.O.W 17 Jul 1916

Pte Edward Roberts : Service number 3034 K.I.A   24 Apr 1916

L/Cpl Alex Robertson : Service number 2238 K.I. 23 Dec 1915

Pte Wm M. Robertson : Service number 1627 D.O.W 6 Nov 1916

Pte George Robson : Service number 4125 D.O.W 31 Oct 1916

Pte Thomas J. Rush : Service number 24085 K.I.A 14 Nov 1916

L/Cpl Ralph Sant : Service number 2589 D.O.W 6 Aug 1916

Sgt Anthony Scott : Service number 340296 K.I.A 27 May 1918

Pte Thomas D. Shale : Service number 164 D.O.W 13 Jun 1915

Pte Ralph Shiell : Service number 241031   K.I.A 24 May 1917

L/Cpl Charles J. Simpson : Service number 1927 Died 24 May 1915

L/Cpl Albert Smith : Service number 240682 K.I.A 26 Oct 1917

Sgt Charles Stoddart : Service number 166 Died 24 May 1915

Pte Michael C. Stoker : Service number 2084 D.O.W 28 Apr 1915

Pte John Storey : Service number 2473 D.O.W 3 Jul 1915

Pte James J. Symington : Service number   4056 K.I.A 11 Sept 1916

Pte Peter Tait : Service number 3369 D.O.W 30 Dec 1915

Pte Henry Taylor : Service number 3668 K.I.A 28 Jan 1916

Pte John Y. Taylor : Service number 240795 Died 26 Oct 1917

Pte James Temple : Service number 4149 K.I.A 14 Nov 1916

L/Cpl William Waddle : Service number 3674 K.I.A 12 Apr 1916

Pte William Walker : Service number 3650 D.O.W 27 Apr 1916

Pte William Warburton : Service number 1912 K.I.A 12 Nov 1916

Pte Frank Ward : Service number 2558 D.O.W 8 Jan 1916

Pte Thomas Warriner : Service number 2080 D.O.W 26 Jan 1916

Pte Frederick Watson : Service number 2253 D.O.W 31 Jul 1915

Pte Thomas Watson : Service number 1696 D.O.W 16 Jan 1916

Pte James Watt : Service number 2935 D.O.W 7 Feb 1916
Drummer Samuel White : Service number 1106 K.I.A 24 May 1915

Pte Henry Whitehead : Service number 3447 Died 20 Jun 1915

Pte George Windlow : Service number 240365 K.I.A 26 Oct 1917

Pte Thomas Wishart : Service number 2559 D.O.W 22 Jul 1916

Pte Robert Wright : Service number 241011 Died 14 Nov 1916

Pte John E Wymer : Service number 2143   K.I.A 25 May 1915

The Officers of the 1/5th Battalion Northumberland Fusiliers, who gave their lives during the Great War.

Major F.O.C Nash	Apr 1915
Capt P.D Forrett	5 Feb1916
Capt W.G Graham	4 Jun 1915
Capt F.H Lawson	24 May 1915
Capt J.C Leask	30 Mar 1918 Military Cross
Capt N.M North	27 May 1918 Military Cross
Capt C.A Patterson	8 Oct 1916
Lieut H.M Anderson	30 May 1918 Military Cross
Lieut D Armstrong	3 Oct 1916
Lieut T.L Bainbridge	29 Apr 1915
Lieut P.H Edwards	24 May 1915
Lieut A.J Field	11 Apr 1918
Lieut M.C Hill	24 May 1915
Lieut & QM R.J Holloway	14 Aug 1916
Lieut A.V Knox	6 Jun 1917
Lieut N.W Lawson	14 Nov 1916
Lieut. A.J. Mawson	4 Dec 1918
Lieut. W.E.S Poole	19 Sept 1917
Lieut. H.T. Richardson	23 Aug 1915
Lieut. E.V. Sargent	27 May 1918
Lieut. F. Winfield	31 May 1915
2nd Lieut. J.H.M. Apps	20 Nov 1917
Lieut. H.M. Belchem*	19 Mar 1915
2nd Lieut. A. Coulson	27 Mar 1918
2nd Lieut J. MacMeeken	27 May 1918
2nd Lieut. W.H.J Markham	27 Mar 1918
2nd Lieut. W.C. May	6 Oct 1917
2nd Lieut. J.H. McMurdo	27 May 1918
2nd Lieut. T.N. Melrose	14 Nov 1916
2nd Lieut. A.E. Moorhouse	15 Nov 1916
2nd Lieut. T. Nettleship	22 Mar 1918
2nd Lieut. E. Phillips	27 May 1918
2nd Lieut. F.C. Phillips	6 Feb 1916
2nd Lieut. J.E. Porrit	27 May 1918

2nd Lieut. W.E. Priestnall	27 May 1918
2nd Lieut. F. Remmer	12 Apr 1918
2nd Lieut. C.L. Richmond	24 May 1915
2nd Lieut. R.B. Ruddock	6 Apr 1918
2nd Lieut. J.B. Slack	27 May 1918
2nd Lieut. R.K. Steel	24 May 1915
2nd Lieut. S. Stones	3 Nov 1916
2nd Lieut. W.G. Verrill	26 Oct 1917
2nd Lieut. O. Willis	20 Jun 1916
2nd Lieut. W. Winkworth	26 Aug 1915
2nd Lieut. W. Wilkin	26 Oct 1917
2nd Lieut. J.H. Young	9 Jun 1918

Lieut. HENRY McDONNELL ANDERSON.

A native of Portaferry, Co. Down, Ireland, he was the son of John and Mary Anderson, of 32, Dargle Rd., Drumcondra, Dublin.

Originally a member of the Black Watch (Royal Highlanders.) The supplement to the London Gazette shows him promoted to Second Lieutenant with the 5th Bn. Northumberland Fusiliers on the 11th September 1915. On his Medal Index Card, the correspondence address is given as 3, Cromwell Road, Belfast, Ireland. Harry landed in France on 5th May, 1915 and died 30th May, 1918.

Lieutenant Anderson was part of 'D Company', 5th Bn. Northumberland Fusiliers, attached to the 63rd Battalion, Machine Gun Corp Corps, and died in an enemy air attack on the hospital he was in recovering from wounds, in at Doullens.

The Irish Times, May 30, 1919: Roll of Honour. Anderson-In loving memory of Lieutenant H. McD. Anderson (Harry), Northumberland Fusiliers, who died in hospital at Doullens, France, (hospital bombed), 30th May, 1918.

Henry is buried in Bagneux British Cemetery, Gezaincourt, in France.

2nd Lieut. JACK HARRY MASON APPS, died on 20 Nov 1917, the first day of the infamous battle of Cambrai; he was 19 years old. The son of Harry Mason Apps and Kate Helena Apps of the Nest, Sutton Valence, Maidstone, Kent. John is buried Croisilles British Cemetery, France.

The battle of Cambrai was where the British, after months of planning, first used tanks on a major scale in an attack. They had made a tentative attempt to use them previously at Flers on the Somme in September 1916 without much success. The attack began with significant gains on the opening day through a combination of effective artillery fire, infantry tactics and tanks. The British forces made an advance of around 5 miles, including recapturing a number of villages. The tank was an undoubted initial surprise approach, but by the end of the day almost half the tanks were out of action and in time it was deemed to be of limited use in offensive operations, cumbersome and prone to malfunction.

Lieut. DENYS ARMSTRONG born 1896, the son of Henry and Maud Armstrong, of 34, Osborne Road, Jesmond. Newcastle upon Tyne. Educated at Bootham School, York and Armstrong College, Newcastle upon Tyne. Denys' father was the secretary of the Young Men's Christian Association (YMCA) in Newcastle upon Tyne.
Prior to his regular military service, Denys attended the University's Officer Training Corps whilst attending Armstrong College. He was commissioned into 5th Battalion Northumberland Fusiliers and was platoon commander of 'B'' Coy. He was killed on 3 Oct 1916, aged 20 and is buried in Warlencourt Cemetery, France.

Supplement to the London Gazette, 1 July, 1915.
5th Battalion, The Northumberland Fusiliers; Cadet Corporal Denys Armstrong, from the Durham University Contingent, Senior Division, Officers Training Corps, to be Second Lieutenant. Dated 12th June, 1915.

The Young Men's Christian Association (YMCA)

Within ten days of the declaration of war, the YMCA had established no fewer than 250 recreation centres in the United Kingdom, providing a cup of tea, sandwiches or other refreshments, perhaps some reading materials. Many of these centres were at or near railway stations or other places where large numbers of troops would be passing.

In November 1914, the first YMCA contingent went to France and organised similar centres at Le Havre. Later, they were also in operation at Rouen, Boulogne, Dieppe, Etaples and Calais (the principal army bases), Abbeville, Dunkirk, Abancourt (railway junction), Paris and Marseilles. Eventually there were numerous such centres in each of the places mentioned, and another three hundred along the lines of communication. Vast quantities of refreshments were served out to troops on the move: for example, one centre at a railway siding at Etaples served more than 200,000 cups of cocoa each month.

On 30 June 1915, YMCA received permission to establish a centre within the area of army operations. It opened a centre at Aire, then the location of HQ of First Army. By the end of the year, small centres were in hundreds of places close to the front. As the pictures on this page show, some of these were very close to the firing line, providing a welcome refuge.

A road side canteen provided by the YMCA, near Wytschaete on 11 August 1917. Although fighting was going on a little to the north in the Third Battle of Ypres, the Messines-Wytschaete Ridge area was at this time relatively quiet. The men on the left and right are two orderlies and two officers of the Australian Medical Corps. Many such small centres located close to Casualty Clearing Stations and dressing stations were in operation at this time.

The YMCA staff was largely voluntary; mostly female but with some male staff who were over military age or below the medical requirements for active service. It appears that the man standing central, with helmet, in the image above is a YMCA worker. At any time, some 1500 YMCA workers were in France and Flanders alone. June 1915 saw the YMCA open a hostel in France for the use of relatives, visiting dangerously ill men. A YMCA car met the visitors at the port and took them to see their soldier relative. There were in the region of 100-150 such visitors each day.

(Article courtesy of 'The Long, Long Trail The British Army of 1914-1918 - for family historian' http://www.1914-1918.net/ymca.htm).

Lieut. THOMAS LINDSAY BAINBRIDGE was born on the 24th April 1882 in Holmwood, Jesmond, Newcastle upon Tyne. He was the son of Mr and Mrs Thomas Hudson Bainbridge of Eshott Hall, Felton, Northumberland and the grandson of the founder of the Bainbridge's Department store; Emerson Muschamp Bainbridge.

Thomas was educated privately at Dr Osborne's, Colwyn Bay, Wales and from there he went on to attend Bede College, Durham. He qualified as an electrical engineer and entered the shipbuilding yard of Swan Hunter and Wigham Richardson, where he was an Assistant Manager. In his spare time, Thomas was a very keen motorist and an all-round sportsman.

His brother Wilfred Hudson Bainbridge a Lieut. with the 6th Bn. Northumberland Fusiliers, was also killed in the war, aged 32 on 15th March 1916. He is buried in Etaples Military Cemetery, France.

Military service:
Prior to his regular military service, Thomas attended the Officer Training Corps at Durham University. He was commissioned into the Northumberland Fusiliers, 5th Battalion, at the rank of Officer Cadet, and then promoted to 2nd Lieutenant on the 23rd December 1911. He received his first post in 1913 as a commander in the signalling section, and was in the Special Reserve of Officers. On the outbreak of war, Thomas volunteered for Imperial service and, after being stationed at Blyth, left for the Front in April 1915. He is cited as being 'a popular officer with all ranks, [...] a keen rifle shot, and in 1913 won the revolver championship of Northumberland."

Death:
Thomas was killed in action on the 26th April 1915 at the aged 33 whilst he was involved in an attack on St Julien, near Ypres.

Memorial:
Thomas is buried in the Birr Cross Roads Cemetery in the Ieper West-Vlaanderen region of Belgium. There is a family headstone in St Andrews Cemetery, Jesmond, commemorating him and both he and his brother are commemorated in the village of Felton, Northumberland on the riverside memorial, near Felton Bridge and at St Michael and All Saints Church. As well as the Armstrong Memorial, he is remembered on the Roll of Honour at Bede College, Durham, where he was a pupil. He is also listed on the 1915 Roll of Honour at his place of work, Swan Hunter and Wigham Richardson, which was held in the company staff institute. Thomas is included in a plaque displayed in the Officers Mess of the Northumberland Fusiliers Drill Hall at Walker. This plaque now resides in Christ Church.

(Sourced from Universities at War. Digital memory book. Newcastle University.)

Swan Hunter and Wigham Richardson shipbuilding yard, erected their own war memorial at a cost of £25.000. Unveiled in 1925 on the Winter Garden and Memorial Hall on Frank Street, Wallsend. A later inscription was added after the Second World War to remember the fallen of WWII.

Lieut. HOWARD MATTHEW BELCHEM*

Howard Belchem was born in Guildford, Surrey, on September 15, 1878 to Capt. Frederick and Mrs. Mary Ann Belchem; the fifth child in a family of four sons and six daughters.

Being from a military background it was pretty much expected that Howard would follow his father in to the Army. After leaving Ardingly College in Haywards Heath, Sussex, he enlisted in the Northumberland Fusiliers and went on to have an illustrious career, serving in the Sudan and South African wars.

It was whilst serving in South Africa that he met Margaret Comer West, at Wynberg. The couple married in 1904 and their two eldest children were born in Bloemfontein, South Africa. His regiment then returned England with the New Mrs Belchem and children in tow. Another four children were born to the couple after their return to England.

In 1911 the family were based in Sheffield, as Howard was now a Quartermaster Sergeant at Hillsborough Barracks in the city.

Promoted to Lieutenant; Belchem was posted to France and on March 19, 1915*, he was killed by a sniper while on active service near Ypres. He was 36 years old. He is buried in the Ramparts Cemetery at Lille Gate, Ypres.

His widow, Margaret, who was living at 'Kylemore', Harrow Road, Haywards Heath, died at Worthing in 1922.

*The 5th Battalion did not land in France until late April, so it is disputable as to whether his unit was recorded correctly. The date is definitely right. Possibly he went ahead of the main contingent of the 50th Division whilst attached to another battalion.

In 1910 Howard was a witness at a Salisbury Coroners court:

Redford, Charles 1910 September 30thWylye
On Monday at Wylye the County Coroner (Mr R A Wilson), with a jury of whom Mr Thomas Dowdell was foreman, enquired into the circumstances attending the sudden death of Charles Redford, a soldier who was engaged in transport duty during the recent manoeuvres.

Howard Matthew Belcham, QMS in the 2nd Battalion Northumberland Fusiliers, said that the deceased was a sergeant in the same regiment. On Saturday about 6.30pm he arrived in the village of Bapton, with the transport. After the horses had been taken out of the wagon, he sat on a roll of blankets holding a mess tin containing either tea or soup, and suddenly he rolled over. Witness went at once for the Medical Officer, who ordered Redford to be removed to the hospital, but he died before he got there. Witness had known him for some years, but intimately for the last six months. He had been poorly for some time, complaining of rheumatism in his back, and indigestion. On the previous Tuesday he was sick and bought a bottle of aspirin in tabloids. He had been riding on the wagons nearly the whole of the time. He was 33 years old.

Roland Sackville Fletch, lieutenant in the Northumberland Fusiliers, said he commanded the company to which deceased belonged, but he had never complained to him of his health. He had seen him constantly during the past few days.

Ronald Martin Davies, lieutenant in the RAMC, stated that he had been on duty with the Northumberland Fusiliers, and had never been consulted by Redford for illness. He was called at six o'clock on Saturday evening, and found him quite unconscious, the appearances being those of sudden heart failure. The heart was very faint, and there was no pulse. He was known to have been ill for some time. It was possible that he might have a larger quantity of aspirin than was good for him.

A verdict was returned according to the quaint formula, that the deceased "died suddenly by the Visitation of God" from failure of the heart's action.
(Article sourced from Salisbury Inquests at wordpress.)

2nd Lieut. ARTHUR COULSON
Military Medal

Former Elswick School boy, Arthur was 22 years old when he died in a German prisoner of war camp on 27th March 1918. The son of Thomas and Caroline Coulson (nee Lawler) of 18 Northbourne Road, Jarrow. County Durham.

On the 1911 census he is recorded as being on 'office messenger boy' at the local Shipyards where his father also worked, as a hand driller. The family, including his six younger siblings lived at 61, Isabella Street, Newcastle upon Tyne.

In the following few years he sought other employment and worked in Bainbridge's store in Newcastle as an office boy. He also worked in the Newcastle Chronicle Office and as a Clerk to a solicitor. Arthur, a keen piano player, along with his family, later moved to Jarrow.

Arthur Coulson volunteered his services on the 29th of October 1914 at the Westgate Road recruiting office in Newcastle. Originally with the 18th Bn. Northumberland Fusiliers, he went to France in January 1916 as Serjeant 18/584 Coulson and was commissioned as a 2nd Lieut. August 1917, transferring to the 1/5th Bn.

Presumably he was awarded the Military Medal while serving as a Serjeant and for his valour in this incident he was put forward for a commission?

The battalion War Diary records Arthur Coulson as having been missing for several months, presumed to having been taken prisoner. Arthur died in a prisoner of war camp in Germany and is commemorated on the Heath Cemetery Memorial, Harbonnieres. France.

Lieut. PERCY HOWARTH EDWARDS was the son of Frederick Henry and Elizabeth Edwards and was born in Elswick, Newcastle upon Tyne, in 1880.

In 1911 the Edwards family are living at 14, Victoria Square, Jesmond, Newcastle upon Tyne; a substantial 14 roomed property. Only two of the couples' eight surviving children (from thirteen births) are living at home; Percy and his sister Julia. Also living at the property are three servants. Percy and his father are both working as 'Explosives Agents'.

Percy was reported 'Missing in action' on 24th May 1915 at the Battle of Bellewaarde Ridge, and is remembered on the Menin Gate (Ypres) Belgium.

From 'The supplement to the London Gazette of 20th October 1914'.
5th Battalion, The Northumberland Fusiliers; the undermentioned to be Second Lieutenants:
Percy Howarth Edwards dated 24th Sept 1914.

Lieut. ALFRED JOHN FIELD died in battle aged 34 on 11 Apr 1918. He was the son of son of Alfred and Anne Amelia Field of Tynemouth and husband of Mary Staniland Field (née Fotherby) of 22, Lesbury Rd., Heaton, Newcastle upon Tyne; whom he married in 1915.

On the 1901 census Alfred was living at home with his parents and siblings at the Esplande, Tynemouth, and working as a Printer, aged 17. By the time the 1911 census was taken, he is recorded as still being single and working as a Commercial Traveller and on the day the census was taken he was staying at a boarding house in Swansea, South Wales.

Alfred has no known grave and is remembered on the Ploegsteert Memorial, Belgium.

Capt. PERCIVAL DONALD FORRETT was born in Belper, Derbyshire in 1884. De Ruvigny's Roll of Honour 1914-1918 (part 3) describes Pericval as being the son of Thomas and Isabella Forrett of Alfreton, Derbyshire. His father Thomas, being the Manager of Secretary of Alfreton Gas Company, for 30 years. Percival was educated at Chesterfield Grammar school *(later on to Armstrong College, Newcastle upon Tyne, where he trained to be a teacher)* and since 1907 had been science master at Dame Allan's Endowed Schools, Newcastle upon Tyne.

Gazetted to a 2nd Lieut. 5th Northumberland Fusiliers from the Durham University O.T.C in December 1910, and promoted to Lieut. on 1 December 1912, and Capt. 11 April 1913. He volunteered for 'foreign service' at the outbreak of war and went to France April 1915. He was badly gassed in the May and invalided home. On recovery he was attached to the 2nd Line Bn. as Second in Command with the temporary rank as Major, but reverted to Captain when re-joining the 1st Line unit in France. He was killed by shellfire on 5 Feb 1916, whilst in the trenches (near Ypres).

Captain Forrett is buried at Maple Copse Cemetery, Belgium.

England & Wales, National Probate Calendar (Index of Wills and Administrations), 1858-1966 for Percival Donald Forrett state that Percival of 214, Portland Road, Newcastle upon Tyne, at probate hearing on 4 April 1916, he left £136 15s 6d to Private Thomas Wallace Forrett of the Durham Light Infantry. (Ancesty.co.uk)

Capt. WILLIAM GEORGE GRAHAM
Mentioned in Despatches.
Son of James William and Jane Graham, of Wallsend, Northumberland; husband of Annie Evelyn Graham, of 14, Lord St., Southport, Lancs.

Captain William George Graham was the son of James William Graham, Manager of the Kowloon Docks, Hong Kong. He was born at Howdon-on-Tyne on 16th May 1890, and was educated at Bede College, Durham. When war broke out he held a mastership at the Stephenson School, Wallsend. On leaving College he joined the 5th Battalion Northumberland Fusiliers and was gazetted Second Lieutenant in November 1913. During the first week of mobilisation he acted as Adjutant and subsequently as Signal Officer, and when the Battalion was ordered to the Front he went to France 24 hours in advance as Captain in charge of his Brigade Transport. Within three or four days of landing they were rushed up to the firing line to the assistance of a Canadian and Middlesex Regiment Battalions. The first day in the firing line his Battalion lost their Brigade Signal Officer and Captain Graham had to take up those duties for a few days. Afterwards they lost their Adjutant, and he was then told to take Adjutant's work till relieved when he re-joined his Company. During the winter of 1914 and spring of 1915 he was mentioned for performing good work. He was tragically killed by a sniper on the 24th June 1915. He is buried in the St. Quentin Cabaret Military Cemetery. He had married in October 1914, and his daughter was born posthumously in November 1915. His father had held a commission as a Lieutenant Engineer in the Hong Kong Volunteers whilst his great grandfather fought at the Battle of Waterloo and was twice wounded.

(Sourced from Bonhams research information complimenting his British War and Victory Medal, which they were selling.)

Lieut. MAURICE CRIDLAND HILL, born 26 Jun 1876, Chester le Street, County Durham; only son of Charles Dennis Hill and Fanny Hill. Educated at Rossall School, Fleetwood, Lancashire and from there went on to Trinity College, Cambridge, where he studied Law. Maurice then returned to Newcastle, where his family now lived, on Osborne Road, Jesmond. He was was now practicing within the city as a Solicitor.

In 1911, and recently married to Alice Mary Pearson he was living at Eland Hall, Ponteland, Northumberland.

Maurice was killed during a gas attack near Ypres, on 24 May 1915, aged 39 and is buried at New Irish Farm Cemetery. Belgium.

His wife Alice Mary Hill, was recorded as living at 25, Front St., Monkseaton, Northumberland, after his death. (*Rossall Sch. Reg.; Law Lists; Univ. War List.*)

From 'The London Gazette of 20 October 1914'.
5th Battalion, The Northumberland Fusiliers; the undermentioned to be Second Lieutenants: —
Maurice Cridland Hill (late Cadet, Rossall School Contingent, Junior Division, Officers Training Corps). Dated 21st September, ' 1914

Record of Service of Solicitors and Articled Clerks 1914-1919 with His Majesties Forces. (P263)
MAURICE CRIDLAND HILL.
Admitted Nov. 1904, practised at Newcastle-upon-Tyne. Joined Sept. 1914 as 2nd Lieut., Northumberland Fusiliers, subsequently promoted Lieut.
Served in France. Killed in action at Ypres May 24, 1915.

Lieut. & Q.M. ROBERT JAMES HOLLOWAY was born on 15 December 1865, Southampton, Hampshire. He enlisted into the Seaforth Highlanders in 1884 and after 10 years' service, transferred as Colour Serjeant to the Durham Light Infantry. Appointed a Serjeant-Major in the 4th Battalion Durham Light Infantry in April 1900, he served with them in the Boer War. The 1901 census show him as living with his wife Katherine, Wingrove Avenue, Elswick, Newcastle upon Tyne.

He was discharged on a pension in 1910; but the same year, appointed Lieutenant and Quartermaster of the 5th Battalion Northumberland Fusiliers. On the 1911 census he describes himself as a retired Army Warrant Officer and now working as a Brewers' traveller and is now living at 4, Grove Street, Newcastle upon Tyne, with Katherine, his wife of 21 years and their 6-year-old son Charles. (One other child having died).

Robert travelled to France with his battalion in April 1915. Suffering a slight wound that month he was soon back in action. In August 1916, he suffered fatal injuries when his horse stumbled in a shell hole and threw him heavily. He was shipped back to England but died at Endsleigh Palace Hospital, London, on 14 August 1916. He is buried in St. John's Westgate and Elswick Cemetery, Newcastle-upon-Tyne.

Lieut. ARTHUR VICTOR KNOX, was the second son of John and Jane A. Knox, of 1, King Edward's Rd, Heaton, Newcastle-on-Tyne. John Knox was a Master Tailor and Arthur had followed in the family tradition and become apprenticed to him.

The supplement to the London Gazette on 15 July 1915 mentions Cadet Lance-Corporal Arthur Victor Knox, from the Durham University Contingent, Senior Division, to the Officers Training Corps. Dated 24th June, 1915.

On 18 November 1915 it records 2nd Lieut. Arthur V. Knox as being made a temporary Lieut. As from 30th Oct 1915. Arthur, of the 5th Northumberland Fusiliers (Territorial) Bn. was attached to the 1st Bn. when he met his death, aged 29, on 6 June 1917. He is remembered on the Arras Memorial.

Capt. FREDERICK HENRY LAWSON

Capt. Frederick Henry Lawson,
5th Northumberland Fusiliers.

Born 23 Jul 1887, he was the eldest son of Frederick and the late Eleanor Lawson, of Field House, Dalton, Newcastle-on-Tyne. He attended Durham Grammar School from 1901-1905. After leaving school he worked for Architects Newcomb and Newcomb, in Newcastle and later for Mr Arthur Stockwell, again in Newcastle.

In 1907 Frederick joined the Northumberland Yeomanry and was gazetted 2nd Lieut. Northumberland Fusiliers in 1909. He became a Lieut. In 1910 and a Capt. 1912. He volunteered for Imperial Service at the outbreak of war and went out to France in March 1917. He was killed in action near St. Jean, Belgium two months later on 24th May 1915. He was 27 years old. His Colonel wrote of him:" He was one of my best officers, thoroughly capable and reliable."
(Sourced from De Ruvigny's Roll of Honour part one 1914-1919)
Frederick is remembered on the Menin Gate (Ypres) Memorial, Belgium.

Lieut. NORMAN WILFRED LAWSON was the youngest son of William Dawson Lawson, Master butcher, and his wife Mary Ann of Waterville Terrace, North Shields. Norman, born 1896 was a former pupil of Tynemouth High School. A Lieutenant in 'B' Company, 1st/5th Battalion, he enlisted in September 1914; was wounded three times and killed in action in the closing stages of the battle of the Somme on 14 Nov 1916, and is buried at Warlencourt British Cemetery, France.

CAPT JAMES CUNLIFFE LEASK 5th Bn. Northumberland Fusiliers, was born in Dublin in 1875 and died in Demuin, France, on the 30th March 1918, aged 43. He, along with a party of men attempted to clear the village to allow the 66th Divison to retreat to Hangard, on the south bank of the river Luce. Leask was awarded the Military Cross for his actions; but lost his life in the venture, allegedly from a direct hit by a shell.
Under command of Lt Col WB Little (D.S.O & M.C) officer in command of the OC 5/Border R- pioneers to the 66th (2nd East Lancs) Division, Leask and his men were sent in to clear the village at 8am, which they did.

The Times Supplement dated 26 July 1918 states the following, regarding the awarding of his Military Cross.

"For conspicuous gallantry and devotion to duty in leading a counter attack through a village. After severe fighting, he successfully cleared the village and enabled a force to extricated, thus greatly assisting the withdrawal that was in progress. He behaved with gallantry and skill."

Lt Col Little put Captain Leask's name forward for a D.S.O (Distinguished Service Order) but this was downgraded to a Military Cross because he was not of field rank. He had joined the battalion prior to Christmas 1917 as a relief officer so that others could take home leave.

Capt Leask's body was never recovered and he was declared dead in December 1918.

James left a wife Mary and two children, a son and daughter. They resided Gosforth, Newcastle upon Tyne, previously having lived Dublin, where according to the 1911 census he worked as an Insurance Superintendent.

Major. FOUNTAIN OKEY COLBORNE NASH

Fountain was born in Hammersmith Middlesex on 19 June 1878, to Joseph and Laura Nash. In 1901 he is working as a Civil Engineer in Rochdale. In 1905 he married Ella Heap Handley and in 1911 the couple were living in Fylde, Blackpool, where they had married. They later moved Birmingham, to 88 Church Road, Mosely. After Fountain died Ella and children Dorothy and Neville moved to 35, Wheeley's Rd., Edgbaston.

Fountain is buried at Birr Cross Roads Cemetery, Belgium.

England & Wales, National Probate Calendar (Index of Wills and Administrations), 1858-1966 for Fountain Okey Colborne Nash: of 88 Church Road Mosely Birmingham major 5th Northumberland Fusiliers Territorial Force died 27 April 1915 in action in North West Europe Probate Birmingham 23 July to Ella Heap Nash widow. Effects £361 14s (Ancestry.co.uk)

Fountain was an associated member of ICE – Institute of Civil Engineers.

Institution of Civil Engineering Obituaries: **Minutes of the Proceedings, Volume 201, Issue 1916**. 1st January 1916, page 409 …..on the North Eastern Railway Extension from Dunston to Gateshead, he went out South America, where he was employed successively on the Buenos Aires Western Railway, the Central Uruguay line and the Central Argentine Railway, returning home to enlist on the outbreak of war. He was elected an Associate Member on the 7th March, 1905. Major FOUNTAIN OKEY COLBORNE NASH was killed in action near Ypres on the 27th April, 1915. Trained under Mr.D. J. Ebbetts, Engineer to the Acton Urban District Council, he was subsequently employed in the engineering departments of Hertford and Rochdale, as surveyor and water engineer of Cockermouth, as assistant to the City Engineer of Newcastle-on-Tyne, and as chief town-planning assistant to the City Engineer of Birmingham..

CAPT NEVILLE MARRIOTT NORTH

CAPT. N. M. NORTH.

Neville North attended Bedford Modern School and later Leeds University; where he graduated with a degree in Civil Engineering. In 1916 when lodging at 2, Chillingham Road, Heaton, Newcastle upon Tyne and on Military Service, he applied to become an associate member of the' Institution of Civil Engineers.' The proposal was accepted on 6th March 1917.

Neville was mentioned in 'despatches' and awarded the Military Cross on 1st January 1916, when still a Lieutenant. His mention in the Times supplement of 16th January 1916 was all but brief, due to at this time Military Crosses being handed out for action that later on would receive possibly no recognition at all due to the increasing intensity of the war and loss of life. The Times simply states. *"Lieutenant (Temporary Captain) Neville Marriott North Northumberland Fusiliers (Territorial Force.)"* Amongst the names of other Military Cross recipients.

Formerly of 5, Goldington Avenue, Bedford, Neville died on 27th May 1918 aged 27, leaving £661 15s 11d to Frances North, his widowed mother. He has no known grave and is remembered on the Soissons Memorial, France.

2nd Lieut. JAMES MACMEEKEN
(Article Published in the Morningside Parish Church, Edinburgh, Scotland. November 2014)

As we mark the centenary of the start of the First World War, I thought it would be interesting to find out more about some of the names on our church war memorials. On the St Matthew's memorial, two of the surnames are the same, and so probably related It turns out that Captain Guy Steel Peebles Macmeeken and 2nd Lt James Macmeeken were indeed brothers, two of the seven children of Rev James Macmeeken, minister of Pettinain Parish Church, Lanarkshire, and his wife Agnes. Born on 13th March 1891, Guy served with the 4th Battalion and later the 12th Battalion Royal Scots Territorial Force, becoming a temporary lieutenant and then acting captain on 20th July 1917. Having been posted to France with his Battalion in July 1916, he won a Military Cross and died of his wounds whilst a prisoner of war in Germany on 5th May 1918 and is buried in Valenciennes (St Roch) Communal Cemetery. The citation for his Military Cross reads: "For conspicuous gallantry and devotion to duty in an attack. Though wounded he led his company to the capture of a strong enemy position with fifty prisoners and three machine guns under heavy shell fire. He showed splendid skill and initiative." His brother James was born on 7th February 1898 and served with the 5 th Battalion Northumberland Fusiliers. He was killed in action at the age of 20 on 27th May 1918, possibly at the Battle of the Aisne. He was buried in Pontavert German Cemetery but his grave there is now lost and there is a memorial to him at La Ville-aux-bois British Cemetery, north of the city of Reims. In connection with his memorial, Mrs M Macmeeken of 12 Comiston Drive, Edinburgh is named as next of kin, which would explain the St Matthews connection. Two other sons of the Macmeeken family also served in the forces during World War 1. The eldest of the seven children, John West Macmeeken, born in 1888, was a civil engineer who originally joined the 38th Battalion of the Canadian Expeditionary Force in Montreal before transferring to Princess Patricia's Canadian Light Infantry in July 1915. He fought at the Somme and was invalided out in April 1918. He died of heart failure, probably as a result of his war experiences, in the USA in 1939 at the age of only 51. The fourth son to fight was Andrew Peebles Macmeeken, in the 4th Battalion (Queen's Edinburgh Rifles) Royal Scots (Lothian Regiment). He was seconded for duty with the Machine Gun Corps in May 1916. He became 2nd lieutenant in October 1916 and then lieutenant in July 1917. He was also acting captain while commanding a section in January 1919, having been made a temporary captain with the Tank Corps in November 1918. He relinquished his command with the rank of captain on 30th September 1921 and died in 1978 at the age of 84. Incidentally, another Rev James West Macmeekn, quite probably their grandfather, was minister at Lesmahagow and produced a history of the Scottish Metrical Psalms.

2nd Lieut. WALTER HENRY JAMES MARKHAM was reported missing on 22 Mar 1918, thought to have been taken 'Prisoner of War' but was later known to have died on 27 Mar 1918 at Bellenglise, France. He is remembered on the Poziers War Memorial, France.

2nd Lieut. JOHN HAMILTON McMURDO was born 1897 in Kilpatrick, Dumbartonshire to Peter and Caroline McMurdo. His father was a Lawyer's cashier and book keeper. The family later moved to Easter Highgate, Beith, Ayrshire. John was 21 years old when he died on the 27 May 1918; the first day of the battle of the Chemin des Dames, on the Aisne. He is remembered on the Soissons memorial, France.

By the spring of 1918, the Allies knew that there would be a major German attack; they just did not know when it would come. The British reinforced their positions near the coast while the French strengthened their positions to the south of the British.

The Third Battle of the Aisne was the third major offensive launched by the Germans on the Western Front in the spring of 1918. The 5th Northumberlands were battle weary, having been involved in all three battles; at the Somme, the Lys and the Chemin des Dames. Unlike the earlier battles, the 50th Division was now in the front line and not held in reserve when the offensive opened on 27 May 1918. The 5th Battalion were hit hard – 59 men dead and many more again wounded.

Despite being described as a diversion, the Germans assembled a massive army for the attack on the Aisne. Forty-one divisions supported by over 4,000 guns were lined up against sixteen Allied divisions, three of which were British divisions moved south for a rest after heavy fighting further north. The battle began with one of the most intense artillery bombardments of the war with over 4,000 guns across a 40 kilometre front. The Germans fired roughly two million shells in four hours on the morning of the 27th. The bombardment was accompanied by GAS attacks, designed to incapacitate defensive guns crews. After which they launched their attack with seventeen divisions owing to the concentration of predominantly British troops in front-line trenches. Casualties from the bombardment were severe, some units being virtually wiped out.

The Allied lines were crushed. The bridges across the Aisne were captured undamaged – even though the Royal Engineers of the 149th had attempted to blow them up, to thwart the Germans advance.

The Germans then broke through a further eight Allied divisions, four British and four French, reaching the Aisne in under 6 hours before continuing their advance towards the Marne. The Germans were able to advance thirteen miles on the first day of the battle, the single biggest advance since the beginning of trench warfare in 1914. By the 30th May the Allies had lost over 100,000 men in the battle with an additional 50,000 soldiers having been captured along with 800 heavy guns.

Captain Sydney Rogerson of the neighbouring headquarters, 23 Brigade, 8th Division, reported that:
'Crowded with jostling, sweating humanity the dugouts reeked, and to make matters worse headquarters had no sooner got below than the gas began to filter down. Gas masks were hurriedly donned and

anti-gas precautions taken - the entrances closed with saturated blankets and braziers were lighted on the stairs. If gas could not enter, neither could the air.[1]

(This quote by Sydney Rogerson is taken from an article regarding a talk by Peter Hart to the Yorkshire branch of the WFA.)

Lieut. ALAN JOHN MAWSON was a native of Newcastle upon Tyne, having been born in Heaton in 1887 to Pharmacist Thomas Mawson and his wife Florence. In 1911 the family were living at 26 Mundella Terrace, Heaton. Alan still living at home, with two of his three siblings was working as a Clerk. Alan returned from the war, he was still alive to hear the news of the Armistice; but sadly died of his wounds on 4 Dec 1918, aged 31. He is buried at St. John's Westgate and Elswick Cemetery, Newcastle upon Tyne.

The England & Wales, National Probate Calendar (Index of Wills and Administrations), 1858-1966 states that Alan; his family now residing 19, East Parade, Newcastle upon Tyne, Lieutenant 5th Northumberland Fusiliers (Territorial) Machine Gun Corps died 4th Dec 1918 at the Military hospital, Belton, Grantham, Lincolnshire. Administration (with will) Newcastle upon Tyne 25th March 1919 to Florence Mary Mawson (wife of Thomas Oliver Mawson). Effects £30 6s 10d. (Ancestry.co.uk)

2nd Lieut. WILLIAM CLARENCE MAY a farmers' son, was born in Bicester, Oxfordshire in 1892 to Thomas and Elizabeth May. They were living at Baynards Green, Stoke Lyne, Bicester at the time of William's death. He was killed on 6 Oct 1917 and is remembered on the Tyne Cot Memorial, Belgium. Only a few short weeks earlier, news of the death of his younger brother, Howard Stanley May, aged 21, a Private, serving with the Oxford and Bucks Light Infantry, killed on the 22 Aug 1917 reached Baynards Green. He too is remembered on the Tyne Cot Memorial, Belgium.

England & Wales, National Probate Calendar (Index of Wills and Administrations), 1858-1966 (Ancestry.co.uk) State that on 27 March 1918 his probate was read in Oxford and he left £225 6s 7d to Thomas May, Farmer.

2nd Lieut. THOMAS NELSON MELROSE. Thomas Nelson Melrose aged 22, of 4 Horsley Terrace, Tynemouth, died on 14 Nov 1916. He is remembered on the Thiepval Memorial, France.

A former bank clerk he had attended Tynemouth High School at same time as Norman Wilfred Lawson (see above). His father Thomas was a self-employed fisherman and boat owner.

As the Somme offensive of 1916 drew to a close, and the final battle of that particular campaign – The battle of the Ancre, brought a heavy loss of life for Northumberland Fusiliers of the 50th Division. The attack began on 13 Nov 1916. It was hoped that the higher ground around Beaumont Hamel and Beaucourt could be seized. However, the incessant machine gun fire created heavy losses and the troops struggled to make any headway.

On the 14th the 2nd Australian Division joined in the attack with support from men of the 149th Brigade – part of the 50th Division and mainly formed from units of the Northumberland Fusiliers and Durham Light Infantry.

The weather was dreadful with snow falls and rapid thaws. The ground became a quagmire and loss of life was heavy. The battle of the Somme came to a miserable end on 18th Nov 1916. The battalion lost 25 men between the 1st and 18th November 1916; most of them occurring on the 14th.

2nd Lieut. ARTHUR EDWARD MOORHOUSE was born in Urmston, Lancashire on 14 Apr 1889 to Joseph, a travelling salesman, and his wife Lily. Arthur lived in Urmston until his late teens, when it is assumed he travelled to Newcastle to take up employment in the coal exportation business, under the watchful eye of his uncle Stanley and Aunt Louisa; the 1911 census it shows him living with his aunt Louisa Sherringham, and her husband Stanley, at 9, Treherne Road, Newcastle upon Tyne.

The supplement to the London Gazette on 17 Nov 1915 states that Arthur was made a 2nd Lieut. on 13 Nov 1915. He died on 15 Nov 1916 aged 27 and is buried at Warlencourt British Cemetery, France.

2nd Lieut. THOMAS NETTLESHIP was born in 1885 in Alnwick, Northumberland and was the son of Charles and Elizabeth Nettleship of 5, Howick Street, Alnwick. On the 1911 census Thomas is aged 25 and single, living at home and employed as a Fishing rod maker.

Thomas Nettleship served in the Northumberland Fusiliers and was killed on 22 March 1918. His brother Mark Nettleship served in the King's Own Scottish Borderers and died 5½ months later on 1 September 1918, aged 25. Both are remembered on the Alnwick War Memorial.

De Ruvigny's Roll of Honour 1914 – 1919 Vol 4 for Thomas N Nettleship.

Thomas, 2nd Lieut. 1/5th (Territorial) Battn. Northumberland Fusiliers. Eldest s. of the late Charles Nettleship by his wife Elizabeth (5, Howick Street, Alnwick), dau. of M. Wilson b. Alnwick, co. Northumberland; 4 Aug 1885; educ. Duke's School there; carried on his father's business as head of the firm; joined the Northumberland Nettleship is as follows.

Hussars Imperial Yeomanry in 1902; on the outbreak of war volunteered for active service, and joined the Northumberland Fusiliers in August 1914; was attached to the 2nd Battn. Served with the Expeditionary Force in France and Flanders from Jan 1915; was wounded at Ypres in the following June and was invalided home; on recovery was attached to the 8th Battn., and sent with reinforcements to Gallipoli in Aug; on evacuation of the Peninsula in Jan 1916; he proceeded to Egypt, and subsequently returned to France the same year; was given a commission and gazetted 2nd Lieut. the 1/5th Battn. of his regiment 30 Oct 1917 and was killed in action at St. Christ on the Somme during the German offensive 23 March 1918. Buried where he fell. His Commanding Officer wrote "Although he was only in my company a few days he had proved himself an exceedingly brave and cool officer, as well as a very efficient one. His loss if felt deeply."

Capt. CHARLES ALFRED PATTERSON. Son of George Nixon Patterson and Jane Ann Patterson, of 26, Osborne Avenue, Newcastle-on-Tyne.

George was a branch manager of an Insurance Company prior to the outbreak of war. The 1911 census shows him as being a visitor to an address in South Shields. Being he was single and his parents at that time living in a large eighteen roomed property at 3, Osborne Road, Jesmond, Newcastle upon Tyne, it is more than probable that his actual address was the same as his parents.

Charles died of wounds on 8 Oct 1916 and is buried at St. Sever Cemetery, Rouen. France.

England & Wales, National Probate Calendar (Index of Wills and Administrations), 1858-196

For Charles Alfred Patterson of 26, Osborne Avenue, Newcastle upon Tyne gentleman a lieutenant in his Majesty's Army died 8th October 1916 at the General Hospital Rouen, France Administration 23rd December (1916) to George Nixon Patterson gentleman. Effects £3087 16s. (Ancestry.co.uk)

2nd Lieut. EDWARD PHILLIPS. Edward Phillips, was killed aged 34 on 27 May 1918 at the battle of the Chemin des Dames.

The son of John and Jane Phillips, of Wanwood Hill, Alston, near Carlisle, he is remembered on the Soissons Memorial, France. (See the part the 5th Bn. played at the Chemin des Dames under 2nd Lieut. JOHN HAMILTON McMURDO). Fifty nine men lost their lives on the 27 May 1918 and many more wounded).

2nd Lieut. FREDERICK CHARLES PHILLIPS, son of Frederick and Margaret Jane Phillips, of 204, Portland Rd., Jesmond, Newcastle-on-Tyne.

Frederick Snr, was a successful Horse Dealer. Frederick Jr, was one of six children. He had been born at High House, North Brunton, Gosforth, where his father farmed as well as running a horse dealership. The family later moved to the above mentioned property on Portland Road; and Frederick Snr ran his business nearby. On the 1911 census Frederick Jr is recorded as being a Clerk.

He died of wounds, aged 21, at a Casualty Clearing Station on 6th Feb 1916 and is buried at Lijssenthoek Military Cemetery, Belgium.

Lieut. WILLIAM EVELYN STANLEY POOLE, was the son of the Rev. George Russell Poole, of 20, Linton Road, Hastings, West Sussex. Born Scarborough, Yorkshire in 1882, but brought up in Sussex. William died aged 35 on the 19 Sept 1917 and is buried at Heniel Communal cemetery Extension, France.

From the London Gazette 30 January 1920.

Re: Lieut. W. E. S. POOLE, Deceased. Pursuant to the Law of Property Amendment Act, 1869. NOTICE is hereby given, that all creditors and other persons having any claims or demands against the estate of Lieut. W. E. S. Poole, 5th Northumberland Fusiliers, late of 20, Linton-road, Hastings, in the 'county of Sussex, deceased, are hereby required to send the particulars, in writing, of their claims or demands to me, the undersigned, the executrix, on or before the 14th day of February, 1920, after which date I will proceed to distribute 'the assets of 'the said deceased amongst ,the persons entitled thereto, having regard only to the claims and demands of Which I shall then have had notice; and 1 will not be liable for the assets of the said deceased, or any part thereof, or distributed, to any person or persons of whose claim or demands I shall not then have had notice. Dated this day 20th January 1920.
CLARA POOLE, 1, Pytches-road, - Woodbridge, 087 Suffolk

2nd Lieut. JOHN ERNEST PORRITT the son of Furnace blacksmith George Porritt and his wife Hannah, was killed aged 28, in the same battle as 2nd Lieut. William Priestnall (see below and 2nd Lieut. JOHN HAMILTON McMURDO for a description of the battle) and many others. John's body was never recovered and he is remembered on the Soissons memorial, France. He was born Grosmont, North Yorkshire in 1889. In 1911 he was living with his parents and sister at 120, Crescent Road, Middlesbrough, and working as a Coal Merchant Clerk.

2nd Lieut. WILLIAM EUSTACE PRIESTNALL. A former Warehouse Clerk from Manchester, William arrived in France on 30 May 1916. The son of William and Margaret Priestnall of 340, Droylsden Road. Newton Heath, Manchester. He was killed at the age of 22, during the bloody battle of the Aisne at the Chemin des Dame on 27 May 1918.

A vile and vicious day for the Battalion. He is buried at La Ville-Aux-Bois British Cemetery, France. (See 2nd Lieut. JOHN HAMILTON McMURDO for a description of the battle).

Lieut. HENRY THOMAS RICHARDSON was born in South Norwood, Surrey in 1878, to John and Frances Richardson. His parents were originally from Durham and had moved south, later to return due to his father's occupation as a Colliery Clerk. In 111 the family were living at 73, Woodbine Road, Gosforth. Northumberland and Henry working as an Insurance Agent.

Henry suffered serious injuries and was transported back to the UK to be treated, where he sadly succumbed to his injuries on 23 Aug 1915; either at a Military Hospital, or at home. He is buried at St. Nicholas Churchyard. Gosforth, England.

The supplement to the London gazette reports Henry made a Lieut. on 14th September 1914.

2nd Lieut. FREDERICK REMMER (or RIMMER)
Formerly of the Lancashire Fusiliers Cycle Corps. Enlisted 4th Aug 1914. 12 Apr 1918, reported missing, presumed killed in action, aged 25. He had been commended for bravery in Feb 1917.

Frederick had been a pupil of All Souls'Church, Heywood, Lancashire, where he later taught as a Sunday school teacher. Prior to the outbreak of war, he had 'Piecer' at Yew Mill. He left behind a sister Kate Remmer who lived at 59, Bradshaw Street, Heywood, Lancashire.

On 23 Aug 1918 his brother Private Harold Remmer of the Lancashire Fusiliers was reported having been taken Prisoner of War.

(Taken from the Heywood book of Remembrance by Michael Dalton. ebook)

2ⁿᵈ Lieut. CUTHBERT LAURENCE RICHMOND

Cuthbert was the son of Richard Frederick and Fanny Richmond, of 'The Laurels' Wroxham, Norfolk. He was born in January 1890 in Lewisham, London. It appears his parents had only recently retired to Norfolk, as in 1911 the family were still living in London. Father Richard describes his occupation on a number of census as 'Manchester Warehouseman'. In 1911 his parents along with Cuthbert, his sister Ethel and a servant named Ellen Bryant, were living at 2, Montague Ave, Brockley, South East London. Cuthbert was working as a Clerk.

He was Educated at St. Dunstan's College, Catford, London. The London Gazette on 4ᵗʰ January 1915 states he was gazetted to 2ⁿᵈ Lieut, on 14ᵗʰ December 1914.

2ⁿᵈ Lieut. REGINALD BARNETT RUDDOCK was with the 5th Northumberland Fusiliers up until 4 Apr 1917 when he was attached to the 4th Bedfordshire Regiment. He arrived at his new battalion with Second Lieutenants Lovatt and Miln in tow. Forty-eight hours later he was dead – killed on 6 April 1917. He has no known grave and is remembered on the Pozieres Memorial to the missing.

Reginald Barnett Ruddock born 1892 in Tynemouth, to Richard, a photographer, and Alice Ruddock. The family are now living at 25 White Ladies Road, Bristol and Reginald is working as a dental salesman.

The supplement to the London Gazette of 6 Dec 1916 records Reginald Barnett Ruddock of the Northumberland Fusiliers being promoted to 2ⁿᵈ Lieut.

The England & Wales, National Probate Calendar (Index of Wills and Administrations), 1858-1966 for Reginald Barnett Ruddock (1918) states that at probate on 27 September in London, to William James Ruddock, surgeon. Reginald left an estate of £355 16s 7d. (Ancestry.co.uk)

Lieut. ERNEST VERNON SARGENT, born Woolwich Kent in 1882, to Thomas and Sarah Sargent. The family later move to 'Tower Lodge' Greenwich and Ernest carves himself a career in the City as a Stockbroker. In 1911 Ernest is recorded as being a visitor at 47, Burnt Ash Road, Lewisham, still working as a Stockbroker.

Formerly Private 3803 with the London Regiment, Ernest was gazetted2nd Lieut. to the 5th Northumberland Fusiliers (Territorial) Force 20th October 1915, along with four other Privates from the London Regiment.

Ernest was killed aged 36 at the Chemin des Dames on 27 May 1918. He is remembered on the Soissons Memorial, France. (See 2nd Lieut. JOHN HAMILTON McMURDO for a description of the battle).

2nd Lieut. JOHN BARNETT SLACK

(The following extract is from the internet: Great War the fallen.)

The birth of John Barnett Slack was registered at Congleton in 1891. He was the son of Henry and Sarah Ann Slack. Henry had married Sarah A. Barnett at St. John's, Buglawton, Cheshire in 1883. By 1891 the couple lived on Bridge Street, Biddulph with their daughter Elizabeth Alice and son, Henry Brindley Slack. Henry senior was a pattern maker who had been born in Buglawton. Sarah and their children were all Biddulph born.

Ten years later the family resided at 66, Tunstall Road. Henry's occupation was given as "mechanical pattern maker" and eldest son Henry, then aged 14, was a chair maker. The family had increased and now included John and his younger sister, Mary.

By 1911 the family had moved yet again although only a few doors away to 90, Tunstall Road. Again, Henry was described as a mechanic and 19-year-old John Barnett Slack was a *"no. checker – North Staffordshire Railway"*. A year later he was a policeman in Manchester.

Before enlisting in the army, John had served as a policeman at Old Trafford, Manchester since 1912. Local sources say he joined the Royal Engineers in November 1915 and after training went to France on January 16th 1916 serving with this unit in Flanders. Though the medal card of John shows he served in the Leicestershire Regiment with a service number of 37869, his battalion is unknown. In January 1917, he again transferred units when he was seconded to the 28th Battalion Artist Rifles (15th Officer Training Battalion). This may well have been at St. Omer in France where the unit had their HQ. John gained his commission and became Second Lieutenant J.B. Slack.

John now returned to the front being posted to the 1/5th Battalion Northumberland Fusiliers (the Fighting Fifth) attached to the 50th Division. He found his new battalion in the Ypres Salient. They had been fighting in the Third Battle of Ypres from July to November 1917. Here the division was decimated during the actions to take the Passchendaele Ridge. John commenced his service with the battalion on November 27th 1917 soon after the battle came to an end. The division spent a cold wet winter holding their front-line trenches until early in 1918 when the division was in action again at St. Quentin and the Battle of Lys. In March, as part of five divisions of exhausted battle disabled troops, they were ordered south for recoup and refit.

A long slow journey by rail was undertaken travelling in cattle trucks of the French railway. Their destination was an area between Soissons and Rheims; a quiet area in beautiful countryside in the valley of the River Aisne and far from the horrors of Passchendaele. The soldiers were to spend two months at rest in this relatively safe and relaxed French sector of the Western Front. The enemy were aware of this and were to take advantage of the situation, for beyond the high ridge of the Chemin-des-Dames, the Germans were secretly amassing a large army.

At 1.00am on May 27th 1918 the enemy bombardment opened with devastating results on the resting troops. At 4.00am the enemy infantry attacked. John's battalion in the 50th Division, who were in position between Craonne and Pontavent, endured a terrible ordeal. Most of these men were already battle exhausted. What an awful twist of fate! This supposedly safe

area became the Battlefield of the Third Aisne. The Northumberland Fusiliers bravely held their lines at first but soon dense waves of enemy troops overwhelmed them. It became a nightmare with many men lost including John.

On May 27th 1918, at the age of 26, Second Lieutenant John Barnett Slack sadly fell on the battlefield. Originally, he was buried by the Germans in their Cemetery at Pontavent and later after the armistice he was remembered in the Ville-Aux-Bois British Cemetery. The CWGC have records which state, "*John is remembered along with a fellow officer, Second Lieutenant James MacMeeken of the same regiment, their headstones lie side by side on the wall of the cemetery.*"

In this cemetery, many of the graves are of 50th Division troops and the cemetery is close to the remains of the WW1 Berry-au-Bois airfield.

The Staffordshire Weekly Sentinel reported on the death of Second Lieutenant Slack.

SEC.–LIEUT. J.B. SLACK, BIDDULPH KILLED IN ACTION

"The sad news reached Mr. and Mrs. Henry Slack, 90, Tunstall Road, Biddulph, on Saturday that their second son, Sec.–Lieut. J.B. Slack, Northumberland Fusiliers, was killed in action on May 27th. Lieut. Slack, who was in his 27th year, enlisted in November 1915 in the Royal Engineers as a Private. Previously he was, for two years, with the County Police, Old Trafford, Manchester. In January 1917, he went to the front, but came home in June to take a commission. He joined the Cadet Corps of the Artists Rifles, and was gazetted second-lieutenant in November.

Mr. and Mrs. Slack's eldest son, Private Harry Slack, Niagara Rangers, is on active service, having come over with the Canadians. Previous to enlisting he was engaged in farming in Canada, where he had been since 1913."

John Barnett Slack is remembered on the memorials at St. Lawrence and also the cenotaph in Albert Square, Biddulph. Michael Turnock and Elaine Heathcote.

2nd Lieut. ROBERT KINGSLEY STEEL. * CWGC states him as being a full Lieutenant.

Robert was the son of John and Alice Steel of Cranford, a recently built property, near Stocksfield in Northumberland. His father was a wealthy coal exporter and shipping broker. Robert after leaving school, worked alongside his father. He had been born in Elswick, Newcastle upon Tyne. The family later moved Tynemouth and then to 'Cranford.'

Robert was comfortably off in his own right and when his probate was read on 15 May 1916, he left £2301 16s 3d to his father. He is buried in New Irish Farm Cemetery, Belgium.

De Ruvigny's Roll of Honour 1914-1919

Lieut., 5th (Territorial) Battalion, Northumberland Fusiliers. Elder s. of John Tinline Steel of Cranford, Stocksfield on Tyne, by his wife, Alice Maria, dau. of Adam Bates and brother to Sec Lieut. J.G. Steel. b. Newcastle upon Tyne 24 April 1888: educ: Mill Hill School: Was a coal exporter and ship broker; volunteered for service at the outbreak of war; obtained a commission as "ns Lieut. Northumberland Fusiliers 15 Sept 1914, being promoted to Lieut. May 1915. Served with the Expeditionary Force in France and Flanders from April 1915 when his regiment was part of the 50th Division, which, although only having arrived in France on the 22nd of that month, was sent in to the fighting line on the 24th to support the Canadians who saved the situation during the second battle of Ypres, when the Germans first used gas. He was killed in action on 24th May 1915, while trying to rescue one of his own men who had been gassed and wounded. Buried at the Irish Farm near Ypres. He earned the praise of a Colonel of the Irish Fusiliers, for the cool manner in which he led the attack on St. Julien. His Sergt. Wrote "He had not a white feather in his wing and could laugh and joke in the face of death."

2nd Lieut. SHEPHERD STONES.

Shepherd Stones was born October 1892 in Sale, Cheshire to Herbert and Elizabeth Stones. He moved to Solihull at a young age when his widowed mother married Joseph Taylor, a manufacturer of gas fittings. On the 1911 census Shepherd was working as a Clerk.

Shepherd is buried at Bazentin-Le-Petit Communal Cemetery Extension, France.

Birmingham Daily Post Friday 10th November 1916.
Sec. Lieut. S. Stones (Killed).

Official notification has been received by Mrs J.P. Taylor of "Ravenswood" Solihull, that her younger son, Second Lieutenant Shepherd Stones, was killed in action on the 3rd inst. He joined one of the Birmingham City Battalions on the outbreak of war and was offered and accepted a commission in the Northumberland Fusiliers in August 1915. He went out to the front last May. He was 24 years of age and was educated at the Rydal Mount School, Colwyn Bay. Mrs Taylor's other son is serving with the Fusiliers.

De Ruvigny's Roll of Honour 1914-1919 Vol 3 carries the following article:

2nd Lieut., 5th (Territorial) Battalion, Northumberland Fusiliers. Son of John Herbert Stones of Sale, by his wife Elizabeth, (Ravenswood Solihull, co, Warwick) 3rd dau. of the late Isaac Holmes, of Lyndale, Southport.b, Sale. co. Chester. 10 October 1892; educ. Mintholme School, Southport and Rydal Mount School, Colwyn Bay; subsequently entered the Birmingham branch of Lloyds bank' volunteered for foreign services and subsequently joined the 1st Birmingham Battn. of the Warwickshire Regt. on its formation in Sept 1914, after the outbreak of war; obtaining a commission in the Northumberland Fusiliers 17th Sept 1915. Served with the Expeditionary Force in France and Flanders from May 1916, where he was Reserve Officer for the Lewis Gun Section and passed through a course of instruction for company commanding, having at previous periods been acting Capt., and was killed in action 3 Nov. Following was buried at Bazentin- Le- Petit.

2nd Lieut. WILLIAM GIBSON VERRILL

Died on 26 Oct 1917 aged 24 and is remembered on the Tyne Cot Memorial, Belgium. The son of John and Elizabeth Verrill of 115, Sidney Grove, Newcastle upon Tyne. He enlisted as a Private in 1914 and was gazetted to 2nd Lieut. on 18th July 1917.

On the 1911 census William is recorded as being a Draper's apprentice and his father as being a Draper's Superintendent.

From the Whitby Gazette – Friday 16th November 1917.
Second Lieut. W.G. Verill

Second Lieut. W.G. Verill, Northumberland Fusiliers whose death was announced in our issue last week, was killed in action, and was the eldest son of Mr and Mrs John Verill, 115, Sidney Grove, Newcastle upon Tyne and a native of Staithes. The deceased officer who was 24 years of age, was also well known in Staithes, being a frequent visitor, and had many friends in the place who deeply regret his death. In a letter of sympathy to his parents, his Major says: "On behalf of the Colonel and brother officers of the battalion, we deeply sympathise with you in the great loss you have sustained through the loss of your son. Second Lieut. W.G. Verill gallantly leading his men in our attack on the enemy's positions. He was sniped through the heart and killed instantly. Although only with us for so short a period, your boy proved himself a splendid soldier and excellent comrade, and he is greatly missed." He joined a local battalion of the Northumberland Fusiliers in September 1914, and went to France with his regiment in November 1915. He was in France for about fifteen months before returning to take a commission and went through part of the battle of the Somme. He returned to England in January 1917, and subsequently received a commission in the Northumberland Fusiliers being gazetted on Jun 27th 1917. On returning to France again in August, he as attached to one of the Territorial units, and was killed in action on October 26th. Previous to joining the army he was in the employ of Messrs. Bainbridge & Co Ltd. Market Street, Newcastle.

2nd Lieut. WILLIAM WHITE WILKIN was the only son of William White Wilkin and Hannah Anderson Wilkin of 7, Vespasian Avenue, South Shields. A former pupil of South Shields Grammar School. On finishing his education, he became a clerk in a ship owner's office. He joined the Quayside Battalion of the Northumberland Fusiliers as a Private, and was promoted to 2nd Lieutenant on 1 Aug 1917. William was reported missing on 26 Oct 1917, presumed to have been killed. He is remembered on the Tyne Cot Memorial, Belgium.

2nd Lieutenant WALTER WINKWORTH,

5th Battalion Northumberland Fusiliers, died of wounds on the 26th August 1915 at 32 years of age and his remains are buried in grave I. C. 130 of Bailleul Communal Cemetery Extension, Nord-Pas-de-Calais, France.
Walter's Army service record is available for a fee at the National Archives and his Medal Roll Index shows that he was posthumously awarded the 1915 Star, Victory and the British War Medals after his father applied for them in 1922. (Photo Courtesy of the IET *Archives*)

The 1911 Census show Walter Snr of 22, Simonside Terrace, Heaton, Newcastle upon Tyne, as Assistant Superintendent, Telegraphs, with the General Post Office in Newcastle and Walter Jr as single and working as an Electrical Engineer. Also in the household are his mother, brother Leonard and sister Elsie.
He was an active Scoutmaster of the 19th Newcastle Upon Tyne Troop, and Divisional Scoutmaster for the East End Division of the Newcastle Upon Tyne Association.
Walter was also a Freemason and member of Lodge Temperance No 2557 which at the time held its meetings in the Old Assembly Rooms, Westgate Road, Newcastle Upon Tyne.

He was educated privately and at Rutherford College, Newcastle-on-Tyne (1895 — 1896). On the completion of his general education, he was, in January, 1897, apprenticed as a Pupil with Messrs. J. H. Holmes & Co., of Portland Road, Newcastle-on-Tyne, Manufacturing Electrical Engineers, and served in that capacity until September, 1903; during this period he passed through the Electrical and Testing Departments at the firm's Works. In 1900, whilst still an Apprentice, he enrolled as a Student at the Armstrong College (now a part of the University of Durham), Newcastle -on-Tyne, and concurrently attended evening classes in electrical engineering subjects: he was awarded prizes in Electrical Engineering in 1900, 1901 and 1905.

He was, on the termination of his apprenticeship in 1903, engaged by Messrs. J. H. Holmes & Co., and employed as a Tester in the Motor-Testing Department. His responsibilities were later increased, and, in May, 1905, he was appointed Assistant to the Chief Tester; he was promoted to the position last named in October, 1912. He relinquished his appointment with Messrs. Holmes & Co. in August, 1914, on the outbreak of war, in order to serve in the Army.

He had, early in his professional career, taken an interest in the Volunteer movement, and, in 1906, enrolled in the Tyne Division Submarine Miners, Royal Engineers (Volrs.). On the creation of the Territorial Force in 1908, in connection with Lord Haldane's Army Reorganization Scheme, he transferred to that Force, and, on the formation of the Tyne Electrical Engineers, Royal Engineers (T.F.) was posted to this unit, in which he attained the rank of Corporal; he resigned from the Force in 1913 on completing five years' service therein.

He enrolled in the Leeds University Officers' Training Corps on August 5, 1914, and proceeded with the Corps into camp at Seaton Delaval, Northumberland, where he was put through a course of military training. He was given a Commission in the Territorial Force in March, 1915, and posted to the 2/5th Battalion the Northumberland Fusiliers an unattached unit, which for a short time was one of the battalions of the 88th Infantry Brigade of the 63rd (Northumbrian) Division. He was employed on Coast Defence duties with this unit at Walker and Seaton Delaval (Northumberland), and at Hollingside, Co. Durham, until he was sent overseas.

He proceeded to France on July 9th with a draft for the 1/5th Battalion of his Regiment, at the time one of the battalions of the 149th Infantry Brigade of the 50th (Northumbrian) Division. This Division had crossed to France in the middle of April, 1915, and its 149th Infantry Brigade had, within a few days of its arrival at the Front, gone into action at the Battle of St. Julien (April 24 — May 4), where it had behaved splendidly in the crisis of the German Gas Attack. When he joined his new unit, his Division was in the Command of the II Corps, which then lay in the Second Army area, and stationed in the Armentières Sector. His Division was at the time on the right of the II Corps front and made junction on its southern flank with the Canadian Division, which formed the left flank of the III Corps. Immediately to the north of the II Corps, the British line was held by the V Corps: on the front of the latter Corps, the enemy, from time to time, showed considerable activity (Actions of Hooge—July 19 and 30, and Aug. 9); otherwise, there was a period of relative calm during the later days of the summer of 1915. Raids and reconnaissance's were, however, being frequently carried out along the front held by the II Corps. On the evening of August 25, he was directed to carry out a night reconnaissance in the neighbourhood of Houplines, and accordingly led his Platoon out of the trenches into No Man's Land to accomplish the duty assigned to him; whilst he was feeling his way forward the enemy put up flare lights and thus located his command. The Germans then suddenly opened a heavy machine-gun fire on his detachment and he was hit in the abdomen and the right arm. He was conveyed at once to the Military Hospital at Bailleul, where he succumbed to his wounds on the following day. He was 32 years old.

His Battalion Commander wrote:

"By this time, you will have received the sad news of your poor son's death, and I, as O.C. 5th Battalion, tender you my deepest sympathy. You have lost a good son, a man to be proud of, and you have some consolation in the fact that he died nobly.

"Every one, officers and men, admired and respected him since he joined us some six weeks ago, and we all mourn his loss.

"Your boy was doing some important patrol work in front of our trenches when he was shot in the body. He was then some hundred yards away and absolutely refused to return until he had had his own back, but Sergeant Coppick, who saw he was badly wounded, carried him back until met by the stretcher party.

"My doctor told me he was one of the bravest men he had seen."

The Officer Commanding his Depot Battalion wrote:-

"Will you please accept my deepest and most heartfelt sympathy with you and your wife and family in the great loss you have sustained in the death of your dear son.

"I cannot tell you how much I regret his early decease. He was such a fine fellow and a great credit to the Battalion, who all mourn his loss.

"Major Luhrs wrote to me saying he had sent you full particulars and spoke in the very highest terms of your son in every way, whose character and abilities were outstanding.

"From what I saw of him before he left for the front, I knew that he would make an exceptionally good officer, and the various officers who have written me all bore testimony to this effect.

"I trust God will strengthen and comfort you all in your great sorrow, and trust the knowledge of his patriotism and sacrifice for his country will be, in some measure, a solace to your grief. Such men can ill be spared just now.

Again assuring you of my sorrow for you all, and of my appreciation of his worth and the good services he rendered to his country."

For sixteen years he taught in the Sunday School, and for some years commanded the Church Lads' Brigade in connection with St. Gabriel's Church, Heaton, Newcastle-on-Tyne: this Brigade was dissolved in 1910, on the formation of the 19th (Newcastle) Troop of Boy Scouts. He became the first Scoutmaster of the latter Troop, which was a very successful unit, being one of the best in the Newcastle-on-Tyne District. In January, 1914, he was appointed District Scoutmaster for the East Section of Newcastle and held this office until he was commissioned in the Army. In August, 1914, at the outbreak of war, he organized the Special Service work for Scouts at the Boy Scouts' H.Q., Newcastle-on-Tyne, supplying boys to the various Hospitals, Schools, Food Depots, etc.; this Special Service organization comprised some 500 Scouts.

Lord Armstrong, Patron of the 19th (Newcastle) Troop, wrote; *"I must write you a few lines to say how dreadfully sorry I was to receive the announcement from you of the death of your noble son.* *"You will have the consolation of knowing that he died the most honourable of deaths, and that he has cheerfully given his life as a sacrifice for his country, and that you have shared that sacrifice.* *"Your son's record has been a splendid one, and with becoming modesty he was always eager to help on the rising generation, and I was always greatly struck by the great influence unconsciously wielded, and I know that there are many men who still mourn his loss and miss his ever ready assistance.* *May the Lord comfort you in your hour of trial."*

From the Newcastle Illustrated Chronicle of Monday 30 August 1915: *5th Northumberland Fusiliers* *Second Lieutenant W. Winkworth, Heaton (killed).* From the Newcastle Journal of Monday 30 August 1915:

Word has been received by his parents at 22, Simonside Terrace, Heaton that Second Lieutenant W. Winkworth, 5th Northumberland Fusiliers, was killed in action on 25th August. Before joining the army he was in the employ of J. H. Holmes and Sons, Electrical Engineers, and was also district scoutmaster, for the east end, in which work he took an active part.

(This edited article was originally published by the 'Institution of Engineering and Technology, Electrical Engineer WWI and WWII Rolls of Honour, 1924, 1949 and later on the published online at the' lodge temperance' website.

2nd Lieut. FRANK WINFIELD is recorded as being a full Lieutenant on his death commemoration by the Commonwealth War Graves Commission. His death was reported in the 'Manchester Courier and Lancashire general advertiser' on Monday 9th August 1915.
Winfield reportedly died of wounds on 31st Jan 1915, again according to the Commonwealth War Graves Commission, but the WW1 Service Medal Award Rolls, show him as being dying on the 31st May 1915, which sounds very much more likely as the battalion didn't set foot in France until April 1915. He is buried in Roeselare Cemetery, Belgium. I have been in contact with the Commonwealth War Graves Commission in regards to correcting the error in their records.

2nd Lieut. OSCAR WILLIS was the son of John Miles Willis, a colliery worker, and Elizabeth Willis of Nether Langwith, Mansfield, Nottinghamshire. He was killed in the Second Battle of Ypres, on June 20th 1916, whilst attacking Mount Sorrel. He is buried in La Laiterie Cemetery, Heuvelland, Belgium.
From the Yorkshire Post and Leeds Intelligencer dated Tuesday 27th June 1916.

Sec-Lieut. Oscar Willis 2/5 Northumberland Fusiliers of Sheffield, has been killed in action by the explosion of a shell. Prior to the war he was for ten years associated with Edgar Allen and Co, steel merchant, Tinsley. When war broke out he enlisted in the Royal Warwickshire's (Birmingham City Battalion), from which he was gazetted to the Northumberlands. He was a native of Longwith but spent his early years in Lincoln.

From the Lincolnshire Post, dated Tuesday 27th June 1916.
Lincoln Lieutenant Killed.
An officer of great promise.
The death in action is reported of Second Lieutenant Oscar Willis 82, Southgrove Road, Sheffield, who was in the Northumberland Fusiliers. He was killed in action on the 20th inst. by a piece of shrapnel. Death was instantaneous. The late Lieutenant Willis who was 26 years old, was the son of the late J.M. Willis of Lincoln, and a native of Langwith in Derbyshire. He spent his early life in Lincoln and later went to Sheffield where he was in the employment of Messrs Edgar Allen and Company, Tinsley.

On the outbreak of war, Lieutenant Willis, who has two brothers at the front – enlisted in to the Royal Warwickshires (Birmingham City Battalion) from which he obtained a commission in the Northumberland Fusiliers.

From the late Lieutenants commanding officer, his brother received the following letter:- "It is with the greatest sorrow and regret that I have to inform you that your brother Second-Lieutenant O.Willis, of the 5th Northumberland Fusiliers, was killed by a shell early this morning. Though he had only been a comparatively short time in the battalion he had during that time, made himself thoroughly liked and respected by everyone, and n-one regrets his death more than I do. Both I and his Company Commander regarded him as a very promising officer and one who, had he been spared, would have gone far and done well. I am assured his death was absolutely instantaneous and it is some slight gratification to think he suffered none of the pain which, unfortunately too often is suffered by the wounds of this war."

Lincolnshire Chronicle Saturday 1st July 1916.
Old technical school boy killed.
Lincolnians heard with regret the death in action of a former Lincoln Municipal Technical
School student, in the person of Lt. Oscar Willis who was killed by a piece of shrapnel on June 20th. Death being instantaneous.
Son of the late J.M Willis of Lincoln, deceased spent the earlier part of his life in Lincoln and then went to Sheffield where he entered the employment of Messrs Edgar Allen and Company, Tinsley. There he held an important position in the steelworks for ten years.
Lieut. Willis enlisted in to the Royal Warwickshires (Birmingham City Battalion) at the beginning of the war and later obtained a commission in the Northumberland Fusiliers. The following letter has been received by his brother from Lieut. Willis commanding officer: "It is with the greatest sorrow and regret that I have to inform you that your brother Second-Lieutenant O.Willis, of the 5th Northumberland Fusiliers, was killed by a shell early this morning. Though he had only been a comparatively short time in the battalion he had during that time, made himself thoroughly liked and respected by everyone, and n-one regrets his death more than I do. Both I and his Company Commander regarded him as a very promising officer and one who, had he been spared, would have gone far and done well. I am assured his death

was absolutely instantaneous and it is some slight gratification to think he suffered none of the pain which, unfortunately too often is suffered by the wounds of this war."

Lieut. Willis two brothers are also serving in the colours. Arthur Willis is a dispatch rider attached to the headquarters staff of the Garrison Artillery and Pte. Cyril Willis is serving in France with the 11th Sherwood Foresters. He has also served at the Dardanelles where he was one of the 30 survivors of his battalions 1,200.

Derbyshire Courier Tuesday 4th July 1916.
LANGWITH LIEUTENANT KILLED.

News has reached his brother, Frank Willis of the Jug and Glass Inn., Langwith, that Second Lieutenant Oscar Willis has been killed by a shell in France. He enlisted when war broke out. He lived in Sheffield and was for ten years in the steel department at Edgar Allen and Co, Tinsley. He was a native of Langwith.

2nd Lieut. JOHN HADDOW YOUNG, a graduate of Glasgow University, was the son of John and Frances Young of 119 Sydney Street, Glasgow. He had originally enlisted in to the 4th Bn. Northumberland Fusiliers, was but later promoted to 2nd Lieut. and transferred to the 5th Battalion.

John died on 9 Jun 1918 and is buried at Melun North Cemetery, France

Here are the traceable men from Walker who received either the Military Cross, Military Medal or the Distinguished Conduct Medal.

Private **THOMAS ATKINSON**   2596   **Military Medal**

Thomas served with the 1st/5th Bn., Northumberland Fusiliers, who died age 23 on 15 November 1916.

Son of Matthew and Margaret Ann Atkinson, of 73, Lamb St., Walker, Newcastle-on-Tyne.

Remembered with honour THIEPVAL MEMORIAL France.

Thomas Atkinson was the son of a Shipyard 'Holder up' and was one of seven children, though three had not survived past infancy.

Thomas and his brother Edward both worked as miners before the outbreak of war. Thomas entered the theatre of combat on 20th April 1915 when the 1/5th Northumberland Fusiliers landed in France. He was awarded the Victory, British and 1915 Star medals - as well as the Military Medal. It appears that Thomas's war records did not survive the German bombings of WW2, so it is not known when he was awarded the Military Medal, or what for.

November 1916: The first Battle of the Somme was drawing to a close, having raged since the 1st July and much fighting in heavy rain in recent weeks had left the ground deep in mud ...."*Snag Trench was full of mud and water with bodies sticking out all along. In fact it was no exaggeration when I say that in our part one had to tread from body to body to get past. Dead from all regiments were there, including our Divisions, and hands, arms and legs were sticking out of parados and parapet where the dead had been hastily buried.*" *A pen picture which may well make future generations shudder!* Excerpt from the Fiftieth Division 1914-1919 by Everard Wyrall.

Thomas would most likely have been killed during the attack on Gird Trench and Hook Sap, which took place between the 13th and 19th November 1916. Orders were given at 6.30pm on the 13th that the attack on the enemy would be carried out by the 5th Northumberland Fusiliers and the 7th Northumberland Fusiliers in support.

Zero hour was to be 6.45pm on the 14th. The objective of the 5th Northumberland Fusiliers was to take Gird Trench from the right of the Division boundary near to the junction with Hook Sap, the 7th Northumberland Fusiliers were to capture Hook Sap and Gird Trench, also Blind Trench.

Heavy rain caused havoc on the night of the 13th and in places men were up to their waist in water, heavy mud that clung onto their boots in masses and made mobility difficult. The battle commenced and the 'Fighting Fifth' were showered in a hail of bullets as they made their way in waves towards their objective. Casualties littered the ground as well as in the captures trench. The fighting continued and objectives were gained though not without many losses of men, both in fatalities and casualties.

Another raid was prepared for the 15th and late on the evening of the 14th a communications trench was dug and three bombing parties went out on raids; verey lights lit their positions and rifle fire forced them to return.

The enemy machine gun fire on the morning of the 15th was exceedingly heavy and Snag Trench and Snag support were very much damaged.

When during this battle, Thomas was injured is not recorded, but it is likely he received his Military Medal posthumously for his actions during this period of heavy fighting.

2nd Lieut. MITCHELL MILLER BRODIE   Military Cross.

Mitchell Brodie was the third son of Alexander and Hannah Brodie of 679 Welbeck Road, Walker. Mitchell Brodie, born Hebburn, was a Clerk in the nearby shipyard offices.

His father had moved down from Scotland to find work in the expanding shipyards of the Tyne, but also found love with North Shields girl Hannah Angus, the daughter of a shoemaker, whom he married in 1879. Mitchell was one of four sons William, Alexander, Mitchell and Robert.

Alexander, who was older than Mitchell by two years, had died in 1894 when he was nine years old.

A Lieut. In the 12th Bn. Northumberland Fusiliers, Mitchell was awarded the Military Cross, some time prior to July 1917, though I am unable to find the specific action in which it was earned.

He died aged 29, on 14th July 1917 as a result of injuries sustained in conflict, at a Military hospital in Rouen, France, and is buried at St Sever Cemetery, Rouen. Six days after his passing his father Alexander died, aged 66, at home. Very likely his death was attributed to hearing the devastating news of his sons death.

Lt/QM RICHARD BROCKETT BROWN   386022
MM MID.

Richard was born in 1882 and served with the 1st Northumbrian Divisional Field Ambulance. He was awarded the Territorial Force efficiency medal on 1st Jul 1912, when he was a Staff Sergeant. He lived with his family at 25 Byker Terrace, Walker – an extensive nine roomed property. His father, John Brown, owned a pharmacy at No's 2/4 Byker Terrace, where they both worked as Chemist's. Richard continued working at the pharmacy after the war. He married Dorothy Oubridge in 1919 and had three children.

Private   JAMES ELLIOTT   34069/26548
Military Medal.

James Elliott, born 18 April 1898 was a junior clerk by occupation, attested on 25 May 1916 and was called up to serve with the Durham Light Infantry on 3rd Mar 1917. He was the son of James and Sarah Elliott – his father a former 'brass finisher' was now working as an insurance agent. Along with his five siblings the family lived at 1420 Walker Road. James was transferred to the Yorkshire Regiment in Oct 1917 and was admitted to hospital on two occasions in 1918 suffering from Trench feet. He was de-mobilised on 10 Oct 1919 and presented with his Military Medal on 14 Feb 1921 by the Lord Mayor of Newcastle.

James, now a 24 year old Customs & Excise clerk, married Jemima Muir (a shop assistant) of 830 Walker Road, St Anthony's on 10 Jun 1922 and died aged 73 in March 1972.

I have unfortunately been unable to trace the action that led to James being awarded the Military Cross.

Private JOHN HOYLE   19716   Military Medal

Private Hoyle of the 10th Bn. Northumberland Fusiliers
Son of Mr and Mrs Hoyle of 6 Back Welsh Row, Walker and husband of Mrs Hoyle, of 2 Cambrain Row, Walker.
London Gazette 23 August 1916.

John Hoyle, who was born at Newcastle-on-Tyne and enlisted at Wallsend-on-Tyne, where pre-war he won a reputation as a boxer. He was killed in action in a trench raid at Ploegsteert Wood on the night of 30-31 August 1916, while serving in the 10th Battalion, Northumberland Fusiliers. The official report of this engagement bears testimony to his bravery, the following posthumous recommendation being penned by his C.O., Lieutenant-Colonel Manners:

'The following N.C.Os and men also showed great gallantry and devotion to duty both in the assault and in bringing in wounded afterwards ...

19716 Private Hoyle, J.: bayoneted a sentry and bombed enemy from parapet. When forced to retire assisted his officer in organising a second attack in which he was wounded. Was last man to leave the trench and was killed on the way back ...'

The attack had been launched in the wake of a British artillery bombardment and gas attack, but only one of our patrols, 'C' Company with Hoyle, penetrated the German lines. Not forgetting their stark pre-operational order to 'kill as many Germans as possible', 'C' Company used its bombs to good effect, 'causing many casualties.'

The Battalion's war diary also reveals that Hoyle had earlier been wounded in the Franvillers sector on 28 January 1916, again while serving in 'C' Company ('Slightly, at duty').

His M.M. had been awarded for earlier gallantry at "Scott's Redoubt" on the Somme between 6-10 July 1916 and he was presented with the riband of the decoration by Major-General Babington at Franvillers on 22nd of the same month.

Hoyle was interred in the London Rifle Brigade Cemetery, Ploegsteert, Belgium.

Private JOSEPH BRUNTON MCNALLY.   110319
Military Medal.

Son of James and Elizabeth McNally of 82 Fisher Street, Low Walker. Joseph married his sweetheart Jane Connon in the early part of 1915, and their first child was born three years later, in 1918. Joe joined the 1/5th Northumberland Fusiliers at the outbreak of war and was later transferred to the 149th Brigade Machine Gun Company which was formed on the 6th February 1916.

The London Gazette published the award of a Military Medal to Pte 23981 J McNally on 21 October 1918. No citation was published.

Joseph was transferred to the Army "Z" reserve on 11 March 1919.

Joe McNally served in the Army with distinction throughout the First World War and unlike many other unfortunate men, managed to see the war through after taking part in many quite slaughterous battles such as the Somme, Ypres, Aisne, Passchendaele, Arras etc. In 1915 he was injured while taking part in the battle of St Julien.

Apparently he was given field punishments number one (being tied to a wheel for up to two hours a day) to deter his apparent *'illegal'* nocturnal raids into German trenches in which he would take 're-possession' of British goods.

He sounds one very brave young man!

On return to Blighty, Joe worked as a Riveter in the shipyards before passing away at the age of 64 in 1952.

Private RICHARD ROBBIE   20008   Military Medal.

Richard was born on 1st September 1895 at 31, Swan Street, Walker, Newcastle upon Tyne and christened at Christ Church, Walker, on 22nd September of the same year. In 1901 he was living with his family at 8, Pearson St, Walker and by 1911, when Richard was 15 years old and working as an apprentice engineer, the family had moved to 65, Church Street – a comfortable 5 roomed property.

Richard married Elizabeth Redhead on 31st December 1915 and they went on to have three children Nora, Richard and Ethel.

Richard had been with the R.A.M.C territorial force since 1911 and therefore was called up at the outbreak of war. In 1923 Richard joined the Royal Air Force as a hospital orderly, but was discharged in 1925 on compassionate grounds.

A member of Walker Presbyterian Chapel, Richard was awarded his Military Medal, sometime prior to mid-1917. Almost certainly for bringing in wounded men, whilst under fire from the enemy.

Company Serjeant Major JOSEPH MYERS ROBSON
Distinguished Conduct Medal. Service Number 303015, 10th
Bn., West Yorkshire Regiment (Prince of Wales's Own) Joseph
Robson died on 20 October 1918 aged 31.
He was the son of Thomas Robson, of Walker, Newcastle-on-
Tyne and husband of Rose Robson, of 91, Salisbury St., Blyth.
Joseph Robson was born in 1887 to Thomas and Mary Ann
Robson. He spent his childhood living at 9 Station Road,
Walker. He was one of ten surviving children, 4 girls and 6
boys. Two other siblings had died in infancy. His elder
brothers all worked in the shipyards like their father. On
leaving school Joseph got himself a job as an 'Office Boy' -
possibly at the ship yard offices, but by the 1911 census, which
found the family now living at 99, Middle Street, Walker;
Joseph was now working as a 'Plater' in the shipyards - a
similar trade to that of all his male siblings.
Citation as to why Joseph M Robson was awarded the
Distinguished Conduct Medal:
30315 CSM JM Robson (Blyth)
For conspicuous gallantry and devotion to duty, when troops on the
flank of his company failed to come forward, he quickly re-organised
the men on the flank of the company, took forward a party of 10 men,
attacked the enemy on the flank, drove him back 200 yards and
secured his own position. 28/03/18

Corporal JOHN TURNBULL   463196
        Military Medal
Cpl Turnbull, of the 50th (Northumbrian) Signal Coy., Royal
Engineers, died age 35 on 12 April 1918. The son of Robert and
Sarah Turnbull, of Walker Rd., Walker, Newcastle-on-Tyne.
John, a former volunteer with the Northumberland Fusiliers
Territorial's, signed up for Military service on the 10th August
1914 at Walker Drill Hall; aged 31 years and nine months. He
was up until that point employed as a labourer at Armstrong
Whitworth Shipyards and residing at 1640 Walker Road. On
the 1911 census he had been living further down the same

road with his parents and siblings, at number 1570.

Here is John's service record in brief: On 10th August 1914 John signed up to defend his King and country for the duration of the war. His medical notes describe him as being 5 feet 7 inches tall, with a fully expanded chest of 35 inches and with an expansion range of 2 inches. His eyesight is good as is his physical development.

Service Record:

3/9/15 It is noted he is in trouble for on the 2/9/15 *'causing a disturbance in his billet from 9 till 10pm.'* Awarded 2 day (illegible - but likely stoppage of pay.) *This is the only incident in an otherwise unblemished career.*

31/3/16 Appointed Lance Corporal, unpaid as of 24/3/16

9/7/16 Granted 'proficient' (1/-) rate of Engineers pay as a Telegraphist, Field Line.

2/8/16 Granted the 'skilled' 1/4 rate of Pay as a Telegraphist, Field Line.

8/9/16 Appointed Lance Corporal (paid.) -also 1699 Smith promoted.

5/1/16 Leave to UK granted from 26/12/16 to 5/1/17

No date - in pencil. Awarded Military Medal - very faint, looks like 7/9/16

16/6/16 Appointed to 2nd Corporal (paid) also 2nd Corporal White

27/10/17 Admitted to hospital on 23/10/17 and then rejoined unit. Was then sent on leave to UK 4/1/18 to 18/1/18

12/4/18 KILLED IN ACTION

Personal items found upon his person were sent back to his family in Walker via the Royal Engineers Record Office at Chatham in Kent. His father signed Army Form b. 104-126 and returned it to the officer in charge, stating that he had received the items listed, namely: 2 letters, 2 pieces of medal ribbon, 2 pocket note books, miscellaneous papers and 3 photo's.

Today John is remembered with honour on the Ploegsteert Memorial, Belgium.

Young man sporting temple wound.

A picture for the wives at home.

The men of the 'Fighting Fifth' Battalion, who I can find recorded as living in Walker at the time of their death.

The address given is that of the next of kin – sometimes the spouse will have a different surname; this is because the wife had re-married after her husbands' death and prior to the list being compiled by the war office. Casualties included are from 4th August 1914 until 11th November 1918. Also, those who died of wounds or illness directly attributed to the war, up until 25th March 1921. This is so that men involved in the battlefield clearances and those who later died as a result of injuries inflicted during the war, are also accounted for.

Private JAMES BAIN 2539, who died age 20 on 02 May 1915 Son of James and Agnes Bain, of 15, Pottery Bank, St. Anthony's, Newcastle-on-Tyne. Remembered with honour PERTH CEMETERY (CHINA WALL) Belgium.

Private DAVID BRUCE 3089/478071, 2/5th Bn. Northumberland Fusiliers, who died aged 43 on 7th Apr 1919, of 44 Fisher Street, Low Walker. Remembered with honour WALKER (CHRIST CHURCH) CHURCHYARD, Newcastle upon Tyne.

Private SAMUEL JOBLING CRAIG 2410004, 1st/5th Bn. Northumberland Fusiliers, who died age 21 on 14 Nov 1916. Son of the late John and Margaret Craig, of 631, Welbeck Rd., Walker, Newcastle-on-Tyne. Remembered with honour THIEPVAL MEMORIAL, France.

Private WILLIAM COATES 2580, 1st/5th Bn. Northumberland Fusiliers, who died age 33 on 27 April 1915. Son of John and Isabella Coates, of Raskelf, Yorks. Husband of Elizabeth Ann Rankin (formerly Coates), of 1619, Walker Rd., Walker, Newcastle-on-Tyne. Remembered with honour YPRES (MENIN GATE) MEMORIAL, Belgium.

Private HENRY DEARDEN 2563, 1st/5th Bn. Northumberland Fusiliers, who died aged 19 on 29 Jul 1916. Native of Walker. Son of the late William and Hannah Dearden; husband of Annie Dearden, of 27, Lamb St., Walker, Newcastle-on-Tyne. Remembered with honour on the ST. QUENTIN CABARET MILITARY CEMETERY, France.

Private D. T. C DODDS 2537, 1st/5th Bn. Northumberland Fusiliers, who died age 32 on 02 May 1915. Husband of Edith Stewart (formerly Dodds), of 44, Byker St., Walker, Newcastle-on-Tyne. Remembered with honour BAILLEUL COMMUNAL CEMETERY EXTENSION (NORD) France.

Lance Corporal T DUNN 2200, 1st/5th Bn. Northumberland Fusiliers, who died age 28 on 22 April 1916. Son of Martha Dunn, of 1570, Walker Rd., Walker, Newcastle-on-Tyne, and the late Patrick Dunn. Remembered with honour LA LAITERIE MILITARY CEMETERY, Belgium.

Private JOHN ELLIOTT 3109, 1st/5th Bn. Northumberland Fusiliers who died aged 45 on 30 Apr 1916. Son of John and Hannah Elliott, Walker, and husband of Allison Elliott, of 1569 Walker Road, Newcastle upon Tyne. Remembered with honour BOULOGNE EASTERN CEMETERY, France.

Private J FERGUSON 2521, 1st/5th Bn, Northumberland Fusiliers, who died age 24 on 28 May 1915. Son of John Ferguson, of 17, Station Rd., Walker, Newcastle-on-Tyne, and the late Eliza Ferguson. Remembered with honour BAILLEUL COMMUNAL CEMETERY EXTENSION (NORD) France.

Corporal WILLIAM GRAY 2926, 1st/5th Bn.
Northumberland Fusiliers, who died age 29 on 27 May 1916.
Son of Ellen Gray, of 1565, Walker Rd., Newcastle-on-Tyne,
and the late John Gray. Remembered with honour
BAILLEUL COMMUNAL CEMETERY EXTENSION
(NORD) France.

Lance Corporal L GOODWIN 5/692, 5th Bn.
Northumberland Fusiliers, who died age 28 on 31 December
1915. Son of John and Sarah Goodwin; husband of Margaret
Goodwin of 16, Mitchell St., Walker-on-Tyne. Remembered
with honour at RAILWAY DUGOUTS BURIAL GROUND,
Belgium.

Private SAMUEL JOSEPH GORMAN 240688, 1st/5th Bn.
Northumberland Fusiliers, who died age 26 on 27 October
1917. Husband of Mary Gorman, of 25, Rhodes St., Walker,
Newcastle-on-Tyne. Remembered with honour on the TYNE
COT MEMORIAL, Belgium.

L/Cpl THOMAS BELL HARDY 1363 1/5th Bn.
Northumberland Fusiliers, who died aged 22 on 2 May 1916.
Son of Mary Hardy of 19 Lamb Street, Walker, Newcastle-
on-Tyne. Remembered with honour on the YPRES (MENIN
GATE) MEMORIAL, Belgium.

Private ROBERT HELLENS 1284, 1st/5th Bn.
Northumberland Fusiliers, who died on 24 May 1915.
Husband of Mary Hellens, of 28, River View, Low Walker,
Newcastle-on-Tyne. Remembered with honour on the
YPRES (MENIN GATE) MEMORIAL, Belgium.

Private ROBERT HENDERSON 1755, 1st/5th Bn. Northumberland Fusiliers who died aged 19 on 28 Apr 1915. Son of Charles and Mary Henderson, Husband of Selina Robinson (formerly Henderson) 6, Birch Terrace, Walker Estate. Newcastle upon Tyne. Remembered with honour on the YPRES (MENIN GATE) MEMORIAL, Belgium.

Private WILLIAM HERON 2565, 1st/5th Bn. Northumberland Fusiliers, who died age 23 on 27 April 1915. Son of John and Mary Jane Heron, of 31, Lamb St., Walker, Newcastle-on-Tyne. Remembered with honour on the YPRES (MENIN GATE) MEMORIAL, Belgium.

Private SAMUEL A HOOD 240707 1/5th Bn. Northumberland Fusiliers, who died age 27 on15 Sept 1916. Husband of Mrs. Hood of 52, Church Street, Walker. Newcastle-on-Tyne. Remembered with honour DELVILLE WOOD CEMETERY, LONGUEVAL, France.

Lance Corporal W LOGAN 240004, 1st/5th Bn. Northumberland Fusilier, Son of Elizabeth Logan, of 166, Church St., Walker, Newcastle-on-Tyne, and the late Walter Logan. Remembered with honour PONT-DU-HEM MILITARY CEMETERY, LA GORGUE, France.

Corporal W LONGWORTH 1764, 1st/5th Bn. Northumberland Fusiliers, who died age 22 on 15 November 1916. Son of W. and Elinor Longworth, of 10, Gibb St., St. Peter's, Newcastle-on-Tyne. Remembered with honour DERNANCOURT COMMUNAL CEMETERY EXTENSION, France.

Private JAMES WALTON LOUGH 2570, 1st/5th Bn, Northumberland Fusiliers, who died age 19 on 27 May 1915. Son of Isabella Scullion (formerly Lough), of 78, Bath St., Walker, Newcastle-on-Tyne, and the late John L. Lough. Remembered with honour HAZEBROUCK COMMUNAL CEMETERY, France.

Private THOMAS LOUGH 240348, 1st/5th Bn, Northumberland Fusiliers, who died age 23 on 12 April 1918. Son of Mrs. Isabella Scullion (formerly Lough), of 78, Bath St., Walker, Newcastle-on-Tyne, and the late John L. Lough. Remembered with honour PLOEGSTEERT MEMORIAL, Belgium.

Private JOHN LOWERY 240708, 1st/5th Bn. Northumberland Fusiliers, who died age 19 on 14 November 1916. Son of Isaac and Jessie Lowery, of 11, Cambrian Row, Walker, Newcastle-on-Tyne. Remembered with honour THIEPVAL MEMORIAL, France.

Private ROBERT LOWES 36113, 1st/5th Bn. King's Own Yorkshire Light Infantry, who died age 19 on 06 January 1918. Son of John William and Margaret Lowes, of 100, Byker St, Walker, Newcastle-on-Tyne. Remembered with honour TYNE COT MEMORIAL, Belgium.

Private DAVID MAIR 2223, 1st/5th Bn. Northumberland Fusiliers, who died age 38 on 31 January 1916. Son of David and Charlotte Mair; husband of Olive B. B. Mair, of 48, Byker Rd., Walker, Newcastle-on-Tyne. Remembered with honour LIJSSENTHOEK MILITARY CEMETERY, Belgium.

Private ANDREW MAUGHAN 3604, 1st/5th Bn. Northumberland Fusiliers, who died age 25 on 04 April 1916. Son of Annie Maughan, of 23, Mitchell St., Walker, Newcastle-on-Tyne, and the late Samuel Maughan; husband of Sarah Anna Maughan, of 156, Dunn Terrace, Byker, Newcastle-on-Tyne. Remembered with honour YPRES (MENIN GATE) MEMORIAL, Belgium

Private ARCHIBALD MAUGHAN 5/1351 1st/5th Bn. Northumberland Fusiliers, who died age 23 on 11 March 1916. Son of Annie Maughan, of 23, Mitchell St., Walker, Newcastle-on-Tyne, and the late Samuel Maughan. Remembered with honour RAILWAY DUGOUTS BURIAL GROUND (TRANSPORT FARM) Belgium.

Private JOE MAUGHAN 5/2013 1/5th Bn. Northumberland Fusiliers, who died aged age 20 on 29 Jan 1916. Son of Mr and Mrs Joseph Maughan of 8 Stephendale Terrace, Newcastle-on-Tyne. Remembered with honour RAILWAY DUGOUTS BURIAL GROUND (TRANSPORT FARM) Belgium.

Private WILLIAM MAUGHAN 2263, 1st/5th Bn. Northumberland Fusiliers, who died age 27 on 25 May 1916. Son of the late Samuel and Annie Maughan, of Walker; husband of Margaret Maughan, of 60, Mitchell Buildings, Low Walker, Newcastle-on-Tyne. Remembered with honour LA LAITERIE MILITARY CEMETERY. Belgium.

Sergeant ARTHUR MELLISH Serjeant 240192, 2nd/5th Bn. Northumberland Fusiliers, who died age 42 on 26 February 1918. Husband of Ellen Mellish, of 26, Hexham Avenue, Walker. Newcastle-on-Tyne. Remembered with honour WALKER (CHRIST CHURCH) CHURCHYARD, England.

Lance Corporal H MOSS 2546, 5th Bn. Northumberland Fusiliers who died age 21 on 26 May 1915. Son of Herbert Henry and Sarah Moss, of Walker Rd., Walker, Newcastle-on-Tyne. Native of Leicester. Remembered with honour BOULOGNE EASTERN CEMETERY, France.

Private MARTIN MURRAY 1898 1/5th Bn. Northumberland Fusiliers, who died age 19 on 18 June 1915. Of 150, Byker Street, Walker. Newcastle-on-Tyne. Remembered with honour YPRES (MENIN GATE) MEMORIAL, Belgium.

Private FRANCIS ARTHUR NAPIER 1269, 5th Bn. Northumberland Fusiliers, who died age 20 on 25 July 1915. Son of Mary and the late Pte. Arthur Napier (6th Bn. Northumberland Fusiliers), of 12, Byker St., Walker, Newcastle-on-Tyne. Remembered with honour BOULOGNE EASTERN CEMETERY, France.

Private CORNELIUS NOBLE 1856, 1st/5th Bn. Northumberland Fusiliers, who died age 19 on 24 May 1915. Son of Mrs. Alice Noble, of 310, Church St., Walker, Newcastle-on-Tyne. Remembered with honour YPRES (MENIN GATE) MEMORIAL, Belgium.

Private SAMUEL VEROW OLIVER 5/1590, 5th Bn. Northumberland Fusiliers, who died age 21 on 09 March 1916. Son of Ralph and Sarah Oliver, of 1577, Walker Rd., Walker, Newcastle-on-Tyne. Remembered with honour RAILWAY DUGOUTS BURIAL GROUND, Belgium.

Private JOHN WILLIAM PURVIS 241893 1/5th Bn. Northumberland Fusiliers, who died age 30 on 14 Nov 1916 (Lived Mitchell Street.) Son of the late Alexander and Isabella Purvis, of 7, Percy Place, Newcastle-on-Tyne; husband of Lilian Purvis, of 7, Percy Place, Newcastle-on-Tyne. Remembered with honour THIEPVAL MEMORIAL, Somme, France. (Previously injured May 1915 and reported in the Newcastle Chronicle.)

Private BENJAMIN 'THOMAS' RATCLIFFE 2091, 1st/5th Bn, Northumberland Fusiliers, who died age 21 on 11 April 1916. Son of John and Rachel Ratcliffe, of 1644, Walker Rd., Walker, Newcastle-on-Tyne. Remembered with honour LA LAITERIE MILITARY CEMETERY, Belgium.

Serjeant CHARLES STODDART 166, 1st/5th Bn. Northumberland Fusiliers, who died age 33 on 24 May 1915. Husband of Florence Stoddart, of 1327, Walker Rd., St. Anthony's, Newcastle-on-Tyne. Remembered with honour YPRES (MENIN GATE) MEMORIAL, Belgium.

Private MICHAEL CHAPMAN STOKER 2084, 1st/5th Bn, Northumberland Fusiliers, who died age 19 on 28 April 1915. Son of Frederick J. Stoker, of 12, Mitchell St., Walker, Newcastle-on-Tyne. Remembered with honour HAZEBROUCK COMMUNAL CEMETERY, France.

Private FRANCIS PATRICK WARD 2558, 1st/5th Bn. Northumberland Fusiliers, who died age 19 on 08 January 1916. Son of Hugh and Mary Ann Ward, of 6, Byker St., Walker, Newcastle-on-Tyne. Remembered with honour LIJSSENTHOEK MILITARY CEMETERY, Belgium.

Private JOHN EDWARD WYMER 2143 1st/5th Bn. Northumberland Fusiliers, who died age 25 on 24 May 1915. Husband of Mrs. Wymer, of 20 Rochester Street, Walker. Newcastle-on-Tyne. Remembered with honour YPRES (MENIN GATE) MEMORIAL, Belgium.

In Memory of the men, who were either born, or lived in Walker and joined Battalion's other than the locally raised 5th Bn. Northumberland Fusiliers; and who met their death in the Great War.

Private JOHN W. ANDREWS G/52209, 23rd Bn, Middlesex Regiment, who died age 22 on 22 September 1917.Son of Mr. and Mrs. Andrews, of 14, Pearson St., Walker; husband of Dorothy Jane Andrews, of 2, Pearson St, Walker, Newcastle-on-Tyne. Remembered with honour TYNE COT MEMORIAL, Belgium.

Private GEORGE H ANDREWS 4209, 2nd Bn. Northumberland Fusiliers, who died aged 22 on 16 Apr 1915. Remembered with honour LA LAITERIE MILITARY CEMETERY, Belgium.

Private JOHN T ANDERSON 97841, 2nd Bn. Sherwood Foresters, who died 16 Jul 1918. Son of Henry and Frances Anderson, of 4, Cambrian Row, Walker, Newcastle-on-Tyne. Remembered with honour COLOGNE SOUTHERN CEMETERY, Germany.
Sarjeant ANDREW ANGUS 16/194, 16th Bn. Northumberland Fusiliers, who died 20 Feb 1916. Remembered with honour AVELUY COMMUNAL CEMETERY EXTENSION, France.

Private ALEXANDER ARNOTT 281742, 10/11th Bn. Highland Light Infantry, who died aged 31on 26 Aug 1917. Son of the late Peter and Charlotte Arnott. Remembered with honour ETAPLES MILITARY CEMETERY, France.

Private JOHN BARNES 18/796, 18th Bn Northumberland Fusiliers, who died aged 31on 30 May 1917. Husband of Ethel Barnes, of 21, Grosvenor Place, Jesmond, Newcastle-on-Tyne. Remembered with honour MINDEL TRENCH BRITISH CEMETERY, ST. LAURENT-BLAGNY, France.

Private GEORGE M BARTON 19112, 13th Bn Durham Light Infantry, who died 5 Aug 1916. Remembered with honour THIEPVAL MEMORIAL, France.

Private ROBERT BARTON 44476, North Staffordshire Regiment, who died age 27 on 11 Sept 1918. Remembered with honour PLOEGSTEERT MEMORIAL Belgium.

Lance Sarjeant JOHN BECK 2103, 1/6th Bn. Northumberland Fusiliers, who died aged 25 on 26 Apr 1915. Late husband of Mary McLoughlin (formerly Beck), of 48, Oak St., Teams, Gateshead. It appears Mary re-married in early 1917. Remembered with honour YPRES (MENIN GATE MEMORIAL) Belgium.

Private THOMAS BECK 28/253, 13th Bn. Northumberland Fusiliers, who died on 18 Oct 1916. Remembered with honour VERMELLES BRITISH CEMETERY, France.

Private WILLIAM BELL 291883, 1/7th Bn. Northumberland Fusiliers, who died age 19 on 17 Apr 1917. Son of the late Thomas and Jane Ann Bell. Remembered with honour ARRAS MEMORIAL, France.

L/Cpl LANCELOT BOX 24183 1st Bn, Northumberland Fusiliers, who died aged 19 on 19 Feb 1918. Son of John and Bertha Box, of 46, Sunningdale Avenue, Walker, Newcastle-on-Tyne. Who is remembered with honour at Bucquoy Road cemetery, France.

Private JOHN S. BIRRS M2/076036, 7th Div. Mechanical Transport Coy. Royal Army Service Corps, who died aged 38 on 14 Oct 1918. Son of John and the late Frances Jane Birss, of Wallsend-on-Tyne. Remembered with honour MONTECCHIO PRECALCINCO COMMUNAL CEMETERY EXTENTION, Italy.

Private BENJAMIN BLAKE T/4/124307, 61st Div. Supply Col. Royal Army Service Corps, who died age 49 on 1 Jun1917. Husband of Jane Blake, of 69, Cannon St., Elswick, Newcastle-on-Tyne. Formerly of 1 Byker Street, Walker. Newcastle upon Tyne. Remembered with honour DAINVILLE COMMUNAL CEMETERY, France.

Private JOHN R. BRADFORD 39162, 2nd Bn. Kings Own Yorkshire Light Infantry, who died aged 19 on 13th Apr 1918. Son of John and Margaret Bradford of 44 White Street, Walker, Newcastle upon Tyne. Remembered with honour WALKER, CHRIST CHURCH CHURCHYARD. Walker, Newcastle upon Tyne.

Private FRANCIS HENRY BRADLEY 16404, 11th Bn. East Yorkshire Regiment, who died age 31on 29 September 1918. Son of Dominic and Catherine Bradley, of Walker; husband of Sarah Jane Bradley (nee Harvey), of 296, Church St., Walker, Newcastle-on-Tyne. Remembered with honour PONT-D'ACHELLES MILITARY CEMETERY. France.

Private JOHN BRADLEY 11080, 9th Bn. Prince of Wales Own (West Yorkshire Regiment,) who died aged 31 on 22 Aug 1915. Son of Dominic and Catherine Bradley, of 30 Mitchell Street Walker. Remembered with honour HELLES MEMORIAL Gallipoli, Turkey.

Private ARTHUR J BRANNAN 10884, 11th Bn. Northumberland Fusiliers, who died aged 31 on 7 Jul 1916. Of 237 Church St Walker Newcastle-on -Tyne. Remembered with honour THIEPVAL MEMORIAL, France.

Private THOMAS BRIGGS 1829, 1/8th Northumberland Fusiliers, who died 26 Apr 1915. Remembered with honour MENIN GATE (YPRES) Belgium.

Lance Corporal RICHARD BRODERICK 16/604, 8th Bn. Northumberland Fusiliers, who died aged 28 on 16 Aug 1917. Son of John and Johannah Broderick, of 182A, Kirk St., South Byker, Newcastle-on-Tyne. Remembered with honour TYNE COT MEMORIAL, Belgium.

Private JAMES BROOKS 15342, 8th Bn. Northumberland Fusiliers, who died 26 Sept 1916. Remembered with honour THIEPVAL MEMORIAL, France.

Private THOMAS G. BROWN 8003, 1/6th Bn. Northumberland Fusiliers, who died on 15 Sept 1916. Remembered with honour DANTZIG ALLEY CEMETERY, France.

Private ROBERT BRYANTON 204279, 15th Bn. Durham Light Infantry, who died aged 21on 23 Oct 1917. Remembered with honour LIJSSENTHOEK MILITARY CEMETERY, Belgium.

Pte MONTGOMERY BRYDEN 16406, 6th Bn. East Yorkshire Regiment, who died on 26 Sept 1916. Husband of Annie Brydon of 49, Grasmere Avenue, Walker Estate, Walker, Newcastle-on-Tyne. Remembered with honour POZIERS BRITISH CEMETERY, France.
Private ROBERT BURGOYNE 30/105, Northumberland Fusiliers, Tyneside Irish, who died aged 29 on 14 Mar 1917. Son and stepson of Jane and James Burgoyne, of North Shields (born Low Walker.) Remembered with honour FABOURG DE'AMIENS CEMETERY, France.

Sarjeant WILLIAM BURNIP 7839, 2nd Bn. Northumberland Fusiliers, who died aged 26 on 22 Feb 1915. Son of James and Dorothy Burnip of Wallsend, Northumberland. Remembered with honour YPRES (MENIN GATE) MEMORIAL, YPRES Belgium.

Private FRANCIS CABLE 11189, 10th Bn. Prince of Wales Own (West Yorkshire Regiment) who died aged 32 on 1 Jul 1916. Brother of Mrs. Abigaile Auchterlonie, of 66, Cuthbert St., Hebburn-on-Tyne. Remembered with honour DANZIG ALLEY CEMETERY, France.

Private THOMAS CALDWELL 204411, 1/4th Bn. Yorkshire Regiment, who died aged 27 on 26 Dec 1917. Son of Henry and Elizabeth Caldwell. 571 Welbeck Road, Walker. Newcastle upon Tyne. Remembered with honour TYNECOT MEMORIAL, Belgium.

Captain HUME SMITH CAMERON 3rd Bn. Norfolk Regiment, who died aged 26 on 4 Sept 1916. Son of Duncan Cameron and Margaret Cameron, who lived at Old Mill House, Walker Gate, Newcastle upon Tyne. Remembered with honour DELVILLE WOOD CEMETERY, France.

Private JAMES CAMPBELL 8535, 2nd Bn. Durham Light Infantry, who died aged 32 on 26 Sept 1916. Husband of Jane Ann Campbell, of 36, Holystone St., Hebburn-on-Tyne, Co. Durham. Remembered with honour THIEPVAL MEMORIAL, France.

Private EDWARD CARROLL 11157, Prince of Wales Own (West Yorkshire Regiment) who died aged 26 on 22 Aug 1915. Son of Mrs. Hannah Carroll, of 35, Pottery Bank, St. Anthony's, Newcastle-on-Tyne. Remembered with honour HELLES MEMORIAL, Gallipoli, Turkey.

Private MATTHEW CARROLL 24/143, 24th Bn. Tyneside Scottish, Northumberland Fusiliers, who died aged 40 on 1 July 1916. Husband of Emma Carroll 983 Walker Road, Newcastle upon Tyne. Remembered with honour THIEPVAL MEMORIAL, France.

Private GEORGE PETMAN CHAMBERS 5761, 6th Dragoons (Inniskilling) B Squadron, who died aged 34 on 8 July 1917. Son of J. W. and Sarah Ann Chambers, of Walker, Newcastle-on-Tyne. Remembered with honour TEMPLEUX – LE GEURARD CEMETERY, France.

Private JOHN CHAMBERS 10817, 9th Bn. West Yorkshire Regiment (Prince of Wales Own) who died aged 22 on 9 Aug 1915. Son of Benjamin and Isabella Chambers of 6, Coutts Road, Walkergate, Newcastle upon Tyne. Remembered with honour HELLES MEMORIAL, Gallipoli, Turkey.

Private JOHN THOMAS CHARLETON 24/302, 24th Bn. Northumberland Fusiliers (Tyneside Irish) who died aged 43 on 1 July 1916. Son of the late William and Elizabeth Charleton of Church Street, Walker. Remembered with honour THIEPVAL MEMORIAL, France.

Private ROBERT CLARK 19965, 11th Bn. Northumberland Fusiliers, who died aged 20 on 15 Sept 1915. Son of John and Maria Clark of 67 Mitchell Street, Walker. Newcastle upon Tyne. Remembered with honour RUE-DE BACQEROT CEMETERY (13th LONDON CEMETERY) France.

Private LAWRENCE CONNOLLY 43048, 9th Bn. Kings Own (Yorkshire Light Infantry) who died 1 May 1917. Remembered with honour WARLINCOURT HALTE BRITISH CEMETERY, France.

Private EDWARD COLLINS 12934, 11th Bn. Durham Light Infantry who died age 46 on 5 Apr 1918. Husband of M.L Patrick (formerly Collins) of 12 Hemels Row, Walker. Newcastle upon Tyne. Remembered with honour ETRETAT CHURCHYARD EXTENSION, France.

Private JOHN CONVERY 11219, 8ᵗʰ Bn. Duke of Wellington, (West Riding Regiment) who died 11 Aug 1915. Husband of Mrs Convery, 1630 Walker Road, Walker. Remembered with honour, HELLES MEMORIAL, Gallipoli, Turkey.

Private GEORGE COOKSON 28/77, 14th Bn., Northumberland Fusiliers, who died age 22 on 28 March 1918. Son of Margaret Jane Cookson, of 9, Diamond Row, Walker, Newcastle-on-Tyne, and the late William Cookson. Remembered with honour POZIERES MEMORIAL, France.

Private A COOPER 4123, 1st Bn., Welsh Guards, who died age 22 on 07 November 1918. Son of Mrs. Jane Cooper, of 16, Potter St., St. Peter's, Newcastle-on-Tyne. Remembered with honour AWOINGT BRITISH CEMETERY, France.

Private JOHN COXON 70816, 15th Bn. Durham Light Infantry (formerly 232033 RFA) who died 27 April 1918. Remembered with honour TYNECOT MEMORIAL, Belgium.

Sarjeant PATRICK COWMAN 27635, 7ᵗʰ Bn. East Yorkshire Regiment, who died aged 30 on 8 Feb 1917. Son of the late Richard and Catherine Cowman of Walker, Newcastle upon Tyne. Remembered with honour THIEPVAL MEMORIAL, France.

Private WILLIAM P CROOKS 14039, 8ᵗʰ Bn. East Yorkshire Regiment, who died on 5 Mar 1916. Remembered with honour YPRES (MENIN GATE) MEMORIAL, Belgium.

Private WILLIAM LOWERY CROWE 879, 1ˢᵗ Bn. Northumberland Fusiliers, who died aged 18 on 18 Jun 1915. Son of J.J and Martha Crowe, 35 Station Road, Walker, Newcastle upon Tyne. Remembered with honour HOP STORE CEMETERY, Belgium.

Private J. CUMMINGS 8092, 14th Bn. Northumberland Fusiliers, who died on 30 May 1917. Husband of Mr M. Cummings 850, Shields Road, Walkergate, Newcastle upon Tyne. Remembered with honour BOYELLES COMMUNAL CEMETERY EXTENSION, France.

Private JOHN CURRAN 9633, Prince of Wales Own (West Yorkshire Regiment) who died aged 29 on 6 Jun 1917. Remembered with honour FAUBOURG D'AMIENS CEMETERY, France.

Private JOHN W CUSKERN 126331, 14th Coy. Machine Gun Corp, who died aged 26 on 21 Mar 1918. Husband of Hannah Cuskern of Walker Road, Walker, Newcastle upon Tyne. Remembered with honour POZIERES MEMORIAL, France.

Pte JOHN DAVIDSON 10868, 9th Bn. West Yorkshire Regiment (Prince of Wales's Own) who died 11th Oct 1914. Son of Mr. and Mrs. Davidson, of Church St., Walker, Newcastle-on-Tyne; husband of Margaret Davidson) of 141, Clifford St., Byker, Newcastle-on-Tyne. Remembered with honour Walker (Christ Church) Churchyard. Newcastle upon Tyne

Private ALFRED DENT 61630, 2/5th Bn. Prince of Wales Own (West Yorkshire Regiment) who died 31 Jul 1918. Son of Luke Dent, of 231, Harbottle St., South Byker, Newcastle-on-Tyne. Remembered with honour CHAMBRECY BRITISH CEMETERY, France.

Private JOHN DEVLIN 3/8461, 1st Bn. Northumberland Fusiliers, who died aged 26 on 9 Apr 1917. Husband of Mrs. I. B. Devlin, of Low Walker, Newcastle-on-Tyne. Remembered with honour BEAURAINS ROAD CEMETERY, France.

Private ROBERT E DIXON 21/546, 21st Bn. Northumberland Fusiliers (Tyneside Scottish) who died aged 26 on 18 Apr 1917. Son of Mary Ann Dixon, of 164, Waggonman Row, Forest Hall, Newcastle-on-Tyne, and the late Richard Dixon. Remembered with honour ROCLINCOURT MILITARY CEMETERY, France.

Private JOHN DODDS 23/321, 23rd Bn. Northumberland Fusiliers (Tyneside Scottish) who died aged 38 on 1 Jul 1916. Remembered with honour THIEPVAL MEMORIAL, France.

Private THOMAS DODDS 6672, 14th Bn. Northumberland Fusiliers, who died on 10 May 1915. Remembered with honour CHESHAM BURIAL GROUND, England.

Lance Corporal WILLIAM DODDS 9800, 2nd Bn. Devonshire Regiment, who died 31 Oct 1916. Son of John and Ann Ellison Dodds, of 13, Prospect Buildings, Walker-on-Tyne, Newcastle-on-Tyne. Remembered with honour GUARDS' CEMETERY, LESBOEUFS, France.

Lance Corporal JOHN J DOICK 26071, Kings Own (Royal Lancaster Regiment) who died aged23 on 7 Jun 1917. Husband of Mrs. R. M. Doick, of 122, Gill Street, Benwell, Newcastle-on-Tyne. Remembered with honour CROONAERT CHAPEL CEMETERY Belgium.

Private LEO PATRICK DOYLE 7931, 'C' Coy 13th Bn. Northumberland Fusiliers, who died aged 25 on 12 Nov 1915. Son of Andrew and Ellen Doyle of 106 Byker Street, Walker, and husband of Annie Doyle of 241 Benson Road, Byker. Remembered with honour CITE BONJEAN MILITARY CEMETERY, France.

Sergeant ALLAN EDGAR 18/662, "C" Coy. 18th (Pioneer) Bn., Northumberland Fusiliers, who died age 24 on 1 Sept 1916. Son of John and the late Ann Edgar, of Walker-on-Tyne; husband of Ann Edgar, of 165, Carville Rd., Byker, Newcastle-on-Tyne. Remembered with honour PEAKE WOOD CEMETERY, France.

Pte ALEXANDER EMINSON 17952, Coldstream Guards who died aged 22 on 10 Oct 1917. Son of Hartley and Mary Jane Edminson, of 1, St. John's Terrace, Dipton, Co. Durham. Remembered with honour TYNE COT MEMORIAL, Belgium.

Private WILLIAM EGERTON 27/1527, 27th Bn. Northumberland Fusiliers (Tyneside Irish) who died on 1 Jul 1916. Remembered with honour THIEPVAL MEMORIAL, France.
Private ROBERT FAIRCLOTH 35506, 8th Bn. Northumberland Fusiliers, who died aged 43 on 29 Sept 1918. Husband of Jemima Faircloth of Walker, Newcastle upon Tyne. Remembered with honour BUCQUOY ROAD CEMETERY, France.

Private JOHN T FAIRHURST 15630, 4th Bn. Royal Fusiliers (City of London Regiment) who died aged 29 on 21 Aug 1918. Son of John and Elizabeth Fairhurst, of 6, Church St. Hesleden, Castle Eden, Co. Durham. Remembered with honour BIENVILLERS MILITARY CEMETERY, France.

Driver OWEN FALLON T2SR/03358, Royal Army Service Corps, who died aged 47 on 18 Apr 1918. Husband of Elizabeth Fallon of 38 Berry Street, Walker, Newcastle upon Tyne. Remembered with honour WALKER CHRIST CHURCH CHURCHYARD, Newcastle upon Tyne, England.

Piper JOHN WILLIAM FELLOWS20/1585, No.1 Coy. 20th (Tyneside Scottish) Bn., Northumberland Fusiliers, who died age 21 on 01 July 1916. Son of William and Martha Fellows, of 29, Weardale Avenue, Walker, Newcastle-on-Tyne. Remembered with honour THIEPVAL MEMORIAL, France.

Private JOSEPH FERGUSON 93288, 20th Bn. Durham Light Infantry, who died on 4 Sept 1918. Remembered with honour TYNE COT MEMORIAL, Belgium.

Private PATRICK FITZHARRIS 11107, 8th Bn. Northumberland Fusiliers, who died 8 Aug 1915. Son of Mr and Mrs Fitzharris of 40 Fisher Street, Walker, Newcastle upon Tyne. Husband of Elizabeth Fitzharris, 11 Thames Street, Wallsend. Remembered with honour HELLES MEMORIAL, Galipolli, Turkey.

Private WILLIAM J FOSTER 16192, 12th Bn. Durham Light Infantry, who died aged 23 on 12 Feb 1916. Son of William and Hannah Foster, of Durham. Remembered with honour BREWERY ORCHARD CEMETERY, BOIS GRENIER, France.

Private NICHOLAS FREARS 1895, 7th Bn. Border Regiment, who died aged 22 on 15 Jun 1918. Son of Joseph and Margaret Frear, Cleator Moor, Cumberland. Born 1895 Walker, Newcastle upon Tyne. Remembered with honour BAGNEUX BRITISH CEMETERY, Belgium.

Private SEPTIMUS FRENCH 20/774, 24th (Tyneside Irish) Bn. Northumberland Fusiliers, who died 28 Apr 1917. Husband of Mary Arm French, of 597, Welbeck Rd., Walker-on-Tyne. Remembered with honour ARRAS MEMORIAL, France.

Private THOMAS GALLAGHER 3/8988, 1st Bn. Prince of Wales Own (West Yorkshire Regiment) who died 14 Mar 1915. Remembered with honour HOUPLINES COMMUNAL CEMETERY EXTENSION, France.

Private THOMPSON GARRETT 18272, 7th Bn. Alexandra Princess of Wales Own (Yorkshire Regiment) who died aged 19 on 12 Jun 1917. Son of Ingram and Martha Garrett, of 21, Low Downs Square, Hetton Downs, Co. Durham. Remembered with honour DUISANS BRITISH CEMETERT, France.

Trooper JOSEPH GILL 426, Household Cavalry and Cavalry of the Line, formerly 1st Life Guards, who died 12 May 1917. Remembered with honour ST NICOLAS BRITISH CEMETERY, France.

Corporal A M GIBBON 267112, 9th Bn. Northumberland Fusiliers, who died on 05 November 1918. Husband of L. Gibbon, of 180, Church St., Walker, Newcastle-on-Tyne. Remembered with honour at AWOINGT BRITISH CEMETERY, France.

Private JOSEPH GILCHRIST 20/1433, 20th (Tyneside Scottish) Bn. Northumberland Fusiliers, who died age 35 on 1 July 1916. Son of the late Anthony and Elizabeth Gilchrist; husband of Jenny Gilchrist, of 12, Heworth View, St. Anthony's, Newcastle-on-Tyne. Remembered with honour on the THIEPVAL MEMORIAL, France.

Private JAMES GILMORE 12040, 1st Bn. Royal Scottish Fusiliers, who died 16 Jun 1915. Remembered with honour YPRES (MENIN GATE) MEMORIAL, France.

Private W GLANVILLE 267096, 1/6th Bn. Northumberland Fusiliers, who died aged 28 on 19 Jan 1919. Husband of Eleanor Glanville, 1 Berry Street, Walker. Newcastle upon Tyne. Remembered with honour WALKER (CHRIST CHURCH) CHURCHYARD, England.

Corporal ALBERT EDWARDS GLASGOW 459290, Royal Engineers, who died age 34 on 13 August 1917. Son of John Glasgow, of Walker-on-Tyne, and the late Mary Rosa Glasgow. Remembered with honour at COWES (KINGSTON) CEMETERY Isle of Wight, England.

Private EDWARD GODFREY 8060, 1/6th Northumberland Fusiliers, who died aged 19 on 1 Oct 1916. Son of William and Jane Godfrey. Remembered with honour THIEPVAL MEMORIAL, France.
(These two men were very likely known to each other – possibly close pals? They have consecutive enlistment numbers. They died two weeks apart. Private John Godfrey – brother of Edward also joined up at the same time.)

Private GEORGE GOODWIN 8059, 1/6th Northumberland Fusiliers, who died aged 27 on 15 Sept 1916. Son of the late John and Sarah Goodwin, of 53, Mitchell St., Walker, Newcastle-on-Tyne. Remembered with honour THIEPVAL MEMORIAL, France.

Private THOMAS GOODWIN 10858, 9th Bn. West Yorkshire Regiment (Prince of Wales Own) who died aged 24 on 09 August 1915. Son of the late John and Sarah Goodwin, of 53, Mitchell St., Walker, Newcastle-on-Tyne. Remembered with honour on the HELLES MEMORIAL Gallipoli, Turkey.

Sapper JOSEPH GRAHAM 151460, 173rd Tunneling Coy, Royal Engineers, who died aged 26 on 30 Jul 1916. Son of Joseph and Sarah Graham, 46 Foster Street, Low Walker, Newcastle upon Tyne. Remembered with honour MAROC BRITISH CEMETERY, France.

Lance Corporal ANDREW GREAVES 12154, 10th Bn. Durham Light Infantry, who died aged 29 on 16 Sept 1916. Remembered with honour THIEPVAL MEMORIAL France.

Private DANIEL HARVEY 12057, 1st Bn. Northumberland Fusiliers, who died aged 25 on 30 Jun 1915. Son of the late John and Margaret Harvey, of Walker, Newcastle-on-Tyne. Remembered with honour BOLOUGNE EASTERN CEMETERY, France.

Private M.H. HACKETT 4310, 8th Bn. Northumberland Fusiliers, who died 11 Aug 1915. Son of Mr and Mrs Hackett of 1563 Walker Road, Walker. Remembered with honour, Helles Memorial, Gallipoli, Turkey.

Private EDWARD HOPKINS 20/178, 20th Bn. Tyneside Scottish, who died 1st Jul 1916 Husband of Mrs Hopkins. 31, East Terrace, Walker. Remembered with honour Ovillers Military Cemetery, France.

Private WILLIAM HOGG 19/1412, 12th Bn. Durham Light Infantry, who died aged 20 on 18 July 1916. Son of Christina Hogg, 21 Fell Street, Walker. Remembered with honour on the THIEPVAL MEMORIAL, France.

Private J. HOYLE   M.M 19716, 10th Bn. Northumberland Fusiliers, who died 31 Aug 1916 age 27. Son of Mr. and Mrs. Hoyle of 6 Back Welsh Row, Walker and husband of Mrs Hoyle, of 2 Cambrain Row, Walker. Remembered with honour LONDON RIFLE BRIGADE CEMETERY, Belgium.

Private WILLIAM HALLIDAY 42366, 2nd Bn. Kings Own (Yorkshire Light Infantry who died on aged 23 on 11 Feb 1917. Son of James G. and Isabella Halliday, of 27, North Rd., Wallsend, Northumberland. Remembered with honour FRANKFURT TRENCH BRITISH CEMETERY, France.

Private RUPERT ARTHUR HARRIS 265900, 1/6th Bn. Northumberland Fusiliers, who died age 22 on 2 Oct 1916. Son of the late Mary Harris, husband of Anne Anna Lowery (formerly Harris) of Foster Street, Walker, Newcastle upon Tyne. Remembered with THIEPVAL MEMORIAL, France.

Private WILLIAM HEANEY 19852, 5th Bn. Alexandra Princess of Wales Own (Yorkshire Regiment), who died aged 18 on 23 April 1917. Remembered with honour WANCOURT BRITISH CEMETERY, France.

Private GEORGE HESLOP 42449, 1/5th Bn. Prince of Wales Own (Yorkshire Regiment), who died on aged 30 on 12 Oct 1918. Husband of Josephine Heslop of Walker, Newcastle upon Tyne. Remembered with honour VIS-EN-ARTOIS MEMORIAL, France.

Private EDWARD HOPKINS 20/178, 20th Bn. Tyneside Scottish, who died 1st Jul 1916. Husband of Mrs Hopkins. 31, East Terrace, Walker. Remembered with honour Ovillers Military Cemetery, France.

Private THOMAS S HUDSON 39864, 9th (Service) Bn. York and Lancaster Regiment, who died on 5 Jun 1917. Remembered with honour YPRES (MENIN GATE) MEMORIAL, Belgium.

Private CUTHBERT HUMBLE 238013, 1/4th Bn. Northumberland Fusiliers, who died aged 18 on 24 Nov 1917. Remembered with honour BOULOGNE EASTERN CEMETERY, France.

Private JOSEPH JOICEY 8045, 12th Bn. Northumberland Fusiliers,who died age 22 on 13 July 1916. Son of Edward and Margaret Jane Joicey, of 8, Diamond Row, Walker, Newcastle-on-Tyne. Remembered with honour on the THIEPVAL MEMORIAL, France.

2nd Corporal ALEXANDER WILLIAM KEITH 457179, 446th Field Coy., Royal Engineers who died age 25 on 12 April 1918. Son of Mr. and Mrs. A. Keith, of 18, Westbourne Avenue, Walker, Newcastle-on-Tyne. Remembered with honour LONGUENESSE (ST. OMER) SOUVENIR CEMETERY, France.

Private F V KELSEY 98617, "D" Coy. 9th Bn., Machine Gun Corps (Infantry) who died on 21 October 1918. Son of Mrs. E. Kelsey, of 182, Church St., Walker, Newcastle-on-Tyne. Remembered with honour HARLEBEKE NEW BRITISH CEMETERY, Belgium.

Private WILLIAM KEMP 33880, 12th Bn. Northumberland Fusiliers, who died aged 19 on 25 Feb 1917. Son of Isabella Kemp, of 10, Charles St., Heaton, Newcastle-on-Tyne. Remembered with honour VERMELLES BRITISH CEMETERY, France.

Corporal MICHAEL KING 2114, 1st Bn. Northumberland Fusiliers, who died aged 26 on 10 Mar 1915. Remembered with honour YPRES (MENIN GATE) MEMORIAL, Belgium.

Private JOSEPH KNOX 240160, 22nd Bn. Northumberland Fusiliers, who died aged 20 on 23 Sept 1917. Son of Joseph and Elizabeth Knox, of 74, Benton Way, Wallsend-on-Tyne. Remembered with honour TINCOURT NEW BRITISH CEMETERY, France.

Private JOSEPH LAMB 10369, 13th Bn. Northumberland Fusiliers, who died 29 Apr 1916 aged 34. Husband of Mrs. Lamb of 42, Middle Street, Walker. Remembered with honour DARTMOOR CEMETERY, France.

Lance Corporal GEORGE LAUDER 34523, 1st Bn. Worcester Regiment, who died aged 39 on 1 Apr 1918. Remembered with honour POZIERS MEMORIAL, France.

Private EDWARD LAWSON 4450, 16th Bn. Northumberland Fusiliers, who died aged 28 on 11 Nov 1917. Remembered with honour BUCQUOY ROAD CEMETERY, France.

Lance Corporal GEORGE LAWSON 21/68, 21st Bn. Tyneside Scottish. Northumberland Fusiliers, who died 1 Jul 1916. Remembered with honour THIEPVAL MEMORIAL, France.

Private JOHN LEIGH 18144, 8th Bn. Northumberland Fusiliers, who died aged 21 on 26 Sept 1916. Son of William and Jane Leigh, Barmston Boat Landing, Washington Durham. Remembered with honour THIEPVAL MEMORIAL, France.

Private JOHN LEONARD 4789, 1st Bn. Northumberland Fusiliers, who died 16 Jun 1916 aged 38. Son of Mrs. Jane Leonard 1613 Walker Road, Walker. Remembered with honour YPRES (MENIN GATE) MEMORIAL, Belgium.

Private W. H. LEWIS 275733, 7th Bn. (Pioneers) Durham Light Infantry, who died aged 21 on 2 Nov 1917. Son of Clara Lewis of 32 Byker Street, Walker, Newcastle upon Tyne. Native of Gillingham, Kent. Remembered with honour DOZINGHEM MILITARY CEMETERY, Belgium.

Private JAMES LIVINGSTON 9704, 1st Bn. Coldstream Guards, who died aged 20 on 19th September 1914. Son of Mrs. J. Livingston (and the late Thomas) of 1, Collin Street, Walker, Newcastle-on-Tyne. Remembered with honour LA FERTE SOUS JOUARRE MEMORIAL, France.

Lance Corporal WILLIAM LIVINGSTONE 10401, 3rd Bn. Coldstream Guards, who died on 28 Mar 1918. Remembered with honour DOUCHY-LES-AYETTE BRITISH CEMETERY, France.

Private GEORGE LAURIE 46029, 13th Bn. Durham Light Infantry, who died 08 October 1916. Remembered with honour THIEPVAL MEMORIAL, France.

Private ALBERT LONSDALE 203064, 4th Bn. Alexandra Princess of Wales Own (Yorkshire Regiment), who died aged 25 on 23 Aug 1918. Son of the late Mr. and Mrs. M. G. Lonsdale, of Walker-on-Tyne, Northumberland. Remembered with honour LA VILLE AUX BOIS BRITISH CEMETERY, France.

Private ROBERT LOWES 36113, 1/5th Kings Own Yorkshire Light Infantry, who died aged 19 on 6 Jun 1918. Son of John William and Margaret Lowes, of 100, Byker St., Walker, Newcastle-on-Tyne. Remembered with honour TYNECOT MEMORIAL, Belgium.

Sapper GEORGE THOMAS LYON 1426, 1st/1st Field Coy., Royal Engineers, who died age 20 on 26 April 1915. Son of Richard and Isabella Lyon, of 552, Welbeck Rd., Walker, Newcastle-on-Tyne. Remembered with honour YPRES (MENIN GATE) MEMORIAL, Belgium.

Driver F MADDISON T4/250368, 2nd Coy. (Northumbrian) Div. Train, Army Service Corps, who died age 30 on 30 January 1917. Son of Lowinger and Elizabeth Maddison, of Gateshead-on-Tyne; husband of Mary E. Maddison, of 64, Church St., Walker, Newcastle-on-Tyne. Remembered with honour DERNANCOURT COMMUNAL CEMETERY EXTENSION, France.

Private ISAAC MADDISON 16001, "C" Coy. 9th Bn., West Yorkshire Regiment (Prince of Wales's Own) who died age 18 on 08 August 1915. Son of Mark Maddison, of 181, Church St., Walker, Newcastle-on-Tyne, and the late Isabella Maddison. Remembered with honour HELLES MEMORIAL, Gallipoli, Turkey.

Private EDWARD MAGEE 4564, 8th Bn. Northumberland Fusiliers. who died on 16 Aug 1915. Son of Mr & Mrs Magee of 1597 Walker Road, Walker. Remembered with honour HELLES MEMORIAL, Gallipoli, Turkey.

Private ROBERT MARTIN 622, 7th Bn. Australian Infantry A.I.F, who died age 29 on 26th Feb 1915. Son of Margaret Ann Martin Elswick, Newcastle upon Tyne. Remembered with honour CAIRO WAR MEMORIAL CENETERY, India.

Private WILLIAM EDWARD MASKELL 12670, 13th Bn. Northumberland Fusiliers, who died age 27 on 22 Sept 1915. Son of the late John and Isabella Maskell, 86 Fisher Street, Walker. Newcastle upon Tyne. Remembered with honour LOOS MEMORIAL, France.

Private GEORGE MASON 18222, Yorkshire Regiment (Prince of Wales Own) who died age 26 on 15 Jan 1918. Son of George and Margaret Mason of 73 Mitchell Street, Walker. Remembered with honour at CHRIST CHURCH CHURCHYARD, Walker, Newcastle upon Tyne.

Lance Corporal WILLIAM McBRIARTY 41439, 9th Bn. Yorkshire Regiment, who died age 28 on 05 October 1918. Son of John and Margaret McBriarty; husband of Margaret Gazley (formerly McBriarty), of 47, Fisher Hill Low Walker, Newcastle-on-Tyne. Remembered with honour GIAVERA MEMORIAL, Italy.

Private WILLIAM McCORMACK 9282, 1st Bn. Northumberland Fusiliers, who died 10 May 1917. Remembered with honour ARRAS MEMORIAL France.

Private JAMES McCULLOCK 1/6th Bn. Northumberland Fusiliers, who died 23 Sept 1916. Remembered with honour THIEPVAL MEMORIAL, France.

Private FRANK McCUE 16507, 8th Bn., East Yorkshire Regiment, who died on 26 Sept 1915. Son of Mrs. M. McCue, of 120, Fisher St., Walker, Newcastle-on-Tyne. Remembered with honour BULLY-GRENAY COMMUNAL CEMETERY, FRENCH EXTENSION, France.

Private HENRY McDAID 11408, A Coy, 12th Bn. Northumberland Fusiliers, who died on 25 Sept 1915. Son of Mr and Mrs McDaid of 70 Fisher Street, Low Walker. Remembered with honour LOOS MEMORIAL, France.

Corporal WILLIAM CAMPBELL McDONALD 2640, 2nd Bn. Northumberland Fusiliers, who died aged 29 on 21 Feb 1915. Brother of George Robert McDonald, of 20, Railway St., Newcastle-on-Tyne. Remembered with honour YPRES (MENIN GATE) MEMORIAL, Belgium.

Private DAN McGEE 24th Bn. Northumberland Fusiliers (Tyneside Scottish) who died on 1 Jul 1916. Remembered with honour THIEPVAL MEMORIAL, France.

Private WILLIAM McGINN 534806, 1st/15th Bn., London Regiment (Prince of Wales' Own Civil Service Rifles) who died age 19 on 01 April 1918. Son of William and Susan McGinn, of 12, Airey Terrace, Walker, Newcastle-on-Tyne. Remembered with honour ARRAS MEMORIAL, France.

Private JOHN McKEE 51772, 1st/4th Bn., Cheshire Regiment, who died age 20 on 03 October 1918. Son of John and Eleanor McKee, of 316, Church St., Walker, Newcastle-on-Tyne. Remembered with honour VICHTE MILITARY CEMETERY, Belgium.

Serjeant DANIEL MALLIGAN 235273, Lancashire Fusiliers, who died aged 39 after discharge as a direct effect of injuries sustained during the war. Husband of Christina Malligan, 308 Church Street, walker. Remembered with honour WALKER (CHRIST CHURCH) CEMETERY, Newcastle upon Tyne.

Private WILLIAM MILLICAN 23837, 2nd Bn. Duke of Wellington (West Riding Regiment) who died aged 30 on 10 Oct 1916. Son of John and Margaret Ann Millican, of 223, Stone St., Newcastle-on-Tyne; husband of Frances Millican, of 2, Sopwith St., Benwell, Newcastle-on-Tyne. Remembered with honour THIEPVAL MEMORIAL, France.

Private GEORGE MORGAN 24/476, Northumberland Fusiliers (Tyneside Irish) who died aged 28 on 21 Nov 1914. Son of Mr. and Mrs. H Morgan, 62 Rochester Street, Walker. Remembered with honour LONGBENTON (Benton) CEMETERY. Newcastle upon Tyne, England.

Private JAMES MOFFAT 20307, 9th Bn., Royal Irish Fusiliers, who died age 22 on 01 July 1916. Son of Robert and Margaret Moffat, of 307, Welbeck Rd., Byker, Newcastle-on-Tyne. Remembered with honour THIEPVAL MEMORIAL, France.

Lance Corporal ROBINSON MURRAY SD/710, Royal Sussex Regiment, who died aged 30 on 18 Dec 1916. Husband of Elizabeth Murray, of 14, Downies Buildings, Newbiggin-by-the-Sea, Northumberland. Remembered with honour DUHALLOW A.D.S CEMETERY, Belgium.

Private ARTHUR FRANCIS NAPIER 3048, 6th (National Reserve) Bn., Northumberland Fusiliers, who died age 56 on 14 December 1914. Husband of Mary Napier, of 85, Byker Terrace, Walker, Newcastle-on-Tyne. Served 16 years with 2nd Bn. Northumberland Fusiliers; also served in the South African Campaign. Remembered with honour WALKER (CHRIST CHURCH) CHURCHYARD, Newcastle upon Tyne, England. (Father of Pte Frank Napier 5th Bn Northumberland Fusiliers and Able Seaman Robert Napier HAWKE Bn. Both also killed in the war.)

Private 38885 FRANCIS NICHOLSON 1st Bn. Gloucester Regt, who died aged 30 on 4 Apr 1918. Husband of Mary Nicholson, of 737, Welbeck Rd., Walker-on-Tyne. Remembered with honour CHAPELLE BRITISH CEMETERY, France.

Gunner JOSEPH NICHOLSON 142640, 92nd Anti-Aircraft Gun Sect. Royal Garrison Artillery, who died aged 40 on 17 Nov 1918. Son of Thomas and Isabel Nicholson; husband of Alice M. Nicholson, of 76, Neptune Rd., Wallsend, Northumberland. Born at St. Anthony's, Newcastle-on-Tyne. Remembered with honour BAGHDAD (NORTHGATE) CEMETERY Iraq.

Private JOHN W NORMAN 50851, 2/9th Bn. Manchester Regiment, who died 9 Oct 1917. Remembered with honour TYNE COT MEMORIAL, Belgium.

Private JOSEPH PARKER 23755, 23rd Bn. Northumberland Fusiliers (Tyneside Scottish) who died 1 Jul 1916. Remembered with honour THIEPVAL MEMORIAL, France.

Private GEORGE W. McK. PEARSON 43362, 10th Bn. Durham Light Infantry, who died age 25 on 22 August 1917. Son of Mr. James Pearson, of St. Anthony's, Newcastle-on-Tyne, and the late Margaret Pearson; husband of Elizabeth Dinning (formerly Pearson), of 795, Walker Rd., Newcastle-on-Tyne. Remembered with honour TYNE COT MEMORIAL, Belgium.

Private H M PLANT 238051, 2nd Bn., South Staffordshire Regiment, who died age 38 on 29 September 1918. Son of George and Margaret Plant, of Walker, Newcastle-on-Tyne, husband of Margaret Jane Plant, of 6, Wharrier St., Walker, Newcastle-on-Tyne. Remembered with honour SANDERS KEEP MILITARY CEMETERY, France.

Private JOSEPH CORNELIUS POTTS 82600, Machine Gun Corps (Infantry) who died of wounds aged 31 on 9th Oct 1917, husband of Jessie Potts. He is Remembered with honour at WALKER (CHRIST CHURCH) CHURCHYARD, Newcastle upon Tyne.

Private HENRY POULTON 2472, 2nd Bn. Northumberland Fusiliers, who died aged 26 on 18 Feb 1918. Son of the late John and Ann Poulton. Remembered with honour YPRES (MENIN GATE) MEMORIAL, Belgium.

Private JOHN PROCTOR 2082, 2nd Bn. Northumberland Fusiliers, who died 4 Oct 1915. Son of Councillor John Proctor – Boot maker 18 Church Street, Walker. Remembered with honour ARRASS ROAD CEMETERY, Rocklincourt, France.

Private ROBERT RAIT 22/817, 20th Bn. Northumberland Fusiliers (Tyneside Scottish) who died on 17 Apr 1917. Remembered with honour HOLLYBROOK MEMORIAL, Southampton, England.

Private ANDREW REID 3030 2/4th Bn. Northumberland Fusiliers, who died of wounds 12th May 1916 aged 38. Remembered with honour Walker Christ Church, churchyard. Walker, Newcastle upon Tyne.

Private J. REYNOLDS 40437, West Yorkshire Regiment (Prince of Wales Own) who died 14 Jun 1917 age 31. Son of Ellen Reynolds, 1 Byker Street, Walker. Newcastle upon Tyne. Remembered with honour WALKER (CHRIST CHURCH) CHURCHYARD, England.

Private JOHN REYNOLDS 14620, 9th Bn. Northumberland Fusiliers, who died 20 Nov 1915. Remembered with honour BIRRS CROSS ROADS CEMETERY, Belgium.

Private JOHN RIPLEY 42376, 2nd Bn. Kings Own (Yorkshire Light Infantry) who died aged 39 on 3 Apr 1917. Husband of Isabella Ripley of Walker Road, Walker. Newcastle upon Tyne. Remembered with honour FORESTE COMMUNAL CEMETERY, France.

Company Serjeant Major JOSEPH MYERS ROBSON D.C.M 303015, 10th Bn. West Yorkshire Regiment (Prince of Wales's Own) who died on 20 October 1918. Son of Thomas Robson, of Walker, Newcastle-on-Tyne; husband of Rose Robson, of 91, Salisbury St., Blyth. Remembered with honour AWOINGT BRITISH CEMETERY, France.

Private JOSEPH ROBSON 23/254, 23rd Bn. Northumberland Fusiliers (Tyneside Scottish) who died aged 19 on 1 July 1916. Son of Thomas and Hannah Robson, 963 Walker Road, Newcastle upon Tyne. Remembered with honour THIEPVAL MEMORIAL, France.

Serjeant DAVID ROCKS 1532, 1/4th Bn. Northumberland Fusiliers, who died aged 27 on 15 Sept 1916. Son of Peter and Margaret Rocks of 110 Byker Street, Walker. Newcastle upon Tyne. Husband of Alice Bland (formerly Rocks) of 49 Lammas Park Rd, Ealing, London. Remembered with honour THIEPVAL MEMORIAL, France

Private JAMES FRANCIS RYAN 24289, 12th Bn, Northumberland Fusiliers, who died age 23 on 16 June 1917. Son of James and Jane Ryan, of 4, Melrose St., Walker Rd., Newcastle-on-Tyne. Remembered with honour   ARRAS MEMORIAL, France.

Private ALBERT SEPTIMUS SCORER 4368, 8th Bn. Northumberland Fusiliers, who died 19 Aug 1915. Brother of Mrs Harrison, of 1580 Walker Road, Walker. Remembered with honour HELLES MEMORIAL, Gallipoli, Turkey.

Air Mechanic 2nd Class HARRY HERBERT AMOS SEABOURNE, 251219 Royal Air Force, Western Experimental Workshops (Cardiff) who died aged 19 on 17th Oct 1918. Son of Margaret Seabourne, of 4, Chilton St., Walker, Newcastle-on-Tyne. Remembered with honour WALKER (CHRIST CHURCH) CEMETERY, Newcastle upon Tyne.

Private JAMES M SIMPSON 114303, Machine Gun Corps, who died age 33 on 11 Nov 1918. Husband of Julia Simpson of Wallsend. Northumberland. Remembered with honour WALLSEND (CHURCH BANK) CEMETERY, England.

Private JOSEPH MAXWELL SIMPSON (CONVEY) 48203, Alexandra, Princess of Wales Own (Yorkshire Regiment) who died aged 19 on 20 Sept 1918. Remembered with honour BERLIN SOUTH WESTERN CEMETERY, Germany.

Private ISRAEL WHITEHEAD SINTON 5577, 8th Bn. Northumberland Fusiliers, Who died age 27 on 19 Aug 1915. Son of George and Isabella Sinton of 108 Fisher Street, Walker. Newcastle upon Tyne. HELLES MEMORIAL, Gallipoli, Turkey.

Private THOMAS FLETCHER SHENFIELD 3/110272, 2nd Bn. Durham Light Infantry, who died aged 32 on 11 March 1915. Husband of Annie Shenfield of 32 Westbourne Gardens, Walker, Newcastle upon Tyne. Remembered with honour HOUPLINES COMMUNAL CEMETERY EXTENSION, France.

Private JOHN SKELTON 23/1078, 23rd Bn. Northumberland Fusilier (Tyneside Scottish) who died 25 Feb 1917. Formerly of 5 Eastbourne Gardens, Walker. (Born Edinburgh). Remembered with honour HAUTE AVENSES BRITISH CEMETERY, France.

Private FRANK WILFRED SKINNER 10250, 1st Bn. Durham Light Infantry, who died aged 26 on 24 May 1915. Son of Herbert Skinner of 19 Woodbine Avenue, Walker. Newcastle upon Tyne. Remembered with honour DELHI MEMORIAL (INDIA GATE) India.

Lance Corporal JOHN SMART 4085, 8th Bn. Northumberland Fusiliers, who died aged 33 on10 Aug 1915. Son of George and Louisa Smart 44 Briarwood Crescent, Walkergate. Newcastle upon Tyne. Remembered with honour HELLES MEMORIAL, Gallipoli, Turkey.

Private EDWARD SMITH 12740, 1st Bn. Northumberland Fusiliers, who died aged 25 on 27 Mar 1916. Son of George and Margaret Smith of 29 Lamb Street, Walker, Newcastle upon Tyne. Remembered with honour (YPRES) MENIN GATE MEMORIAL, Belgium.

Q.M.S ROBERT SMITH 9, Royal Army Medical Corps (Territorial Force) who died aged 31 on 1 Aug 1916. Husband of Margaret Smith, formerly of 190 Byker Street, Walker. Newcastle upon Tyne. Remembered with honour BAILLEUL COMMUNAL CEMETERY EXTENSION, France.

Private THOMAS KEATS SMITH 18616, 13th Bn. Northumberland Fusiliers, who died aged 23 on 22 Sept 1916. Son of Ann Keats Smith, 65 Back Fisher Street, Low Walker, Newcastle upon Tyne. Remembered with honour THIEPVAL MEMORIAL, France.

Gunner WILLIAM SMITH 32102, Royal Horse Artillery and Royal Field Artillery (Res Brigade) who died aged 58 on20 May 1916. Father of Mrs. Mary E. Grugan, of Pear Tree Cottages, Blackhall Mill, Hamsterley Colliery, Co. Durham. Remembered with honour NEWCASTLE UPON TYNE (ST ANDREW'S JESMOND) England.

Private THOMAS WILLIAM SNOWBALL 40927, 6th Bn. South Wales Borderers, who died age 29 on 29 May 1918. Husband of Frances Snowball, 11 Kirk Street Byker, Newcastle upon Tyne. Remembered with honour TERLINCTHUN BRITISH CEMETERY, France.

Private W.W. STEELE 27228, 23rd (Tyneside Scottish) Bn. Northumberland Fusiliers, who died aged 28 on 29 Apr 1917. Son of Mrs. J. A. W. Steele, of 1, Mills Yard, Walker Rd., Newcastle-on-Tyne. Remembered with honour. BROWN'S COPSE CEMETERY, France.

Private   GEORGE STEPHENSON 17975, 1st Bn. Coldstream Guards, who died 31 July 1917 aged 22. Son of George Henry and Annie Mary Stephenson, of 6, Jackson St., Walker, Newcastle-on-Tyne. Remembered with honour (YPRES) MENIN GATE MEMORIAL, Belgium.

Private GEORGE HENRY STEVENS 13873, 9th Bn. Northumberland Fusiliers, who died aged 26 on 3 Aug 1916. Son of Emily Stevens, of 30, Co-operative Terrace, New Delaval, Newsham, Northumberland; husband of Sarah Lennox Kirkup (formerly Stevens), of 18, Disraeli St., Cowpen Quay, Blyth, Northumberland. Remembered with honour THIEPVAL MEMORIAL, France.

Private THOMAS STONEHOUSE 3253, 1/7th Northumberland Fusiliers, who died aged 24 on 26 April 1915. Brother of John Stonehouse, of 14, Seaham St., New Seaham, Co. Durham (formerly North Road, Wallsend. Northumberland). Remembered with honour (YPRES) MENIN GATE MEMORIAL, Belgium.

Private GREENER TELFORD S/11919 8th Bn. Seaforth Highlanders. Died of wounds aged 32 on 22nd Oct 1916. Formerly of Gateshead, Greener, a shipyards plater, was married with a young family. It appears likely the family had moved to Walker after the 1911 census was taken, as he is buried in Walker (Christ Church) Churchyard, Walker.

Private GEORGE THOMPSON (served as ELLITSON) 10727, 6th Bn., East Yorkshire Regiment, who died aged 19 on 9 Aug 1916. Son of George and Annie Thompson, of 275 Back, Church St., Walker, Newcastle-on-Tyne. Remembered with honour HELLES MEMORIAL, Gallipoli, Turkey.

Private ROBERT THOMPSON 267100, 1/6th
Northumberland Fusiliers, who died aged 35 on 26 Oct 1917.
Son of Elizabeth Ann Thompson, of 42, Burdon Main Row,
North Shields. Remembered with honour TYNE COT
MEMORIAL, Belgium.

Private WILLIAM THOMPSON 63736, 1/6th Bn. Prince of
Wales Own (Yorkshire Regiment) who died aged 18 on 11
Oct 1918. Son of Robert and Rebecca Thompson, of 13,
Sixteen Houses. Shotton Colliery, Co. Durham.
Remembered with honour VIS-EN-ARTOIS MEMORIAL,
France.

Acting Corporal JAMES TIPPING 60541, 17th Bn. Royal
Welsh Fusiliers, who died aged 25 on 24 May 1918. Son of
Annie Tipping, of 24, Prudhoe St., North Shields, and the
late Jackson Tipping of Wallsend. Northumberland.
Remembered with honour ST SEVER CEMETERY
EXTENSION, France.

Private JACK (JOHN LEIGHTON) TODD 101529, 13th Bn.
Durham Light Infantry, who died aged 23 on 14 Oct 1918.
Son of Forster Fawcett Todd and Alice Eleanor Todd, of 39,
Hadrian Rd., Wallsend-on-Tyne. Remembered with honour
ROISEL COMMUNAL CEMETERY EXTENSION, France.

Sarjeant GEORGE TONES 42509, 24th Bn. Northumberland
Fusiliers (Tyneside Irish) who died aged 32 on 28 Apr 1917.
Husband of Charlotte Tones of South Shields. County
Durham. Remembered with honour ARRAS MEMORIAL.
France.
Corporal JOHN TURNBULL M.M. 463196, 50th
(Northumbrian) Signal Coy., Royal Engineers who died age
35 on 12 April 1918. Son of Robert and Sarah Turnbull, of
Walker Rd., Walker, Newcastle-on-Tyne. Remembered with
honour PLOEGSTEERT MEMORIAL, Belgium.

Serjeant ROLAND STEPHEN TWEDDELL 25/1301, 25th (Tyneside Irish) Bn. Northumberland Fusiliers, who died age 21 on 24 April 1917. Son of Roland Stephen Tweddell and Sarah Jane Tweddell, of 64, Mitchell St., Walker, Newcastle-on-Tyne. Remembered with honour ARRAS MEMORIAL, France.

Private Michael Walsh 21300, West Yorkshire Regiment (Prince of Wales Own) who died age 35 on 25 August 1918. Son of Martin and Bridget Walsh of York. Husband of Frances Walsh of 18 Foster Street, Walker, Newcastle upon Tyne. Remembered with honour TERLINCTHUN BRITISH CEMETERY, France.

Private SEPTIMUS WALTON 17577, Alexandra Princess of Wales Own (Yorkshire Regt) who died 28 September 1915. Remembered with honour LOOS MEMORIAL, France. Private WILLIAM WARD 37080, 1st/4th Bn. Essex Regiment, who died age 20 on 03 November 1917. Son of Robert and Jane Ward, of 57, Fisher St., Low Walker, Newcastle-on-Tyne. Born at Wallsend-on-Tyne. Remembered with honour GAZA WAR CEMETERY, Israel and Palestine.

Corporal PHILIP WARD 12753, 10th Bn. Durham Light Infantry, who died aged 32 on 28 Aug 1916. Husband to Christiana Ward of 20 Water Street, West Hartlepool, Durham. Remembered with honour DELVILLE WOOD CEMETERY, France.

Private FREDERICK J. WATSON 19/1836, 9th Bn. Northumberland Fusiliers, who died aged 21 on 9 Nov 1916. (Formerly lived 29 Eastbourne Gardens, Walker.) Brother of Mr. J. R. Watson, of 16, Murton Row, Percy Main, North Shields. Remembered with honour BIENVILLERS MILITARY CEMETERY, France.

Private JOHN WATSON S/3648, 11th Bn. Princes Louise's Argyll and Southern Highlanders, who died 4 Nov 1915. Remembered with honour LOOS MEMORIAL, France.

Driver EDWIN WEAR 224481, Royal Army Service Corps, who died aged 23 on 21 Jan 1919. Son of Mr. and Mrs. John Wear, of 11, Westbourne Avenue, Walker, Newcastle-on-Tyne. Remembered with honour ISMAILIA WAR MEMORIAL CEMETERY, Egypt.

Private THOMAS NESBIT WHITE 23/1312, 23rd Bn. Tyneside Scottish, Northumberland Fusiliers, who died aged 37 on 1 Jul 1916. Husband of Elizabeth White of 1353 Walker Road. Newcastle upon Tyne. Remembered with honour THIEPVAL MEMORIAL, France.

Private EDWARD WINTER (Served as Charlton) 30/123, 30th Bn. Northumberland Fusiliers (Tyneside Irish) who died aged 40 on 17 Aug 1918. Eldest son of Robert and Barbara Winter, Newcastle upon Tyne. On 17 Aug 1918 Remembered with honour TANNAY BRITISH CEMETERY, France.

Private JAMES WHELAN 11134, 10th Bn. Prince of Wales Own (West Yorkshire Regiment) who died aged 29 on 1 Jul 1916. Son of Patrick and Catherine Whelan. Remembered with honour FRICOURT NEW MILITARY CEMETERY, France.
Private JAMES WHELAN 8625, 1st Bn. Northumberland Fusiliers, who died 4 Mar 1917. YPRES (MENIN GATE) MEMORIAL, Belgium.

Private JOHN THOMAS LOWERY WHITE 20484, 2nd Bn. York and Lancaster Regiment, who died aged 17 Oct 1915. Husband of Isabella White, of 423, New Cross Row, Wingate, Co. Durham. Remembered with honour LIJJSENTHOEK MILITARY CEMETERY, Belgium.

Private THOMAS WHITE 28074, 12th Bn. Northumberland Fusiliers, who died aged 25 on 13 Jul 1916. Son of James and Margaret White, of 5, Tweed St., Hebburn, Newtown, Co. Durham. Remembered with honour THIEPVAL MEMORIAL, France.

Private RALPH WIDDRINGTON 19839, 9th Bn. Alexandra Princess of Wales Own (Yorkshire Regiment) who died aged 40 on 20 Feb 1917. Husband of Mary Agnes Widdrington, of 156, Milburn Rd, Ashington, Northumberland. Remembered with honour HERSIN COMMUNAL CEMETERY EXTENSION, France.

Serjeant FRANK WILKINSON 2612, 2nd Bn. Northumberland Fusiliers, who died age 24 on 4 Oct 1915. Son of Frank and Ann Wilkinson of 3 Blackwell Ave, Walker, Newcastle upon Tyne. Remembered with honour LOOS MEMORIAL, France.

Sarjeant HENRY YEATS 23/792, 23rd Bn. Tyneside Scottish, Northumberland Fusiliers, who died aged 42 on 1 Jul 1916. Remembered with honour THIEPVAL MEMORIAL France.

Private William Bell. Service Number 291883 1/7th Bn. Northumberland Fusiliers.
Killed in action 17th April 1917 aged 20.

William Ellerington Bell was born in September 1896 at East Terrace, Low Walker, to Thomas and Jane Anne Bell (née Judge) and was baptised at nearby St Christopher's Mission Hall, Fisher Street, on 1st October of the same year. The family later moved 41, Clyde Street, Wallsend.

William's parents had married in 1884 and had eight children; three sadly dying in infancy and later a son David, who died aged 21 in 1909. William's mother had already passed away - aged 39 in 1902, whilst giving birth to her youngest child, Thomas.

William's father, also called Thomas, died just before the outbreak of war in 1914 at the age of 61. William was survived by sisters' Jane and Elizabeth and brother Thomas.

"Mind how you go folks, keep to the left and watch out for the uneven ground. Most importantly; keep together. Billy makes sweeping movements with his hand as he guides the group along the busy trench ......Stop ... Move in, move in (everyone shuffles to the right of the trench)...*let the wiring party through; that's it let them past.....right, where were we? Oh aye, you wanted to know a bit about me didn't you? Well, I've been out here near on two years now – came out April '15, part of number 4 Company. I've been home once on leave......aye, just the once.*

Anyway - before the war I worked as a chippie – a carpenter. We lived in a flat on Clyde Street, Wallsend - number 41. There was me, my two sisters, my Da and our Tommy. Da died just before the war started......... You might know Clyde Street, it's got the picture theatre at the end of the road.

I was born in Walker – East Terrace. It's just by Angus Buildings down by the river – beside the big crane and the slipway.

I went to East Walker School at the bottom of Welbeck Road. In the summer we used to play down by the slipway or in the fields on the other side of the railway line, by the allotments. It was a canny childhood, had nowt and wanted for nowt.

Our Jane brought 'us up... Ma died when I was five, when she had our Tommy; a difficult birth the doctor said. She was 39 and it was her eighth bairn. She'd already lost four babies. It was sad really. The doctor didn't expect our Tommy to pull thorough, but he did.

Jane was only 12 but she had no choice other than to step into Ma's shoes and keep home for us all. She learned to do the cooking and cleaning and with help from Auntie's and neighbours did well in bringing up little Tommy...... She didn't go to school again after Ma died..."

"CYRIL GET DOWN!"

Everyone ducks as huge chunks of dirt fly through the air .... A hushed silence follows – broken only by the distant sound of a bombardment somewhere to the left. *"Damn...I tried to tell him* (shakes head) *come on let's move to a quieter spot, the First Aid party will be along soon and they'll clear the mess up"*

Loud crumps and thuds are heard as shells begin to land near to the trench and the ground begins to shake. Small mounds of snow that had gathered in the nooks and crannies of the trench walls begin to dislodge and fall to the ground. Troops hunker down, keeping themselves as safe and discreetly hidden as possible. A head pops out from behind an inconspicuous but tatty canvas curtain, which covers the entrance to a damp and dingy candlelit dugout. *"Bring em' in 'ere Billy lad, till it quietens down; we don't need no extra casualties"*

Billy escorts the party through and continues his tale. *"Now y'all saw what happened there – it's happening all over the battlefield, every second, so take heed and keep your head down……don't worry about the clarty ground, you'll get used to it."*

The party stay in the dank, but reasonably safe dugout until the 'all clear' is called.

"Howay folks – let's get moving, let's get you's all out of here." Billy ventures outside, the group follow – one chap begins to examine what looks like a bone with some cloth attached, sticking out through a gap, blasted between some sandbags which line the trench wall.

Further along Billy stops to point out some features. *"You'll notice the fire step is on the wrong side of the trench, that's because this is an old German trench, our lads have been busy digging out new fire steps so we can keep up with Fritz. We've found a few souvenirs here – look there's a helmet over there."* Jimmy Robson, with cigarette hanging from his lips, waves a spiked pickelhaube towards the group.

"Oh aye, watch out for the rats, where there's death there's always rats and out here I've seen 'em as big as rabbits; I kid you not."

(Murmurs in the group as they continue on their tour.)

"Me Da died just before the war broke out. It was tough 'cos we lost his wage, it was just me earning after that. Da was a hammer man at the shipyards, that's a type of blacksmith to you. I joined up not just 'cos I wanted to do my bit for King and Country, but also because…well, it looked exciting and different – the uniform, the parades, going abroad, escaping the drudgery of Tyneside… eeeh, I'd love to see a bit o' Tyneside now."

More clumps of mud fly overhead, showering the group and the 'Battlefield Tours' guide books that they held over their heads.

"Howay, quickly now, best get you lot out of here before the next bombardment starts; follow me and mind your step, these duckboards are quite slippery….. Like I was saying (more loud booms) *Come on keep up!…. I've been through some tough times I can tell you and lost a good few mates. It's not nice, it's not what I expected…Now let's get you all into this dug-out and you can wait here till the worst of it's over."*

A voice in the distance calls "Private Bell – into position. Jumping off in two minutes…bayonets ready. "

"I've got to go folks, it's nearly time, remember just keep your heads down………………"

Many of the officers kept personal diaries throughout the duration of the war. Captain F. Buckley of the 7th Bn. Northumberland Fusiliers took excerpts from these diaries after the war and put them together in a 'War History' dedicated to the men of the battalion who laid down their lives in the Great War.

Here are some excerpts relating to the battle in which William Bell was killed.

12 April 1917 (O.G. Line, Arras. Reserve position.)

We were yesterday billeted in a small village (Wanquentin) and suddenly received orders to move. We were on the road in about two hours' time, about 5.45p.m. It started to snow, and snowed very hard indeed for about three hours. We passed through a very famous town (Arras); and after innumerable delays caused by the indescribable traffic on the roads, we arrived in the present German trench about 3 a.m Things are going successfully. Prisoners are streaming in, and I can see from the battlefield how small our casualties have been.

18th April 1917
We have been in action and are now out for a bit. Things are going well for us about here, and the Boches are having a bad time. Prisoners are coming in every night. And also a lot of deserters; and we are hoping for great events shortly. The havoc about here is simply appalling, and one honestly feels sorry for the Boches. Some prisoners we took yesterday were nearly in a state of lunacy when we got then into our dug-out. The C.O. went up to one to give him a cigarette, and he just shrank like a dog that expects to be kicked. There is no doubt they believe in many cases they will be shot when captured.

19th April 1917

On the 16th we were ordered to proceed to the front line and relieve another battalion of our brigade. At the time we were occupying an old German trench captured a day or two before, and about a thousand yards in rear of our advanced troops. We had been there for a couple of days in the most beastly weather you can imagine. Rain, snow and frost; and six inches of mud everywhere. Far too many shells flying about; and nothing but "iron" rations, which means bully beefand biscuits. Water was bad to get, as the Boches if they have no time to poison the wells empty all the nearest filth into them. What water we get is brought up on pack mules, and it reeks of petrol, being carried up in petrol tins. The battalion began to move up about 8p.m. I took two companies up myself, and got them posted in the support position, the bank of a sunken road about five hundred yards behind the front line. I then returned to send the other two companies to the front line, and had just got back to Battalion Headquarters (a hole in the ground some six feet square) when the most frightful racket started. All the guns in the place got going, and they are pretty thick about here; and all kinds of rockets were going up in the front line. The only thing we were positive about was that the Boches were attacking; but at what part of the line or in what numbers of course, it was impossible to say. The road past battalion Headquarters was packed with men from half a dozen different regiments. It was pitch dark, and to make matters worse the rain started coming down in torrents. Every telephone wire was cut by shell-fire, and every now and then people were getting knocked out. I wonder if you can picture the indescribable confusion? There was nothing to do but wait till things cleared up a bit; so we just sat down in our hole and waited. The next thing we heard was someone shouting, "Where's Battalion Headquarters?" and a man in the last stage of exhaustion fell into our hole and gasped out "The Germans have taken Tower Trench!" That is all he knew, but it was valuable information, as we now knew where to look for trouble.

The C.O decided to go himself, and also decided to take me with him; so off we went, and I do not think I shall forget the journey. We fell into every shell-hole we could find; and in five minutes were wet to the skin, and mud from the soles of our feet to the top of our tin hats. We reached the support line and found it still held by the men I had already guided up there previously. Everything was in a state of pandemonium of course, but eventually we found one of our Company Commanders (Captain Outhwaite) who had got a grip of things. He had crawled up to within fifteen yards of the captured trench and had come to the conclusion that about one hundred and fifty yards of it was occupied by the enemy. He was of the opinion that we might make a bombing attack and recapture it. He was promptly given the job. I went back to get a supply of bombs for him, and the C.O went to Battalion Headquarters. Having got the bombs up I was sent to report to the General, and I was about fagged to death when I got there. The General gave me a large whisky and soda and a lump of cake; and then I told him how much I knew. I got back to Battalion headquarters and sat down to wait for our bombing attack to develop. It came off about midnight. It was a failure. One officer killed and Outhwaite was wounded in the face, a bullet going through his tin hat. He walked back to Battalion Headquarters and gave us a lot more useful information, and was then packed off to hospital. In the meantime, we learned Captain Swinney was missing. He was last seen standing on the parapet firing at the Boches with his revolver when they closed round him. We did not find any trace of him afterwards. Our first attack having failed, it was decided to make a bigger one on a larger scale with artillery preparation. I was sent up to organize it; and it was about the worst job I have ever had. I was given two companies and told that the artillery would bombard the captured trench for five minutes, commencing at twelve noon. It was not pleasant having to order these people over the top, when they were all wet and tired and hungry; but it had to be done. I sent the two companies across to a bank about two hundred and fifty yards from the Boches, and made them crawl by twos and threes over the open, so as not to excite suspicion. How we got them there without being spotted I cannot tell. Anyway, all got forward up behind the bank ready to give the go at a given signal. I got to a place where I could see a whole show and waited for the result, and very trying it was. Well, things went like clockwork. Our men attacked as if they were drilling. I saw them get into the trench with very few casualties; and the next thing I saw was some prisoners being sent back, so I concluded everything was alright. Later we heard that most of the Boches had legged it before our men could get at them with a bayonet. Well, we were relieved late that night, and to-night we go further back and hope to get some dry clothes and a decent rest.

22nd April 1917 Arras (G.S.J)

We have had ten days of it, and to some purpose. It is not often that a single battalion is singled out by a Corps Commander for Congratulations, but in reality, it was a one battalion show. The most forward point in the advance – an observation post of the utmost value, the possession of which was necessary for any further progress – had fallen into the enemy's hands. We received orders to take it, the zero hour was fixed for 12 midday. The men had been out in the open for nearly thirty-six hours, the weather was abominable, rain and sleet all the time; and for more than a week we had nothing more than iron rations. We had about two hundred and fifty yards frontage. The barrage was to be a five minute one. But as the ground was so sticky and the men not so fresh I decided to jump off two minutes before zero. The risk was that they might be observed by enemy before the barrage came down, more particularly as the left company had in the first instance to move to a flank. Still I decided to risk it, and for the first two minutes the men were ordered to crawl. My calculations turned out as I had hoped, and when the barrage started the two attacking companies were in position, three waves of at thirty paces distance and about two hundred yards from the objective. I was able to watch the attack from behind, and (though I did not know it at the time) so also were practically the whole staff of the three Divisions. The men went forward splendidly, as well as or even better than they have ever done in training. The barrage was very fine, three

Brigades of field artillery being at work. One shell fell very short and the troops dropped, but only for a moment, and when the barrage lifted (zero+5 minutes) they rushed the position, and Wancourt Tower was ours. It was a fine show, which might readily have ended it disaster. I do not think I have ever spent five minutes in such intense excitement in my life; and we had a very anxious time of it for the next twelve hours till we were relieved, as the Boches were threatening to counter-attack, and we were anxious to get on with the consolidation. We only got four prisoners as the Boches scuttled as hard as they could, and did not give our men much chance to use the bayonet. They had, however, to pass through our back barrage before regaining their trenches, and I do not think many would survive. Our casualties were very small.

That last sentence – *'Our casualties were very small.'* .... in terms of a battle, they were small. To Private William Bell's family that small loss was a massive void, a huge never to be filled crater that had just blown up and shattered their lives. Billy would never walk through the door again; there would be no more letters or cards asking after his sisters and telling Tommy to be a good lad. Billy Bell, the lad from Walker was gone, aged 20 and in his prime. His life taken in a war that was supposed to end all wars. There was no grave to visit; there was nothing recognisable left of Billy Bell.

Sister Elizabeth 'Lizzie' Bell married Adam Bell, from Willington, Wallsend, at St Luke's Parish Church, Wallsend on 25th January 1919.
Jane Marshall Bell married William Murray in 1933 aged 43. I have been unable to find any further information on his brother Tommy, though it is possible he died 1972 in Northumberland.

Published in the Newcastle Journal – 30th September 1915.
Family of soldiers.

The King's letter to a Walker woman

It recently came to the knowledge of the Lord mayor of Newcastle that Mrs Livingston, of 1, Collin Street, Walker, had five sons serving in the Cameron Highlanders, that a sixth son; serving in the Coldstream Guards, had been killed in action in September 1914, and that a seventh was engaged on war munitions work at Elswick arsenal. His lordship at once placed himself in communication with Lord Stamfordham in order that this extremely patriotic family might be brought to the notice of the King, and His Majesty has graciously caused the following letter to be sent to Mrs Livingstone;

Privy Purse Office, Buckingham Palace, S.W.,
10th September, 1915
Madam,- I am commanded by the King to convey to you an expression of His Majesty's appreciation of the patriotic spirit which has prompted your six sons to give their services to the Army. The King was much gratified to hear of the manner in which they have so readily responded to the call of their sovereign and their country, and I am to express to you and to them His Majesty's congratulations on having contributed in so full a measure to the great cause for which all the people of the British Empire are so bravely fighting- I have the honour to be, madam, your obedient servant,

F.M Ponsonby, Keeper of the Privy Purse.

Mrs Livingston.

In Memory of
Private 9704 **JAMES LIVINGSTON**
1st Bn. Coldstream Guards
who died 19th September 1914 aged 20

Son of Mrs. J Livingston (and the late Thomas) of 1, Collin Street, Walker, Newcastle-on-Tyne.
Remembered with honour on the LA FERTE-SOUS JOUARRE MEMORIAL France.

James Livingston, was one of the first few hundred soldiers to die in the Great War. When war broke out six of the nine battalions forming the Brigade of Guards were on the list for active service, according to the mobilisation scheme then in force. Four of which composed the 4th Brigade and two part of the 1st Brigade.

Thus, the Coldstreams commenced mobilisation with the rest of the Army on receipt of orders on the night of the 4/5th August 1914. The battalion arrived at Le Harve, France, a few days later and from there they en-trained on an 18 hour journey to the village of Le Nouvion, where they spent the night of the 15th. At each stop on the journey, crowds of locals would gather and cheer, throw bouquets of flowers at the soldiers and cheer 'God Save the King.'

From there they marched to the village of Boué, near Etreux - where the 1st Guards Brigade were billeted and they remained there until the 21st. From this point on they marched and rested and 'practiced' at war, until 23rd August when they became involved in full active service. In September the Coldstream Guards were involved in the Battles of the Marne and Aisne; it was at the latter that James met his death.....................

Printed in the Newcastle Journal, Thursday 09 November 1916.
The Fighting Fusiliers.

Some years ago our Government was seized with sudden
fears
Of spending too much money, so reduced the Fusiliers –
The old Fusiliers, the bold Fusiliers, cut down a whole
battalion of the Fighting Fusiliers.
But time will have its changes, and produced some other
fears;
Not of spending too much money, not of lack of Fusiliers –
Old Fusiliers, bold Fusiliers; they called for more battalions of
the Fighting Fusiliers.
When the Northmen heard the calling they responded with
their cheers;
And something more substantial came to join the Fusiliers –
The old Fusiliers, the bold Fusiliers, rolled up in their
thousands for the Fighting Fusiliers.
From the plough and from the office, from the mine came the
volunteers,
From all sorts of occupations to enlist as Fusiliers.
Old Fusiliers, bold Fusiliers, flocking to the Colours of the
Fighting Fusiliers.
And they're fighting like the heroes who, in all the bygone
years,
Made the glorious reputation of the County Fusiliers –
Old Fusiliers, bold Fusiliers, every day they're adding laurels
to Fighting Fusiliers.
Mat God protect the soldier laddies in the time of blood and
tears,
Who are battling for our country in the ranks of Fusiliers –
Old Fusiliers, bold Fusiliers, heroes of Northumberland the
Fighting Fusiliers.

R,O'D,R,L.

Field Punishments

method of tying feet

Filed Punishments Number 1:
When flogging came to an end in 1881 a new way of dealing with soldiers found guilty of minor offences such as drunkenness was introduced. This was called Field Punishment Number 1 and consisted of the convicted man being shackled in irons and secured to a fixed object, often a gun wheel or similar. He could only be fixed in this position for up to 2 hours in any 24, and not for more than 3 days in 4, or for more than 21 days in his sentence. This punishment was often known as 'crucifixion' and due to its humiliating nature was viewed by many as unfair.

Field Punishments Number 2:
Field Punishment Number 2 was similar except the man was shackled but not fixed to anything. Both forms were carried out by the office of the Provost-Marshal, unless his unit was officially on the move when it would be carried out regimentally i.e. by his own unit.

Died whilst in service with the Royal Navy, Mercantile Marine or Royal Marines.

** Not from Walker but buried in Walker Churchyard.

Fireman   **THOMAS BLACKWOOD**
       12 Sept 1917
S.S. GIBRALTAR (Mercantile Marine)
Back Sumerson Buildings, Walker. Newcastle upon Tyne.

Stoker Petty Officer   **BOLTON BRADLEY 825**
.V(CH)   **23 Jun 1917**
H.M.S. MACEDONIA   (Royal Naval Reserve.)
Wife resided North Shields.

Able Seaman   **ERNEST BULLOCK**
       K.P/320   **4 Jun 1916**
ANSON BATTALION   Royal Naval Division
Son of Mary Ann King of 2 Airey Terrace, Walker. Newcastle upon Tyne.

First Engineer   **WILLIAM CARMICHAEL**
       3 Jan 1918
S.S. BIRTLEY (Newcastle)
Son of the late Thomas and Mary Carmichael of Walker.
Husband of Isabella Carmichael (née Mowatt) 5, Brannen St, North Shields.

Private   **GEORGE CHAMBERS**
       Deal/2372   **20 Jan 1918**
ROYAL MARINES   Royal Naval Division
Resided 291 Church Street, Walker. Newcastle upon Tyne.

Able Seaman   **PETER DUFFY**
K.P/610   **5 Jul 1915**
ANSON BATTALION   Royal Naval Reserve.
Resided 45, Howard Crescent, Walker. Newcastle upon Tyne.

Able Seaman   **NORMAN DIXON**   **200859**
           10 Jun 1915
H.M.S. TORPEDO BOAT 12
Brother John Dixon, 36 Middle Street, Walker. Newcastle upon Tyne.

Engine room Artificer WILLIAM DOBINSON
       M.32114   **20 Jul 1918**
H.M.S. VICTORY
Mother Margaret Dobinson, 83, Middle Street, Walker. Newcastle upon Tyne.

Private   **THOMAS FISACKERLY   PO/510**
      13 Jul 1915
ROYAL MARINE LIGHT INFANTRY (Portsmouth battalion.)
Resided 99, Walker Road, Walker.   Newcastle upon Tyne.

Able Seaman   **HENRY G GARDNER**   **207143**
         23 Jan 1916
H.M.S. COCKATRICE
Born Northampton.

Chief Artificer   **CHARLES F JOHNSON   **270756**
       14 Feb 1919
H.M.S. DOLPHIN
Born Gainsborough.

Leading Stoker   **JOHN W ROBSON**   **S.S.100413**
       10 Apr 1917
H.M.S. P26

Resided 71, Sutton's Model Dwellings, Walker. Newcastle upon Tyne.

Boy 1st Class   CHARLES SHARPE   J/54193
2 Aug 1917
H.M.S. ST. GEORGE
Son of Wm and Mary Sharpe, 46 Scrogg Road, Walker. Newcastle upon Tyne.

Engine room Artificer   GEORGE SOULSBY 426.E.B
7 Mar 1917
H.M.S. SPEY
Resided Hull.

Carpenter   JOHN WALSH
11 Mar 1915
S.S. BANYO
Mother Annie Walsh, 80 Church Street, Walker. Newcastle upon Tyne.

Fireman   JOHN WARREN
12 Sept 1917
S.S. GIBRALTAR   Mercantile Marine
Husband of Ann Warren, Back Sumerson Buildings, Walker. Newcastle upon Tyne.

Signalman   ROBERT WILLIAMSON
12 Aug 1917
Tyneside/Z/48 R.N.V.R
Son of John and Margaret Williamson, 30 Diamond Row, Walker. Newcastle upon Tyne.

Able Seaman   JAMES ALEXANDER WOOD
SS6940   2 Aug 1918

H.M.S. ARIEL
                     Son of James and Martha Wood of Falmouth
Road, Heaton, Newcastle upon Tyne (born Walker.)

Able Seaman   GEORGE WOODMAN   KP/503
                     3 May 1915
ANSON BN.   Royal Naval Volunteer Reserve
Husband of Alice Woodman, 44 Back Church Street, Walker.
Newcastle upon Tyne.

This is an interesting group, as they didn't all die at sea as you
would expect due to the arm of the service they served in. For
example, Peter Duffy and Ernest Bullock of Anson Battalion
fought alongside the Army on land in Gallipoli, as did
Thomas Fisackerly. George Chambers fought in Gallipoli but
survived, only to fall on the battlefields of France.

Ernest Bullock and Peter Duffy both sailed from England in
early February 1915 and arrived in Malta some 10 days later.
They then again set sail for the Dardanelles (Turkey.)
Many people see Gallipoli as an ANZAC war, but in fact, both
the British, and the French army contingents on Gallipoli
outnumbered the ANZAC's in terms of men deployed and
casualties lost. There were appalling losses of life - estimates
are that the Turkish army suffered 300,000 casualties
(including the many sick) and the Allies, 265,000. The
resulting effect of diverting troops and supplies sorely needed
on the Western Front is impossible to measure.
Conditions on Gallipoli were horrendous at best. The terrain
and close fighting didn't allow for the dead to be buried and
flies and other vermin flourished in the heat; thus creating an
epidemic of sickness. The winter of 1915, with storms and
blizzards followed by a calamitous thaw, caused casualties of
around 15,000 British soldiers.

Of the 213,000 British casualties on Gallipoli, 145,000 were due to sickness; chief causes being dysentery, diarrhoea, and enteric fever.

Both Ernest and Peter were killed in action at Gallipoli. Peter in June 1915 aged 25 and Ernest in July 1916 aged 23. Ernest has no known grave and is remembered on the Skew Bridge Cemetery Memorial, Cape Helles, Gallipoli. Peter is buried in Lancashire landing Cemetery, also at Cape Helles, Gallipoli.

Private Thomas Fisackerly (PO/510) Aged 26, a former wood cutting machinist at the shipyards and living at 56, Church Street, Walker, joined the Royal Marines at the outbreak of war. His widowed mother Martha must have been even more heartbroken than many mothers on hearing of his death as she had already lost four of her 6 children before they reached the age of six; as well as losing her husband at the early age of 45 in 1901. Martha was living at 99, Walker Road when she received the news of Thomas's death.

Thomas, like Peter and Ernest also fought in the hellish Gallipoli battlefields with his Light Infantry (Portsmouth) battalion. They set sail from Portsmouth on 12 Jan 1915 and joined the Middle Eastern Force on 28 Feb 1915. Thomas was killed in action on 13th July of the same year. He has no known grave and is remembered on the Helles Memorial – Gallipoli, Turkey.

"In the attacks of 12th and 13th July, the French had placed some thirty or forty guns and howitzers under British command, and on account of the shortage of British ammunition their guns undertook the whole of the artillery preparation, our artillery confining itself to covering fire during and after the Infantry advance. The counter-attacks were so violent and the calls for artillery support were so incessant that towards the afternoon of the 13th July the British gun ammunition began to get alarmingly low, until finally only about 5,000 rounds of 18-pr. ammunition, including all rounds in Battery charge, remained at Helles. The French were reluctant to supply

*further artillery support, fearing further attacks on themselves. This was the most anxious night I spent on the Peninsula all but a limited number of rounds were withdrawn from most Batteries and were placed in horsed ammunition wagons, which perambulated from one side of the British position to the other according to where it seemed most likely the next Turkish attack would take place.***"**
'GALLIPOLI DIARY' BY GENERAL SIR IAN HAMILTON, G.C.B. 1920

Charles Sharpe, aged seventeen – Boy 1st Class, one of the youngest to die. His vessel HMS ST. GEORGE along with HMS ERMINE, were sunk by enemy submarine action in the Aegean Sea on 2nd August 1917. His parents William and Mary Sharpe, lived at 46 Scrogg Road, Walker. Newcastle upon Tyne. He is remembered with honour MIRKA BRITISH CEMETERY, KALAMARIA. Greece. His father was an engine fitter, as were his older brothers William, James and Henry. He also left behind two younger siblings Joseph and Hilda.

Pte George Chambers, a former miner and Royal Navy volunteer reservist of 291 Church Street, Walker, enlisted 25 Nov 1914. He transferred to the Royal Marine Divisional Train in March 1915 and was drafted to the Mediterranean in December the same year, joining the Divisional Train at Mudros and participating in the Gallipoli campaign. In August 1918 he was attached to the 188th Brigade HQ. George was killed in action and is buried at Metz-en-Couture communal cemetery British Extension, Pas De Calais, France.

Four lives were lost when the Mercantile Marine vessel 'SS GIBRALTAR' was struck without warning by a torpedo from an enemy submarine 100 miles SE ½ S from Cape de Creus, Spain. The torpedo obviously hit the engine room, as neighbours from Back Sumerson Buildings, Low Walker; and more than likely good pals before offering their services for their country; John Warren and Thomas Blackwood, both in their 40's and who were serving as Firemen aboard the vessel, were killed.

H.M.S. P26, in which 23-year-old Leading Stoker John Robson served, was actually a hospital ship 'H.S. SALTA'. She was mined on the morning of the 10th April 1917, just outside Le Harve, there were no patients on board. 5 officers, 9 nursing sisters, and 37 other ranks were lost with the ship.
Twenty four bodies were recovered and now rests in Ste. Marie Cemetery in Le Harve. John was not one of these bodies. His name is remembered on the Chatham War Memorial in Kent.

Brother and sister.

Mercantile Marine reserve John Walsh, a ships carpenter, died aged 32 when the S.S. BANYO was torpedoed by a submarine in the Clyde. He left behind a widowed mother Annie and three siblings. His mother having already lost four children as infants, and her husband in recent years. John is remembered on the Plymouth War Memorial in Devon.

Robert Williamson, a 24 year old Signalman aboard the Drifter 'HM DEWEY', a patrol boat. He died on 12th Aug 1917 along with ten others on-board when the boat was involved in a collision in the English Chanel. He is remembered on the Chatham War Memorial in Kent.

Stoker Petty Officer Bolton Bradley a 45 year old Royal Navy Reservist died while his ship H.M.S. MACEDONIA was berthed in Brazil on 23rd June 1917. His death is recorded as 'Killed or died by means other than disease, accident or enemy action.' Could his death have been murder?
He is buried at Gamboa British Cemetery in Rio De Janeiro, Brazil.

Thirty-two-year-old Norman Dixon of Middle Street, Walker, is buried in Walker Churchyard. He died as a direct result of enemy action. At 15.30 in the afternoon on 10th June 1915 in the North Sea, Torpedo Boat 12 felt a large explosion under her bows, believed torpedoed at the time (later confirmed mined) she stayed afloat as other Torpedo Boats came to her rescue. The crew abandoned ship when Torpedo Boat 10 came alongside to tow her to safety, but Torpedo Boat 10 now suffered an explosion and sank. A Trawler took over the towing of Torpedo Boat 12, assisted by the destroyer H.M.S. CYNTHIA. Slowly Torpedo Boat 12 gradually settled, sinking at 10.55 (presumably on the 11th.) Her commander Lt Bulteel and 22 ratings lost.

By strange coincidence William Dobinson aged 20, also of Middle Street and also buried Walker Churchyard died of 'disease', likely at Walkergate Hospital which during the war years was the 'City hospital for Infectious diseases.' He had been a crew member of H.M.S. VICTORY, which was in actual fact a shore establishment at Portsmouth Dockyard and not the historic ship of the same name on which Nelson served.

Spare a thought for poor Able Seaman Henry Gardner aged 31 who served on board H.M.S. COCKATRICE and is buried in Walker Churchyard and who was a native of Northampton. He is not a Walker lad or even a Newcastle lad, nor did he die in battle or his death caused by enemy action.

He drowned in the cold dark murky depths of the River Tyne on the 23rd January 1916. Henry was an experienced sailor with 16 years' service, man and boy behind him. Whether he fell in to the water from the quayside or from overboard I do not know. Varying reports say he drowned in the Tyne others the North Sea but the likely hood is he fell overboard.

James Alexander Wood served in the Royal Navy from 5 Feb 1916 until 2 Aug 1918.

George Woodman, age 28 and a father of three, of 44, Back Church Street, died of wounds on 3rd May 1915, after being in battle with the Royal Naval Volunteer Reserve Anson Bn. Royal Naval Division in the Dardanelles. He was the son of the late George and Henrietta Woodman, of Howden, Yorkshire and husband of Alice. Alice re-married early in 1917 to a chap called James Goldsworthy and they moved to 28 Tynevale Terrace, Walker. He is remembered on the Chatham War Memorial, Kent.

First Engineer William Carmichael was born at 136, Dean Street, Walker, in 1859. The family later moved to Tyne Street. It was while living here, at the age of 12, he was apprenticed into the trade of a boiler-smith. Possibly once his apprenticeship was fulfilled, he joined the merchant Navy and on the 1881 census was to be found working as a 'Fireman' aboard the ELECTRA, which was docked in Middlesbrough at the time.

William Married Isabella Mowatt in 1898, when he was 38 and she was 23. They had six children, Mary Jane, Isabella, Francis, Lilian and Margaret. Another child died in infancy.

His name is recorded on the Mercantile Marine Memorial, Tower Hill, London. The memorial register states the following: CARMICHAEL. 1st Engineer. William. S.S. Birtley (Newcastle). Presumed drowned 3rd Jan., 1918. Age 63. Son of the late Thomas and Mary Carmichael; husband of Isabella Carmichael (née Mowatt). Of 5, Brannen St, North Shield. Born at Walker Newcastle upon Tyne.

Engineering Artificer Charles Johnson aged 37, another non-local but buried in Walker Churchyard. Its' probable Charles was taken ill on board his submarine H.M.S. DOLPHIN and it made a trip up the Tyne to deposit him ashore, from whence he was admitted to Walkergate Hospital, as he reportedly died from Disease. His family obviously did not have the money to have his body brought back to his home town of Gainsborough in Lincolnshire and he was therefore buried locally.

Another Engineering Artificer George Soulsby aged 34, born Walker but now living in Hull, was killed on 7 March 1917, not by enemy action but when his boat the harbour tender H.M.S. SPEY was run down by a sludge vessel in Chatham Harbour. Twenty men lost their lives. His body was recovered and he is buried in Western Cemetery, Spring Bank, Hull.

H.M.S. Spey was operating her usual role in the Thames estuary between Southend and Sheerness on 7th March 1917. Contemporary newspapers reported the sinking but, due to wartime restrictions, could only refer to 'one of the smaller vessels of HM Navy'.

On that Wednesday afternoon, Lt Ernest Humphreys RNR was in command of the diving operations when the winds increased to gale force and the Spey lost an anchor. Humphreys decided to return to Sheerness. While still in the main Thames Channel a larger ship was seen to be coming down river, dead ahead, but not necessarily on a collision course. She was the SS Belvedere – a mud-hopper owned and operated by the London County Council. She carried 1,000 tons of sludge on regular journeys down river on the ebb tide to dump the waste at sea; she then returned to London docks on the flood tide.

At about 3.40pm the Belvedere was seen to alter course towards the Spey and the Diving Tender, doing her maximum of 6 knots, responded with two blasts on the siren and turning to port. It was too late to avoid a collision. Although the Belvedere had her engines astern by then she struck the Spey a glancing blow on the starboard side. The forty-year-old Gunboat did not recoil well from the jolt. Numerous riveted seams sprung open and the sea rushed in, sinking the ship in about three minutes. Most of the thirty-seven men on Spey knew of the impending collision just before it happened but events moved so quickly, and few could have expected their ship to sink so quickly.

Thirteen men got away quickly on the Carley raft and thirteen more managed to safely launch the cutter. The only other boat, a skiff, was the last to leave with only four men aboard. That left seven men to await rescue or take to the water, the two officers, two Royal Marine divers and three seamen. These men probably expected to be rescued by the Belvedere which had lowered one of its own sea-boats and was hove-to about half a mile away. The Second Officer of the Belvedere had been on watch during the accident and his first actions were for the safety of his ship and crew of twenty-three men. He ordered the discharge of the ship's load and 1,000 tons of sludge and mud were dropped through the ship's bottom into the sea. That operation took six valuable minutes during which time the wind had blown Belvedere well away from the Spey. The Belvedere's sea-boat was lowered and rowed towards the now sunken Spey but the crew were soon exhausted in the gale. They did meet the skiff and take one man from that before returning to Belvedere, unable to find any more survivors.

Other Naval vessels were in the vicinity and a search and rescue operation was soon under way. The City of Belfast, an Armed Boarding Ship, actually saw the Spey sink and radioed the news to Sheerness Signal Station. The emergency tug immediately left for Sheerness and, from Southend pier, came a destroyer. None of these ships had any success, however, although they searched long into the evening using searchlights.

Spey's skiff was eventually blown on to mud flats off the Isle of Grain at about 5.30pm. The three exhausted survivors waded ashore and were thankfully found by men of the nearby RN Air Station. The Carley raft also drifted on to the Grain mud flats later the same evening but all thirteen men had died. The raft must have been swamped soon after leaving the Spey but continued to float, although half submerged. The men had all succumbed to the wet and cold.

The cutter, however, was a good sea-worthy boat and the thirteen men who got away from Spey in that all survived. They had to constantly bale out as waves broke over them but, by five o'clock, they had reached the safety of Sheerness Dockyard.
The other seven men's bodies were found at intervals much later. A Coroner's Inquest into the deaths of the sailors was held at the Royal Naval Hospital, Gillingham on 10th, 12th and 17th March 1917 and found that death was due to drowning following a collision at sea. What the Admiralty made of it in their enquiries is not known. **This excerpt courtesy of Chatham Dockyard Historical Society.**

Jolly group of sailor's on board ship (Author's own collection.)

Serviceman from HMS POWERFULL, sporting a broken arm hidden beneath his jacket. (Authors own collection).

HMS VICTORY shore establishment, Portsmouth. (Authors own collection.)

HMS VICTORY, Portsmouth Shore establishment, Portsmouth. (Authors own collection).

Royal Navy / Reservists and Mercantile Marine men born in Walker and awarded Campaign medals for their service during the Great War.

The Royal Naval Reserve was established with the Naval Reserve act of 1859 as a reserve force of seamen, extended to include officers in 1862 and men, for deep sea merchant ships who could be called upon during times of war or crisis to supplement the forces of the Royal Navy. (National Archives.)

PATRICK CONWAY born 20th Feb 1893   (Royal Naval Reserve)   Service Nos: V1186   T2513 S 276

RICHARD CUNNINGHAM born 17th Dec 1884   (Royal Naval Reserve)   Service Nos: V1380   U2350 T2984   S966

PATRICK MCELWEE born 15th Aug 1881   (Royal Naval Reserve)   Service No: T 2038

JOHN EDWARD THORNTON born 14th Jan 1889   (Royal Naval Reserve)   Service No: ST 2637

JAMES TERENCE BOWDEN born 1897 (Merchant Navy)

RICHARD BLENKINSOPP born 14 Sept 1893 Service No: M17375

Richard Blenkinsopp, a former miner Served with the Royal Navy from 20 Nov 1915 and was demobilised 5 August 1919 His first ship being HMS PEMBROKE I and his last HMS GANGES.

EDWIN BOUCHER born 28 Aug 1888   Service No: SS107672M

Edward Boucher served in the Royal Navy from 1st Nov 1908 until 1918. His first ship being H.M.S. NELSON and his last H.M.S. BIRMINGHAM

WILLIAM BRITT born 20 May 1896   Service No: K32556

William Britt served in the Royal Navy from 25th April 1916 until 21 Aug 1918. His only ship being H.M.S. PEMBROKE II

HUBERT GODFREY DICKINSON born 4th Oct 1897 Service No: M32514

Hubert Godfrey Dickinson served in the Royal Navy from 2nd Jul 1918 until 9th April 1919. His first ship was H.M.S. PEMBROKE II his last H.M.S. PRINCE GEORGE.

THOMAS GRADWELL born 8 Jan 1887   Service No: 227395

Thomas Gradwell served in the Royal Navy from 24th Aug 1903 until 28th Nov 1917. His first   ship was H.M.S.CALEDONIA and his last H.M.S. PEMBROKE I. (Invalided out.)

JAMES GREWAR born 19 Jul 1985   Service No: M21931

James Grewar served in the Royal Navy from 1st Jul 1916 until 3 May 1919. His first ship was H.M.S. ASSISTANCE and his last H.M.S. VINDICTIVE.

JOHN WILLIAM HAXON born 28 Sept 1892   Service No: M17366

John William Haxon served in the Royal Navy from 20 Nov 1915 until June 1919. His first ship was H.M.S. PEMBROKE I and his last H.M.S. PEMBROKE I.

ROBERT NAPIER   T/Z4868

Killed 13 Nov 1916 RNVR HAWKE BN. Mother Mary, 85 Byker Terrace, Walker. His father and brother were also killed during the Great War (see Families at war)

NORMAN PARK born 19 Jan 1897   Service No: M17639

Norman Park served in the Royal Navy from 20 Nov 1915 until 22 Feb 1919. His first ship was H.M.S. PEMBROKE I and his last H.M.S. SATELLITE.

HENRY CAMPBELL SCOTT born 17 Apr 1899   Service No: J52515
Henry Campbell Scott served in the Royal Navy from 16 Apr 1916 until 25 May1919. His first ship was H.M.S. GANGES and his last H.M.S. PEMBROKE I.

GEORGE HENRY SCOTT born 5 Apr 1899   Service No: SS8157
George Henry Scott served in the Royal Navy from 16 May 1918 until 15 May 1923. His first ship was H.M.S. VIVID I and his last H.M.S. DOLPHIN.

JAMES DANIEL SMITH born 1883   (Merchant Navy)
Former Shipwright, born Walker.

Signalman   ROBERT WILLIAMSON
          Tyneside/Z/48 R.N.V.R
K.I.A   12 Aug 1917   HM DEWEY
Son of John and Margaret Williamson, 30 Diamond Row, Walker. Newcastle upon Tyne.

The Church Street boys.

These men were neighbours; they lived in a close community and more than likely most were known to each other. They would have attended meetings at the Mechanics Institute together. The families would all have attended Church or Chapel. They bought their produce in the same local shops; Hassan's the butcher, Nevin's the fruiterer's. Bought fish suppers from Hugh Ross and black bullets and liquorice root from Mr. Nickel's sweet shop.

Many of the men worked side by side at the many shipyards that graced the length of the Tyne, or possibly at the local Ann Pit.

At the outbreak of war in 1914, not a single one of them had any idea that they were about to participate in the most depressing and vile war the world had ever seen. By November, three months of bloody warfare across France and Belgium had settled into a complete deadlock. A continuous 600-mile network of frontline trenches had been established, running from the North Sea to the Swiss border. Both sides had now dug themselves into impenetrable positions that over and over again, had proved impossible to capture.

Lord Kitchener had warned the Government and the public, just days after Christmas, when the war was supposed to have ended, of an "eternal stalemate" following months of fighting and of "slaughter on an industrial scale." A fear that soon came to be realised on the western front. "After three or four months of the most tenacious fighting, involving very heavy losses, the French have not at any one point on the line gained a couple of miles. Would the throwing of an additional half a million men on this front make any real difference?" he asked.

As 1915 dawned there were less and less men prepared to risk leaving their families and homes and 'volunteer' themselves for a life in the trenches; with a good chance of being shot at, maimed or possibly killed.

If you read the article on the 'Recruitment process during WW1' you will see that men, once thought not suitable for the Army or Navy were later called up and sent to abroad, or to do war work on UK soil.

"Now let us take a walk along Church Street – picture the houses and shops on our excursion. The sounds of the trams, and of the horses and carts as they trundle along the cobblestones. You'll probably recognize some of the family names. If you're lucky we may even bump into one of your ancestors.

We'll start on the corner by the Methodist Chapel, at the junction with Welbeck Road and Westbourne Avenue. Our first stop is outside of number 8…

Private **ROBERT WALTON** (Service No 15435) attested to the East Yorkshire Regiment on 9 Nov 1914 at Sunderland, aged 24 years. His address was 47 Double Burdon St, Ryhope, Sunderland. He was a miner by trade and married to Martha Walton (née Carr.) They had 2 daughters - Mary Elizabeth born 1912 and Sarah born 1913.

Robert was posted to the 3rd Bn. East Yorkshires on 13 Nov 1914 and later drafted to the 2nd Bn. in May 1915 ready for its embarkation to France on 19 May 1915. After a short spell in France the regiment made their way to Marseilles, from where they set sail on 25 Oct 1915 and joined the Mediterranean force in Alexandria, Egypt on 2 Nov 1915.

He suffered a knee injury on 6 Jun 1916 and in Sept 1916 was admitted to hospital with diarrhoea. He died, likely of dysentery on 27 Sept 1917.

Widow Martha was awarded a pension of 22s 11d for herself and two children, as from 16 Apr 1917

Robert Walton is remembered with honour at Salonika (Lembet Road) Military Cemetery, Greece.

After his death, his wife is recorded as living at 8 Church St, Walker, Newcastle-on-Tyne. Could this be her family address? Number 8 Church Street consisted of two properties (flats) having 2 rooms each. On the 1911 census the amount of rooms in each property was counted – the kitchen was to be counted as a room, but not the scullery, landing, lobby, closet, bathroom, nor warehouse, office or shop.

I have added Robert because he does have some connection to Church Street, possibly his wife moving here prior to his death to be closer to her family?

Now let's walk a little further on …… the premises and home of John Proctor – Councillor and Boot maker, number 18/20 Church Street, Walker; a 5-roomed property.

Son - Driver **ALBERT EDWARD PROCTOR** (Service No 205116) of the Royal Regiment of Artillery (Royal Field Artillery) helped out here before being called up at the age of 19, as did brother John. His two sisters Myra and Harriet also help out in the shop. Albert & John worked as a boot repairers. Albert served 'at home' from 5 Feb 1917 until 16 May 1917 when he was posted to France. He was there until Feb 1918 when he came home on leave and was subsequently admitted to the 1st Northern General Hospital in Newcastle, suffering from bronchitis. He was well enough though, to return to his unit in France on 21 March, where he stayed until 3 April 1919 when he was posted to Germany, until 17 Aug 1919.

His brother **JOHN PROCTOR** (Service No 2082) was not so lucky, he was declared missing and later confirmed dead, having been killed on 4 Oct 1915. He served with the 2nd Bn. Northumberland Fusiliers and is buried at Arras Road Cemetery, Roclincourt, France.

Private **JOHN THOMAS CHARLETON** (Service No 24/302). John's father William (deceased) had been a butcher – at No 3 Walker Road in 1881. In 1911, mother Elizabeth was living at number 1705 Walker Road with her niece Iris Allan. John Charleton address at the time of his death was recorded as being Church Street, Walker. John was killed on the 1st July 1916 when he went over the top with his Battalion the Tyneside Irish, at La Boiselle on the Somme; he was 43 years old. Remembered with honour on the Thiepval Memorial, Somme, France.

Private **RALPH OLIVER (**1354) joined the 5th Bn. Northumberland Fusilier Territorial unit in 1912 aged 21, and therefore, being a reservist was called to the Colours as soon as war was declared. He was transferred on a number of occasions to different companies within the 5th Battalion and was in September 1916 released to do 'War work' at Armstrong Whitworth's Walker yard. Finally, being discharged from the Army on 10 Feb 1917. Ralph served in France between 25 March 1916 and 2 Sept 1916. He lived at 28, Church Street with his wife Lillian and his parents Ralph and Sarah Lived at Number 34, Church Street, Walker. During his service Ralph committed a number of minor offences – often being late for evening tattoo or overstaying leave. His main punishment was confined to barracks with one occasion incurring 2 days loss of pay.

Here we pass the fried fish shop at number 30 "*Hello Mr Jones*". He seems fairly busy with the lunchtime rush, we'll not disturb him. Let's move on. Oh, watch out Sir – yes the horses do go to the toilet on the road; you need to be careful where you're walking.

Sergeant **PATRICK COWMAN** (13540/27635) formerly of 146, Byker Street, Walker, Patrick attested on the 13 Oct 1914 at Beverley in Yorkshire to the 7th Bn. East Yorkshire Regiment. He quickly moved up the ranks being made a lance Corporal in 1914, a full Corporal in 1915 and a Sergeant in early 1916. It all started to go wrong though in June of that year when he began to miss parades, stay out overnight, etc. He went missing for 2 days in August 1916 and was reduced to the rank of Corporal as punishment. Further to this he had a severe reprimand for over sleeping by two and a half hours. Luckily, in time, he got himself sorted out and got rated back up to being a Sergeant.

On leaving school Patrick had worked as an office boy. His widowed mother Maggie had taken on a job as a teaching assistant. Patrick had five older siblings and a brother Frank, who was several years younger.

In 1891 the family were living at 36, Church Street, Walker. His father Richard was working as a shipyard labourer at this time.

Patrick was killed on the Somme 8 Feb 1917 and is remembered on the Thiepval Memorial, France.

Able Seaman **GEORGE WOODMAN** (KP/503) 44, Back Church Street, died, aged 28 of wounds on 3rd May 1915 after being in battle with the Royal Naval Volunteer Reserve Anson Bn. Royal Naval Division in the Dardanelles. He was the son of the late George and Henrietta Woodman, of Howden, Yorks. He left behind a widow Alice and three young children. Alice re-married early in 1917 to James Goldsworthy (a former miner, and Royal Navy seaman from 1914 until 1920 when he was discharged, his records citing he was suffering from neurasthenia). The Goldsworthy/Woodman family moved to 28 Tynevale Terrace, Walker.

George is remembered on the Chatham War Memorial, Kent.

At number 52 we stop outside the front window of the home of Private **SAMUEL HOOD** (240707). Samuel, a former house painter, was posted missing on 1st of Sept 1916 and was later declared to having died. His body being found some days after his death and interred at Delville Wood Cemetery, Longeuval, France. Samuel was born in Gosforth in 1887. Whilst living at 18, Shieldfield Green in Newcastle, he met and married nineteen-year-old Sarah Cowen of White Street, Walker. They wed in in 1913 and their daughter Margaret was born the following year. Another daughter Jane, was born posthumously, a short few weeks after his death in 1916. Sadly, her life was to be savagely cut short, like her fathers; she died aged 2 in early 1919.

Private **THOMAS WINSHIP FISACKERLY** (PO/510) was born on 1 Oct 1890, Byker, Newcastle upon Tyne. A former wood cutting machinist at the shipyards, he was living with his mother and sister in one room at 56, Church Street, Walker, when he enlisted to the Royal Marines at the outbreak of war. His widowed mother Martha must have been doubly heartbroken on receiving the news of his death as she had already lost four of her six children before they reached the age of six as well as losing her husband Andrew, at the early age of 45 in 1901.

Martha, now living alone and with only one surviving child, Ethel, a domestic servant for a family in Benton, moved away from the former family home and was living at 995, Walker Road by 1920.

Thomas fought in the hellish Gallipoli battlefields with his Light Infantry (Portsmouth) battalion. They set sail from Portsmouth on 12 Jan 1915 and joined the Middle Eastern Force on 28 Feb 15. Thomas was killed in action on 13th July 1915 aged 24. He has no known grave and is remembered on the Helles Memorial – Gallipoli, Turkey.

"In the attacks of 12th and 13th July, the French had placed some thirty or forty guns and howitzers under British command, and on account of the shortage of British ammunition their guns undertook the whole of the artillery preparation, our artillery confining itself to covering fire during and after the Infantry advance. The counter-attacks were so violent and the calls for artillery support were so incessant that towards the afternoon of the 13th July the British gun ammunition began to get alarmingly low, until finally only about 5,000 rounds of 18-pr. ammunition, including all rounds in Battery charge, remained at Helles. The French were reluctant to supply further artillery support, fearing further attacks on themselves. This was the most anxious night I spent on the Peninsula all but a limited number of rounds were
withdrawn from most Batteries and were placed in horsed ammunition wagons, which perambulated from one side of the British position to the other according to where it seemed most likely the next Turkish attack would take place."
'GALLIPOLI DIARY' BY GENERAL SIR IAN HAMILTON, G.C.B. 1920.

Sapper **GEORGE WILLIAM HEWITT** (Service No 545299) the 21-year-old son of Jane Hewitt, 62 Church Street, Walker (formerly 1, Staiths St, Walker) attests to the Royal Engineers on 10th Dec 1915. George is described as being employed as an 'Engine man' standing 5ft 8½ inches tall and with a 36½ chest with an expansion of a further 3 inches. He begins his service as an 'Engine driver' on 12 June 1916 with the 90th Field Coy Royal Engineers. In 1917, he is transferred to the 7th Bn. York and Lancaster Regiment but is soon transferred back in to the Royal Engineers *'for the benefit of the service'* at a base depot. In October 18, he re-joins his unit from hospital (no record of injury or illness) and is sent on 14 days home leave 2-16th October 1918.

His demobilisation medical is held in Stockheim, Germany on 8 Sept 1919.

Private **HERBERT BICKER** (Service No 3502) a single man, 38-year-old crane driver Bert was lodging with his sister, Mrs Hewitt at 1 Straits Street, Low Walker. He attested in Newcastle on the 8th March 1916 and joined the Labour Corps. He served in England until 3 Nov 1916 and was then sent to France with the British Expeditionary Force on 4 Nov 1916. Demobilised on 3 May 1919 he was awarded a pension of 5/6 as from 4 May 1919 due to a 20% disablement attributed to his war service. He was now living at 62 Church Street, Walker, with the same sister; Mrs Caroline Hewitt and nephew George (see above.)

Next door neighbour……
Private **GEORGE SAMUEL ROBINSON** (Service No 68057) an apprentice 'Plumber' at Armstrong Whitworth's. George of 64 Church Street, Walker, attested in to the Army on 2 Jun 1916 at the age of 17. He is described as being 5ft 8½ inches tall, weighing 124lb, with brown hair, blue eyes and a fresh complexion.
George was attached to the King's Own Yorkshire Light Infantry, transferred to the Lancashire Fusiliers for a short time then back to the King's Own Yorkshire Light Infantry. He didn't travel to France until 30 Oct 1918 and returned 21 Jan 1919 when he was demobilsed.
Also at the same address – this was a property of multi occupancy, each family having 2 rooms. (*In 1911 newly-weds George and Eleanor Muir rented two rooms as did James Rayner and his wife Annie alongside their baby son, Sydney. It is likely that these rooms were very basic and therefore cheap and affordable for young couples starting out.*)

Opposite the Robinson's lived the Robbie's at number 65; Peter and Sarah and three of their offspring. Their property is one of the larger on the street spread over two floors; unlike many of the cramped 'Tyneside' flats on the street. By the 1860's the industrialisation on Tyneside was booming and its population overcrowding the accommodation available. The idea was thought up to build houses and flats that would be affordable for the tenants and prove profitable for the landlords in high population density areas. The 'flats' looked just like any other standard row of terraced houses, the only difference being the pairs of front doors - one leading to the ground floor, the other opening onto a staircase to the flat above.

Each flat had a separate entrance, exit and small back yard. The yard to each 'house' being divided in half and having a separate coal house and outside toilet.

The upper flat has a stairway leading directly from the front door. The lower flat using the area beneath this as storage space.

Housing of this period was often constructed as a mixture of two-storey terraced houses and single-storey Tyneside flats, to accommodate the varying size of families and their incomes.

Richard Robbie *(Picture provided with kind permission of Rosemary O'Day)*

Private **RICHARD ROBBIE** (Service no 20008) a Military Medal recipient, was born 1st September 1895 served with the Royal Army Medical Corps during the war. An apprentice engineer, he had been with the Army Medical Corps Territorials since 1911 and therefore was called up immediately war was declared.

Richard married Elizabeth Redhead on 31st December 1915 and they went on to have three children Nora, Richard and Ethel.

In 1923 Richard joined the Royal Air Force as a hospital orderly, but was discharged in 1925 on compassionate grounds.

A member of Walker Presbyterian Chapel, Richard was awarded his Military Medal, sometime prior to mid-1917. Almost certainly for bringing in wounded men, whilst under fire from the enemy. Brother Frederick Robbie is also serving on the front line; he lived on Mitchell Street with his wife Mary and young son Reuben. (**See families at war**).

Driver **FREDERICK MADDISON** (Service No T4/250368). Frederick joined the Northumbrian Div. Train, Army Service Corps. Son of Lowinger and Elizabeth Maddison, of Gateshead-on-Tyne and husband of Mary E. Maddison, of 64, Church St., Walker, Newcastle-on-Tyne. Frederick was born in 1886 at Gateshead and married Mary Ethel Ridley on 2nd May 1914, although on the 1911 census it states that he has been married to Mary for three years (at that time they had a 2-year-old son, also called Frederick). His Army papers are a little more honest and name the real date of marriage. A second son Norman was born in 1915. There is a 'visitors report' made after Frederick's death regarding his son Frederick Jr – stating that the child is the illegitimate son of Mrs. Maddison and Frederick Maddison. Up to the date of their marriage Frederick Senior paid 5/- a week towards his son's upkeep.

Frederick, prior to the outbreak of war was working as a porter/carter for A.E.R. Railways. His medical notes describe him as being 5 feet 6 inches in height and being of good physical development. He had a tattoo on the back of his right forearm displaying clasped hands and a cross with the words 'IN MEMORY OF MY MOTHER,'

Fred got himself into bother on 2 occasions – both times with harsh penalties. On 13 Jan 1916, he neglected to obey and order and left some horses un-attended. The penalty was loss of ten days pay. Then on 4 Jul 1916, he went absent without leave from 5p.m. and didn't return until 6.15.a.m. on 6 Jul 1916. Penalty 15 days Field punishments No1***

The Army Service Corps (A.S.C.) was responsible for the dispatch and supply of food, water, fuel, and general domestic stores such as clothing, furniture and stationery. "Lines of communication" was an army term used to describe what today we might call the army's logistics: the supply lines from port to front line, and the camps, stores, dumps, workshops of the rear areas. It is difficult to comprehend just what supply to an army that in France alone built up to more than 2 million men actually means. Goods were taken via sea Ports, rail, horse and man to the front lines.

Frederick died aged 26 on 1 Oct 1918 and is remembered with honour on HELLES MEMORIAL, Gallipoli, Turkey Private W. Rae of 2 Coy 50th Div, Train A.S.C. was also injured in the incident that killed Frederick and he died later the same day from his wounds.

Wife Mary died in 1969 aged 81. Their son Frederick Jr. emigrated to Coupar, N.S.W. Australia and died at the age of 67 in 1976.

Let us walk a little further along the street. Ah, here is Annie Walsh's house. The curtains are drawn, poor Annie……she looks so much older than her 65 years………….

Carpenter **JOHN WALSH** along with his brothers Allan and William worked in the shipyards. They lived at home with their recently widowed mother Annie. Annie, a mariner's wife knew the hardships of worrying about a loved one at sea. The Walsh's now resided at 80 Church Street and had lived in the Walker area since the 1870's. Both Annie and her deceased husband Edward, originated from Berwick upon Tweed, but had settled in Walker after their marriage. Annie had given birth to eight children but 4 had died before reaching adulthood. On 11th March 1915, she lost a fifth child when the S.S. Banyo was torpedoed in the Clyde, off the west coast of Scotland.

Let's cross the road ......Number 85. Here we have George Robson's house. George and his wife Jane are in their late 60's. They have six surviving children, from nine live births. Their youngest two sons George and James are still living at home. George Senior was a 'Farm Labourer' in 1911 but by 1914 he had changed trades and become a cart man. Son James had also been a labourer in 1911 and he too had changed occupations and joined his father in the family carting business. Private **JAMES ROBSON** (Service No 227356) James, was 27 years old when he was conscripted in to the Labour Corps in June 1917. He was discharged in November of the same year as he was cited as not being physically fit to serve as he suffered from chronic bronchitis.

 Private **WILLIAM LEWIS** (Service No 43292) was previously employed as a 'holder up' at Armstrong Whitworth and Co Ltd. Forty-four-year-old William of 70 Rochester Street, Walker. A single man with no ties, he attested in Sept 1914. He is described as being 5 feet 5 inches in height with grey/brown hair and with tattoos on both arms.

His records state that in 1915 he is sentenced to 19 days imprisonment by the civil Police for being drunk, assault and willful damage.

Formerly a member of the 3rd Bn. Royal Scottish Militia William originally enlists into the Tyneside Scottish Bn, but is then transferred to the 250th Protection Company of the Royal Defence Corps. On 19 Apr 1916, he is appointed L/Cpl but this is later reverted back to Private. His address at this point in time is 88, Church Street, Walker.

On 5 Mar 1918, he is transferred to munitions work with Wright Anderson and Co Ltd, Gateshead.

Staff Sergeant **WALTER COX** (Service No A2999) along with two of his brother's William and Colin participated in the Great War. They survived pretty much unscathed and were able to return to their homes and to their families after the war.

Walter's parents, William and Mary had both been born in Yorkshire but had moved north at an early age and their children were all born in Walker. John, William, Thomas. Joseph, Walter and Colin.

Walter was a 'watchmaker' living at 90 Church Street, Walker, formerly of 2, Eastbourne Gardens and 84, Byker St, Walker. Twenty-five-year-old Walter was called up in Dec 1915 to the Royal Army Ordnance Corps; attached to the 50th (Northumbrian) Division – the same month as his marriage to Robertina Train. Walter is described as being 5 foot 7 inches in height, weighing 155 lb and having false upper teeth. He returned to watch-making after the war and proved to be a successful businessman who ran a shop on Church Street for many more years.

Here we stop outside the home of John Box – Beer retailer and Bar Manager. The door is open; let's pop in for a swift half. *"Ah, hello Bertha, two beers please."*

Look, there's adopted daughter Irene Carter doing some homework and Harold Box helping her." (*In 1915 Irene would be 7 and Harold 12*). Elder brother Lancelot aged 20 is working as a shoemaker.

Private **CYRIL BOX** (Service No 135405) enlisted at Alnwick, though his family address was 122, Church Street, Walker. Cyril who was 22 and working as a 'Footman' for Lord Percy at Alnwick Castle in Northumberland, when he signed his attestation papers on 29th Oct 1915.

Lord Percy's own family were heavily involved in the war. His sons. Earl Alan Percy (later the 8th Duke of Northumberland) and Lord William, both served with the Grenadier Guards. His youngest son, Lord Eustace, was working in the diplomatic corps in Washington trying to bring the USA into the war on the allied side. Daughters' Ladies Margaret and Victoria, helped out on the 'Home Front' including aiding with the organisation of Red Cross facilities.

Cyril would have seen the camps being built near to the Castle; the home to a number of Northumberland Fusilier battalions, including the 16th Newcastle Commercials and the Tyneside Scottish and Irish. As well as the camp, soldiers from the 7th Battalion were billeted in the town and camped on Alnwick Moor. He had previously been employed as a 'Hall boy' by Edward Joicey Esq, at his 39-roomed property at Blenkinsopp Hall near Haltwhistle. Incidentally, Edward Joicey, lost his son Captain Clive Montagu Joicey to the Great War, on 5 June 1917. Clive served with the 4th Bn. Northumberland Fusiliers and is buried at Brown's Copse Cemetery, Roeux, Pas de Calais,France.

Cyril joined the Royal Army Service Corps, attached to the 31st Field Ambulance Unit. Having passed his Motor Learners test in Jan 1916, he spent time with the Mediterranean Expeditionary Force as well as in the UK and with the British Expeditionary Force in France. He got himself in to trouble on a couple of occasions and had his pay deducted; On 13 Sept 1918, he absented himself by 24 hours after missing the leave train when returning to his unit: Forfeit 3 days' pay. On 3 Aug 1919, He failed to comply with orders to proceed to H.Q and instead went to Bethune where he stayed the night and did not report until 10.30am the following day. Forfeit: 10 days' pay.

Private **NORMAN WILSON** (Service No 27831/447182) was born in Tweedmouth, Northumberland but was living at 111, Church Street, Walker, and working as a 'Joiner' when he attested to the Army in Dec 1915. He was held in reserve and not called forward until Sept 1916 to join the 29th (Res) Bn. Northumberland Fusiliers. The heavy losses on the Somme battlefield had left many battalions desperate for replenishment of troops. He was soon after transferred to the 1/4th King's Own Yorkshire Light Infantry and then finally to the Labour Coy, Royal Engineers after being gassed in July 1917. Norman was also hospitalised twice with a thigh injury –firstly in Nov 1916 and then again in Nov 1917.

On leaving the Army, Norman knocked 5 years off his real age (30) and boarded the 'Grampian' at Glasgow docks in October 1919. He sailed to Canada to return to a life he had begun there 10 years earlier; in Vancouver, British Columbia as a Carpenter. Like many other men who had left Britain to find work overseas; he returned to his homeland to serve his country during its' troubled time. On the Canadian 1921 census he is living with his wife Amelia.

Private **FREDERICK WILLIAM ARMSTRONG** (Service No 158479). Frederick was born at 118, Church Street; a four-roomed property, and was still living there when he volunteered his services to the 5th Bn. Northumberland Fusiliers on 4 Aug 1915 aged 15. His father Robert – an iron riveter at the shipyards, had now passed away and he was living with his widowed great-aunt Hannah, his mother Mary Ann, cousin Violet, and two male boarders.

His service record states than on enlistment he was 5 feet 5 inches tall and with a chest expansion of 33½. He had dark brown hair, a fresh complexion and grey eyes. Ideally suited to the Army – though if you re-read above, you will see he was underage (no proof of real name or age was required). Frederick went off with his battalion to train and eventually sailed to France with them. Sometime later his mother discovered what he had done, and in despair sent a letter and young Fred's birth certificate to the Army, to prove his real age. Frederick was then swiftly returned from the battlefields of France and transferred to a training reserve unit as a 'Boy Private'. He was made a full Private on 18 April 1918 and was demobilsed on 19 March 1919 at York. Unable to settle into civilian life he re-enlisted in to the 5th Bn. Northumberland Fusiliers on 3Aug 1920. On re-joining the unit his medical describes him as being 5 feet 11 inches tall and weighing 154 pounds. This was very tall for a chap living in the industrial North at that time. His chest measurement was 37 inches with a further 2 inch expansion. The Army certainly had made a man of him physically.

Now we walk past the Mechanics Institute and Library, the Walker and Byker Industrial Permanent Building Society and the Picture House. Next door is the Registrar of Births and Deaths office, look Mr Trewick is sitting at his desk (*waves through the window.*) Next door we have the North-Eastern Banking Co. Then there's the Walker Poor Rate Office; Mr Brown being the overseer and Poor Rate collector. We then pass the Presbyterian Church – Mr Howatson being the Minister.

We'll quickly pop in to the Drill Hall – the home of the 5th Bn. Northumberland Fusiliers and say 'Hello' to Captain G.A.J Soltau-Symonds…….

Sapper **WILLIAM BAMBER** (Service No 75117 / 194137). William, originally from Barrow-in-Furness and son of John Bamber, was 23 years and 7 months old when he attested on 1 Dec 1915. He was living at 155, Church Street and employed as a 'riveter' at Armstrong Whitworth's William was the tallest soldier I have come across in Walker – standing 6 feet 1 inch tall. He weighed 161 pounds and had a 39 ½ chest with an expansion of another 3 inches. William's records are very fragmented and burnt from the WWII bombings on the storage facility where the records were housed, so it's difficult to decipher much from them. Prior to moving to Walker, William had been a member of the Kings Own Royal Lancashire Fusiliers (Territorials). I see he was engaged firstly with the Royal Garrison Artillery and then transferred to the Royal Engineers with the Railway Operation Transport Department. He was posted to Salonika in 1917 and was hospitalised with malaria soon after arriving. In Jun 1917, he was under close arrest and given 14 days Field Punishments number 1 for causing a disturbance in camp. He was de-mobilised in February 1919.

Private **WILLIAM DAVIDSON** (Service No 8005 M/404338) a woodcutting machinist, also living at 155, Church Street, Walker, William attested to the Military on 28 June 1918 at the age of 20. He was first attached to the West Yorkshire Regiment then transferred to the Royal Army Service Corps, where he was employed in the motor transport section as a driver. In 1919, he sailed to Port Said in Egypt where he stayed until de-mobilization in April 1920. He stayed on as a territorial soldier with the Northumberland Fusiliers, service number 4260968. He was finally discharged from Military service at the age of 31 in 1929.

On the 1911 census William was living a few doors further along the road, at 159, Church Street; a two-roomed property. His father John was a ship's joiner and mother Janet a housewife. The couple had parented eight children, six of whom were still alive (a brother John having died on war service in 1914 and buried Walker). Five of those surviving children with ages ranging from six to twenty-three were still living at home. There is no mention of the occupations of the older siblings. Brother Private **JOHN DAVIDSON** (Service No:10868) died 11th Oct 1914, aged 26. A member of the West Yorkshire Regiment (Prince of Wales's Own). Husband of

Margaret Davidson) of 141, Clifford St., Byker, Newcastle-on-Tyne. Likely died in the illness or injury sustained in training, he is buried at Christ Church cemetery, Walker.

Now lets' cross back over the cobbled road and a few doors along. Now be careful you ladies in high heels; we've already had one mishap today – we don't want to be having to take one of you to Walker Park hospital with a sprained ankle.

Lance Corporal **WILLIAM LOGAN** (Service No 240004) was the son of Elizabeth Logan, of 166, Church St., Walker, and the late Walter Logan. He was a member of the 1st/5th Bn. Northumberland Fusiliers and died aged 30 on 10 Apr 1918. He is remembered with honour Pont-Du-Hem Military Cemetery, La Gorgue, France.

mother and six of his seven surviving siblings; three others had died in infancy.

William was killed during a very intense period of fighting. The Battalion War Diaries state: 10th April……. *"At 3. 15 p.m. the 5th & 6th Northumberland Fusiliers moved into position in support of the 150th Brigade. The line of the River Lys & River Lawe to be held at all costs. At 9.10p.m the 5th N.F. were ordered to take up position in strong points near Trou Bayard where they joined the 4th N.F. Soon after daybreak fighting began again."*

The 5th Northumberland Fusiliers who were now holding Pont Levis (They had relieved the 4th E. Yorkshires earlier) were heavily attacked under cover of violent artillery fire. In spite of fine resistance put up by the Fusiliers the enemy forced his way across the bridge, though a dozen machine guns, firing from Trou Bayard, gave him a warm reception. Only his prodigious numbers carried him through.

The Divisional History also gives an account of the relief of the 4th E. Yorkshires where 2 companies (5th N.F.) had relieved A & B companies of the E. Yorks. 2 platoons of 'A' company went astray and were reported as lost.

2.a.m. on 11th April the 5th N.F. held the right of the line Estaires to Neuf Berquin Rd. to just West of Trou Bayard. Very heavy fighting again at 7a.m. the enemy was reported to have occupied Trou Bayard. At 9.35 the 5th N.F. was heavily attacked. The 151st brigade had been forced back exposing the right of the 149th brigade and so the 5th N.F. were withdrawn.

Private **JAMES BRADLEY** (Service No 3/212204) lived at 173 Back Church Street, he attested to the Northumberland Fusiliers on 30 Sept 1914 aged 34 years old. It was a bit of a rash decision as James, a fireman at Walker Colliery, really was not cut out for the Military way of life. There is no record of when he left the service….saying that, he was never really there:

Absent for 15 days from 4 Jul 1915 to 18 Jul 1915 awarded 28 days Field Punishment No 2 *** and 43 stoppage of pay.

As soon as his Field punishments were completed he again went absent without leave, this time for 10 days; from 22 Aug 1915 to 31 Aug 1915 and was on this occasion awarded 28 days loss and pay and Field Punishment No 2 (unclear of for how many days).

Things quieten down for a while as he works for free – paying back all his 'fines'. He is then transferred to the East Yorkshire Regiment on the 30 Nov 1915. Old habits return and on 24 Jan 1915 until 1 Feb 1916 he again goes absent without leave. He forfeits 9 days' pay and is returned to the Northumberland Fusiliers. He's now had enough and deserts the following day and is absent for a total of 69 days. Likely-hood is he was found at home by the Military Police and is eventually returned to his old unit. He goes absent again 17 Jul 1916 until the 7 Aug 1916, a total of 22 days. His punishment is fairly lenient at 14 days 'duty.'

On 7 Jan 1917, he goes missing for 10 days returning on 16 Jan 1917 and again on the 27 Jan 1917 he becomes absent, this time for 12 days. Returning (or being returned) to his unit on 7 Feb 1917.

James was married to Mary and they had eight children – Mary, James, Elizabeth, Janet, Frank, Margaret and Catherine. Previous addresses include Mitchell Street and Caledonia Street – where they were living during the 1911 census, along with widowed Aunt Janet Summerville, aged 70.

It would be interesting to find out what happened to James Bradley the 'not too happy' soldier after the war. More than likely he is the James Bradley who died in Tynemouth parish in 1937 aged 56.

Private **RICHARD JESSOP HENZELL** (Service No 300058). Richard was 41 when war broke out, and was living in a 2 roomed property at 176, Church Street, Walker, along with his wife and 6 children. He was working locally as a Dairy Farmhand. He signed up to the Royal Field Artillery and served with 'D' Battery, 317 Brigade – part of the 63rd Division. He later was moved to the Labour Coy. Richard was discharged on de-mobilisation on 4 Mar 1919. In 1920, he signed up to the 5th Bn. Northumberland Fusiliers Territorials.

Private **ISAAC MADDISON** (Service No 16001). Isaac was the son of coal miner Mark Maddison, of 181, Back Church St., Walker, Newcastle-on-Tyne, and the late Isabella Maddison. He joined "C" Coy. 9th Bn., West Yorkshire Regiment (Prince of Wales's Own) and died aged 18 on 8 August 1915. He is remembered with honour on the Helles Memorial, Gallipoli, Turkey.

(The memorial takes the form of an obelisk over 30 meters high that can be seen by ships passing through the Dardanelles.)

In 1911 at the age of 14 Isaac was attending the Industrial School on Jubilee Road, Newcastle. It's likely he had been a bit of a 'bad lad' and was sent by the courts to the 'reformatory' school to try and straighten him out. Isaac had seven siblings, though two had died in infancy, his mother Isabella passed away in 1913 aged 43.

The 9th Bn. West Yorkshire Regiment, sailed on the 1 July 1915 from Avonmouth for Gallipoli, via Mudros, and landed at Suvla Bay on 7 August 1915.
A letter written to the Times of London in October of 1923 by Mr. John Still, adjutant in the 6th battalion describes the battle in which Maddison and Ellison (see further down) died;

Publish but please read it eliminating all self-praise radically. As there was no self-praise, cutting out was not necessary. I am IAN HAMILTON, 1 Hyde Park Gardens W2 Dear General Hamilton, - You will not remember meeting me on the occasion of a dance held upstairs in this office about a dozen years ago. But I do not write as secretary of this association, but as an officer who served under you on Gallipoli. I have just read your Gallipoli Diary, and read it with an extraordinary interest; for rather an extraordinary reason for it so happens that I am perhaps the only person in the world who can throw light upon some of its greatest puzzles. In your map of the Suvla area, square 105 F/K, you give a position on Scimitar Hill occupied and withdrawn from, apparently without your knowledge for two years! I was there. I know exactly what happened, why, and when. For I was adjutant of the 6th East Yorks Regiment on that hill after Estridge (the regular adjutant) had been wounded. I was also signaling officer. And if I may say so, I was the only officer on that hill who had spent years in jungle and on hills and was in consequence able to appreciate things accurately. We had been ordered to take up that position on the map and we took it up. I fixed our exact position by prismatic compass. We fought all day there and had a good few casualties including two officers (or three), and then we were taken off again at night "because the regiments to right and left of you have not been able to get up". That was the night of August 8. On our right were a sergeant and two men only of another regiment, lost and refound by us. I forget their unit, but I can still see the identifying mark on their backs in my mind's eye: it was a sort of castle in yellow beyond them there was a gap right away to Chocolate Hill. On our left was not as you state another regiment, but only a weak half company of the West Yorks with two officers of whom one was killed, and the other – Devenport (sic) – severely wounded. And this left us in the air. Your orders given to General Stopford at 6pm never reached us on Scimitar Hill. Why? They knew where we were, for I was in touch by day with Brigade H.Q. signallers on Hill 10 or close to it. By night I lost contact for both my lamps failed me. As you justly say, anyone with half an eye could see Tekke Tepe was the key to the whole position. Even I, a middle-aged amateur who had done a bit of big game shooting and knocking about saw it at once. We reconnoitered it, sent an officer and my signaller corporal to climb it, and got through to Brigade H.Q. the message giving our results. I sent it myself. The hill was then empty. Next morning you saw or heard that troops had actually reached the top of Tekke Tepe. Yes, they had. A worn and weak company, D Company of my regiment together with my Colonel (Moore). Major Brunner, of the R.E., and myself started up that hill. About thirty got to the top: of them five got down again to the bottom, and of those three lived to the end of the war. I was one of them. You wonder why we did not dig in (pages 78 and 79 of your Volume II) as we had lots of time. There, Sir, is where that war was lost. You set a Brigade at that empty hill on the afternoon of the 8th. Actually, owing to staff work being so bad, a battalion received orders to attack and did not receive those orders until dawn on the 9th. I received them myself as adjutant. The order ran to this effect: "The C.-in-C. considers this operation essential to the success of the whole campaign". The order was sent out on the late afternoon of the 8th, when we were on scimitar hill. It reached us at dawn on the 9th in a Turkish trench at Sulejik. In the meanwhile, for those hours more precious to the world than we even yet can judge, the Brigade major was lost! Good God why didn't they send a man who knew the country? He was lost, lost, lost and it drives one almost mad to think of it. Excuse Me. Next morning (from the order) at dawn on the 9th you saw some of our fellows climbing cattle tracks. You don't place theme exactly where I think you really saw them, but as I know there were none just precisely where you say you saw them, I am pretty certain it was us you saw from the ship, only we were half a mile north of where you describe. Then we climbed Tekke Tepe. Simultaneously the Turks attacked through the gap from Anafarta.

Their attack cut in behind D Company and held back the rest of the battalion who fought in the trench, with the Duke of Wellington's on their left. We went on, and, as I said, not one of us got back again. A few were taken prisoner. I was slightly wounded, and stayed three years and three months as a prisoner. Later that morning we who survived were again taken up Tekke Tepe by its northern ravine on the west side. Turkish troops were simply pouring down it and the other ravines. On the top of Tekke Tepe were four field guns camouflaged with boughs of scrub oak, and a Brigade H.Q. was just behind the ridge. I had a few minutes conversation there with the Turkish Brigadier in French. But I am coming home on leave in March or April next. May I have the honour of meeting you and going over it on the map? I think much might be cleared up that was still obscure when you wrote your book. There are one or two things one prefers not to write. Please let me know your wishes in this matter. I loved your book and I want to do any small thing possible to complete your picture. Yours truly (Sd) JOHN STILL Victoria Commemoration Buildings, Nos 40 and 41 Ward Street, Kandy, Ceylon Sept 19.

Private **MARK MADDISON** (Service No 124306) a coal miner and father of Isaac above and also of 181, Back Church Street, Walker. Having previously served 6 years with the 3rd Bn. Durham Light Infantry Militia, Mark Maddison a 45-year-old widower, attested on 25 June 1915. He was posted 2 days later to a 'reserve' position so that he could retain his civilian employment and be available to be called up if needed. Mark no doubt hoped to get called up so that he could avenge the death of his son in August of the same year. He was released from the Army as being 'surplus to requirement' on 14th Dec 1918.

Private **FRANK VANHEE KELSEY** (Service No 98671). Frank was the illegitimate son on Edith Kelsey, of 182, Church St., Walker, Newcastle-on-Tyne. He died on 21 Oct 1918, aged 22. Frank had been born four years before his mother had married – father unknown. His grandparents had helped with his upbringing as his mother was financially unable to cope on her own. It is very possible that Frank was born in the Newcastle Union Workhouse on Westgate Road, Newcastle. Frank Vanne Cornish is recorded on the 1911 census as living with his parents George and Edith Cornish (nee Kelsey) at 182, Church Street, Walker. Both George and Frank work at a colliery. George and Edith had married in 1900 at Durham. On the 1901 census they are living at Framwellgate, Durham – while Frank is living with his Grandparents in Rosehill, Wallsend.

Frank served with "D" Coy. 9th Bn., Machine Gun Corps (Infantry) and was killed in the closing weeks of the Great War. He was likely wounded at the river Lys near Harlebeke, on the night of the 19th/20th October, when there was intense fighting. He is remembered with honour at Harlebeke New British Cemetery, Belgium.

At the outbreak of war, each army infantry battalion and cavalry regiment had two machine guns. In November 1914, a Machine Gun School opened in France and in England the Motor Machine Gun Service formed at Bisley in Surrey, originally by the Royal Field Artillery with motor cycle mounted machine gun batteries. By 1916, 36 companies had been raised and trained, using a range of guns and ammunition such as the Hotchkiss Machine Gun, The Maxim and the Vickers Machine Gun Mark II. The Transport sections of horse and mule drawn limbers to move the guns and ammunition was actually larger than the Infantry battalion's transport.

Private **HUGH ROSS** (Service No 404587) was a 21-year-old 'Fish Merchant' living and working at 193. Church Street, Walker; from where his widowed father, also named Hugh – ran a Fried Fish shop. No 193 was a three-roomed property and in 1911 several family members lived there including Hugh's brother Matthew and his new wife.

When Hugh attested to the Army on 11 Dec 1915, his physical description states that he is 5 feet 5½ inches tall and has a 37½ inch chest with an expansion of a further 2 inches. He joined the West Yorkshire Regiment and was later transferred to the Labour Corps in 1918 after being wounded for a second time; a gun-shot wound to the hand. In December, the same year he contracted Flu and was hospitalized in Etaples, France. He was also hospitalized with 'epilepsy' in Oct 1917 – presumably a one-off seizure? On 25 Jun 1917, he was confined to barracks for 7 days for the offence of having a 'dirty rifle.'

Careful now, watch the trams......let Mrs. Dodds cross over the road with her perambulator. Poor Johnny hates getting bounced all over on the cobbles.

Corporal **PATRICK HASSAN** (Service No 146510). Twenty-seven-year-old Patrick joined the Army Service Corps (69th Field Butchery Corps) in 1915. Living at 40, Rochester Street; he ran his own successful butchery business from 216, Church Street, Walker, ably assisted by his younger brother John. Patrick was single and lived with his widowed father, also called Patrick. Brothers Joseph and John and sister Mary Jane and Lizzie Ann. His mother Mary (Née Diamond) had passed away in 1908.

Patrick is described as being 5 feet 7 inches tall and having a 'spare but muscular' build. He attested on 5th Nov 1915 and was sent to Aldershot for training on the 8 Nov 1915.He was soon to depart UK shores on ship from Devonport (Plymouth), Devon, and arrived Mombasa, Kenya on 15 March 1916 as part of the East African Force.

On 12 March 1919, he embarked on the Hospital troop ship 'SALAMIS' at Dar-es- Salam and returned to England to be demobilised and return to work in his shop.

There is one misdemeanour recorded in Patrick's documents, though no chastisement is recorded; On 18 April 1916 "When on active service, urinating outside of Garrison Institute about 9p.m."

Patrick died in 1945 aged 57.

Private **JAMES EAGAN** Service number   43901

James was a 27-year-old miner living at 207 Church Street when he attested on 9 Dec 1915. He was married to Ellen Holland (on 1st Jan 1913) and had a son John born 1913, but died as an infant during the war and a daughter Ellen, born 3 Jun1916. James was attached to the 8th Bn. York and Lancaster Regiment. He was discharged on 15 Oct 1918 due to having tuberculosis of the lungs, attributed to active service. He was awarded a pension of 22/- a week from 16 Oct 1918.

His service was as follows:

Home 9 -12-15 1 day

Reserve 10-12-15 to 19-3-17

Home 20-3-17 to 19-6-17

France 20-6-17 to 9-11-17

? 10-11-17 to 23-6-18

Home 24-6-18 to 15-10-18

Gunner **THOMAS GRANT**   Service No 106703

Gunner Grant of the 2nd Brigade Royal Field Artillery, was originally 'Private 27478 Durham Light Infantry' when he joined in July not 1915, but was transferred to the R.F.A on 4 Sept 1915. Thomas a coal miner of 228 Church Street, Walker was 26 years old when he attested to the army. He spent a lot of the war in France and Flanders and was admitted to hospital on a number of occasions; three times in 1916 with varying ailments: dental caries, diphtheria and diarrhoea.

On the 9 May 1918, he was awarded 14 days Field Punishment No1*** with 21 days deduction of pay for "DRUNKENESS" (written in capitals) in the field.

On 31 May 1918, he was wounded – shell splinters and gas and when his condition was stable enough he was transported back to England on the hospital ship 'St David' on 29th June 1918.

His 'Clothing and necessaries' were packed up and sent on ahead, they included:

Boots 1,Cup SD (*service distribution*) 1, Greatcoat 1, Drawers woollen1, Jacket SD 1, Pantaloons cord 1, Puttees pairs 0, Waistcoat cardigan 0, Rifle RFA 0, Badges cap 1, Braces pairs 1, Brushes shaving 1, Brushes tooth 1, Cap comforter 0, Combs hair 1, Discs identity 2, Rifle clasp lanyards 1, Steel helmet 1, Bottle water 0, Housewife 1, Blankets GS 2, Fork 1, Holdall 1, Knife table 1, Laces pairs 1, Razor case 1, Shirts 1, Socks worsted 1, Spoon 1, Spurs jack 0, Towel hand 1, Vests woollen 1, Gloves woollen 1, Dressing field 0, Pay book 1, Haversack 1, Tin mess 0, Bandolier 0, Box respirator 1.

Thomas was granted leave from 17th to 24th Dec 1818, he was then to report to Ripon discharge centre (a rail warrant was issued) where he would have transferred to 'reserve' to go back to work in the coal mines.

Private **ARTHUR BRANNAN** lived at 237 Church Street. One of his brothers traded as a confectioner. His two other brothers Nicholas and Francis were ship's riveters like himself, and his sisters – Susannah and Alice, both were 'domestics at home' on the 1911 census and likely helped out in the shop too. The Brannan's lived in a comfortable 4 roomed property. Arthur died on 7th July 1916, aged 31, while serving with the Northumberland Fusiliers.

Gunner **WILLIAM LUCAS**   Service No143319

William a 27-year-old 'newspaper dispatcher' was married to Annie and living at 239 Church Street, Walker when he attested on 7 Dec 1914 – his first wedding anniversary. He wasn't called for until March 1917 when he was allocated to the Royal Garrison Artillery and posted to Bexhill, in Sussex. His only recorded misdemeanour appears to be when he overstayed his first leave home. He was due back at his barracks on 4 May 1917 (a few weeks in to his service) and overstayed by 2 days and 19 hours. He was confined to barracks for 7 days and made to forfeit 6 days' pay. He didn't do it again.

On 10 June 1917 William landed in France and was immediately sent to join his new unit - the 113 Siege Battery. He spent 7 days sick in hospital in Sept 1918.

He stayed in France until Sept 1919 helping with the battlefield clearances.

Here we shall have a ten-minute break so that you can venture into Mr Nickles' Confectionery shop at number 241, and buy an ounce of black bullets, sherbet pips or aniseed balls. Maybe some liquorice root will take your fancy? His assistant will weigh out your choice and put it in a nice paper twist for you to take home and enjoy at your leisure.

Please – if any of you would like to make purchases at the other shops; such as Nevins' fruiterers or Howeys' Drapers, please let me know and we can extend the break.....it will be interesting for you to mingle with the local residents and business folk. Gallon's Grocer's at no 252 come highly recommended, as does Corby's Butcher's at 297 – next to West Walker School.

Sapper **WILLIAM PRESTON**   Service No 2485

William was a 49-year-old miner, when he enlisted in 1917 and was posted to the Royal Engineers (Pioneers) to join the 303 Road Construction Company. He lived at 256 Church

Street, Walker, with his wife Alice Seaton whom he married in 1891 at Walker Parish Church, and their five daughters. Alice, Olive, Lily, Flora and Eleanor.

William was de-mobilized Jan 1919 at Clipstone, Nottinghamshire aged 51.

Private **GEORGE THOMPSON** (served as **ELLITSON**) Service No 10727

George Thompson was the son of George a coal miner, and Annie Thompson of 275 Back Church Street, Walker. He, along with his elder brother also worked in the mines. His father was a 'waiter on' brothers Joseph and John coal miner 'putters' and George a coal miner 'driver'. (Brother John's middle name was Ellison from census info.) In 1901 the family were living at 238 Church St. In 1911 the family had moved to 1640 Walker Road and by 1915 the family at Back Church Street.

George was posted to the 6th Bn. East Yorkshire Regiment and sailed with them to Gallipoli via Mudros, and landed at Suvla Bay 7 August 1915.

 He was killed, aged 19, on 9 Aug 1915. He is remembered with honour on the Helles Memorial – Gallipoli Penninsula.

Near neighbours George Thompson of the East Yorkshire Regiment and Isaac Maddison of the West Yorkshire Regiment, died day apart thousands of miles from home.

Private **JOHN HENRY GODFREY** Service number   061896 John, aged 24 is living at 289 Church Street, Walker. He joined the Royal Army Service Corps as a Horseman/ Driver, having been a former Cartman. He joined the expeditionary force in France on 12 April 1915 and was demobilised 13 June 1919 suffering from Dermatitis. John's brother Thomas, also a 'Cartman' and living at 37 Rhodes Street, Walker, joined the Royal Army Service Corps at the same time as John.

Private **GEORGE CHAMBERS**   Service No DEAL/2372

Private George Chambers, a former miner and Royal Navy volunteer reservist of 291, Church Street, Walker, enlisted 25 Nov 1914. He transferred to the Royal Marine Divisional Train in March 1915 and was drafted to the Mediterranean in December the same year, joining the Divisional Train at Mudros and participating in the Gallipoli campaign. In August 1917, he was attached to the 188th Brigade HQ. George was later killed in action in France on 20 Jan 1918. Little information surrounding his death can be found. He had served with the Royal Marines R.N. Division. He is buried with honour at METZ-EN-COUTURE COMMUNAL CEMETERYBRITISH EXTENSION, Pas De Calais, France.

Private **JAMES BEATON**

Residing at 296 Church Street Walker, a 'Labourer' by trade he joined the Army aged 27 on 5th June 1916. A married man, James had previously served 4 years with the 5th Bn. Northumberland Fusiliers (Territorials).

James sailed with his unit to Salonika in 1917 (the Salonika campaign was fought in northern Greece, Serbia and Albania during 1915-1918.) He was admitted to hospital on a number of occasions with diarrhoea and Malaria. In 1916 he became a Lance Corporal but was deprived of his stripe by order of the C.O for overstaying his pass from midnight 3 Aug1916 until 8pm on the 6 Aug 1916. He then went absent again for 8 days in Sept from the 10th to 17th 1916. In March 1918, he was transferred to the 2/9th Durham Light Infantry. Discharged as a Private on 18 Mar 1919 and re-enlisted into the Labour Corps on 10 May 1919.

Private **FRANCIS HENRY BRADLEY**   Service No 16404

Francis was also residing at 296 Church Street when he was killed on 29 September 1918 aged 31. He was attached to the 11th Bn. West Yorkshire Regiment.

The son of Dominic and Catherine Bradley, of Walker; husband of Sarah Jane Bradley (nee Harvey), of 296, Church St., Walker, Newcastle-on-Tyne.

Remembered with honour PONT-D'ACHELLES MILITARY CEMETERY, NIEPPE, France.

On 4 March 1916 - John Harvey (37) – brother of Sarah Bradley was killed in an accident at the Armstrong Whitworth Walker shipyard. Some men from Pearson's Works at Wallsend had been sub-contracted to fit a fan to a ship there. They raised the fan 15 feet on wire ropes which were strong enough to hold 2 tons (as had done with 2 previous fans safely.) When within 3 feet of the fixed position the rope was substituted for an independent rope which then snapped and the fan fell, crushing John and another man, who were working in the boiler room below. John was injured about the head, back and legs and he succumbed the following day, Thursday 2nd March 1916.

Private **CORNELIUS NOBLE**   Service No 1856

A native of Walker, Cornelius was born in 1896 to John, an' Iron moulder' and Alice, his wife. The family live at a number of addresses in Church Street and I first find them at no 268 on the 1901 census. Brother George 17 is a ships' 'rivet heater'. Thomas 10, Deborah 8 and Cornelius 6 are scholars and sister Elsie 2 is at home. Sarah Glass aged 77 is a boarder. By 1911 they have moved to cramped two
roomed accommodation at 314 Church Street. Father John is 59 and still working as an iron moulder, Alice still has all her children at home George, Thomas and Cornelius are all general labourers at the shipyard. Mary Egan aged 15 is a servant.

John Noble passed away early 1914. Alice had given birth to 9 children - 4 of them dying in infancy.

 At the time of his death, Cornelius's family were living at 310 Church Street, Walker.

After leaving West Walker Council School, Cornelius joined the 1st/5th Bn., Northumberland Fusiliers on 1 Jun 1913 and volunteered for Imperial service on 5 Aug 1914. He went to France on 20 May 1915 and was killed in action aged 19 on 24 May 1915. He is remembered with honour on the YPRES (MENIN GATE) MEMORIAL.

The 1st/5th Bn., Northumberland Fusiliers were raised in August 1914 at the call of the outbreak of war, part of Northumberland Brigade, Northumbrian Division.
Having landed in France mid-April 1915, Cornelius Noble's war lasted a little over 4 weeks.
Excerpt from 'The Fiftieth Division' 1914-1919 by Everard Wyrall 1939

Battle of Bellawarde.

The discharge took place from opposite our line near Hooge, thence northwards nearly to Turco farm. It was so violent that, even through the roar of guns, the hissing from the gas cylinders could be heard from across No Man's Land where the British and German trenches lay close together, i.e , especially astride the Menin Road. The effect of the gas was felt later some twenty miles behind the front line, so that what it must have been in the latter

can be imagined. The gas clouds soared as high as forty feet and were so dense as to blot out houses and farms.

But the wind being favourable, many officers in the front line were on the alert and, as a surprise attack, the gas failed. Nevertheless, owing to the proximity of the opposing lines in certain places, the troops had little time in which to adjust their primitive respirators before the fumes overcame them.

The enemy infantry assaulted immediately but, met by a withering fire from machine guns and rifles, experienced a heavy and costly repulse. Only in one part of the line, i.e., at Mouse Trap farm, held by two platoons of the Royal Dublin Fusiliers, did he succeed in over-running our position. At this point the opposing trenches were only thirty yards apart, and the Germans were in the "farm" (now only a rubble heap of bricks and mud) ere the garrison had an opportunity of putting up a defence. South of Mouse Trap Farm, however the struggle continued for many hours. With dogged courage and a tenacity which surprised and thrilled even those who expected them to make a stand, those units of the Old Army, reinforced by partially-trained reinforcements, upheld the great traditions of the past and "Ypres '15" was fought with the glorious spirit of "Ypres '14"

Serjeant **DANIEL MALLIGAN** Service number 235273, of the Lancashire Fusiliers, a former labourer, died on 28th April 1920 aged 39, at home and after discharge. His death was said to be caused as a direct effect of injuries sustained during the war. Husband of Christina Malligan, of 308 Church Street, Walker (1911). He left behind at least three children. Remembered with honour WALKER (CHRIST CHURCH) CEMETERY, Newcastle upon Tyne.

Private **JOHN HICKS McKEE**   Service No 51772
John was the son of a bricklayer/builder, also called John. His elder brother David worked in the newspaper offices as a 'Point Shifter.' John himself was described as being a 'Newsboy.' On completion of his schooling he chose to work for the railways as a Locomotive cleaner. Possibly he hoped one day to be an Engine Driver?
John also had a younger sister Anne and a younger brother Isaac. Two other siblings had died in infancy.

John at first was attached to the North Staffordshire Regiment and travelled to France with them in October 1917 but was soon posted to the Cheshire Regiment. He was reported missing between 21/30th March 1918 but was then returned to his battalion in April – where he had been I have no idea, though a hospital admission is a possibility. He was gassed on 27th May 1918 and it looks as though he was transported to Rouen in France to a Military Hospital. He re-joined his old battalion on 8 Aug 1918. He was back in action and at the front line at The Battles of the Soissonais and the Ourc and the capture of Baigneux Ridge. Sadly, while taking part in the Final Advance in Flanders, weeks before the Armistice, John McKee was killed in action, aged 20 on 03 October 1918. The son of John and Eleanor McKee, of 316, Church St, Walker, Newcastle-on-Tyne, he is remembered with honour at VICHTE MILITARY CEMETERY Belgium.

Private **GEORGE YOUNGER**   Service no 22929

George lived on Church Street, Walker but at what number I have no idea as his service records were badly damaged and difficult to read. I could make out that he had lived there with his brother.

George, who followed the Presbyterian faith, was born in 1896 and was 19 years and 10 months old when he attested to the Army in February 1916, or should I say conscripted. He had previously been working as a Tram Conductor.

 George was sent to the 3rd Bn. King's Own Scottish Borderers. He wasn't cut out for Military life though and deserts from his unit on 21 March 1916 at Dover. He then took himself off and somehow had himself landed in France in April 1916 with the 7/8th British Expeditionary Force. He had *'joined the expeditionary force by his own accord but was returned to the 3rd Bn. after 38 days.'* (Taken from his service record). He was then admitted to hospital in Rouen sometime later the same month. He deserted again on 14th June 1916 and declared a' deserter' two days later.

In July, he was admitted to hospital again, this time at Etaples. Here his mental condition appeared to be in a very bad way and he was transferred to the Royal Victoria Hospital in Netley, Hampshire, on 18 Aug 1916. They then transferred him to Dykebar War Hospital in Paisley, Scotland.

A memorandum sent to his battalion from Dykebar War Hospital on 17th April 1918 states the following: *'I beg to acknowledge receipt of discharge documents of George Younger of 3rd Bn. K.O.S.B's. This man is shortly to be transferred to an Asylum. But it has not yet been fixed to which one he will be going.'*
                    Major RAMC o/c

George was discharged from the Army in May 1918 as considered 'No Longer physically fit for Military service.' He was awarded a pension of 5/6 a week for 13 weeks as from 4 May 1918 and to be reviewed after the 13 weeks expired. A Telegram to the Pension Issue Office states he is discharged due to his 'mental imbecility.'

Having researched a variety of records I'm pretty sure George lived until the ripe old age of 87, dying in 1984 in North Tyneside.

Many of those who returned from the battlefields were very different in character to the person they were when they left. They tried to pick up their lives where they had left off, but it wasn't that easy. Even those who stayed at home and worked in munitions, or the women who took on jobs previously filled by men, were affected. No family was left untouched, be it directly or indirectly. Sons, husbands, brother, colleagues, neighbours, friends – everybody knew someone who would not return. Gone forever, remembered only by letters and sepia tinged photographs; and later as a name carved onto a memorial stone far away from home. It wasn't possible to go back to 'normality.' The new 'normality' was different; maybe similar, but certainly different.

THE CALL OF THE PIPES.

The call of the pipes.
The fiery cross is out, now
There's a beacon on each hill,
The Scottish pipes are sounding,
'Tis the slogan wild and shrill.

Refrain:-
Don't you hear the pipes a calling?
Don't you hear the martial strain?
O'er Tyneside the sound is falling, Scottish pipes ne'er call in
vain.

Clansmen your country calls you;
You are wanted over there,
Midst shriek of shell and bullet
You will gladly do your share.

You've come from hill and hamlet,
City street, the village green;
Eager to serve your country
As the Scots have always been.
Onward! The Tyneside Scottish,
"Scotland for Ever" crying;
Still in face of every foe
We'll keep the old flag flying.

W.B.L. (written WW1)

The Tyneside Scottish and Tyneside Irish on the 1st July 1916.

Newcastle was a hugely industrial city at the start of the Great War, people came from all over the United Kingdom to work for the shipbuilding, coal mining, iron and steel and engineering works that ran the length of the Tyne. A vast number of the men who worked in the shipyards had come down from Scotland. Looking on the 1911 census you will see families will parents and often older children who were born in the shipbuilding ports of Scotland, such as the Clyde.

On 8th September 1914, a proposal was put forward for raising a Tyneside Scottish battalion. The appeal was made directly to Scotsmen living and working in Newcastle. A letter was dispatched to the War Office by Sir Thomas Oliver – who's idea it was to raise the battalion. He also requested that the men be allowed to wear kilts, as *"so distinguishing a dress would bring in a better class of recruit."*

The War Office turned down the proposal to raise a Scottish battalion, they also refused to sanction the raising of an Irish battalion. Letters passed too and forth from Newcastle to the War office, while eager recruits joined other units.

On 10 October 1914 Lord Haldane, the Lord Chancellor visited Newcastle. He inspected troops and visited the wounded at Armstrong College and the Royal Infirmary. He then went on to see the crowds gathered in their thousands as bands played, people sang and patriotism shone through. The Lord Chancellor then gave a speech in which he said Lord Kitchener had agreed to the raising of a Tyneside Scottish, a Commercial and hopefully an Irish battalion too.

A shop at 17, Grainger Street, Newcastle upon Tyne was used as a recruiting office. Recruitment began on 14th Oct 1914 and by 19th Oct, 250 men had enrolled. It was hoped that they would soon have the 1100 needed by opening recruiting offices in other places including South Shields, Wallsend, Hebburn and Jarrow.

The Tyneside Irish were not as yet recruiting but were accepting names of those wishing to enrol.

List of the names of men enlisted would appear in the newspapers daily. By the 22nd Oct 1914 enough men had come forward to make it possible to recruit a second Tyneside Scottish battalion. By 25 Oct 1914, one thousand one hundred and fifty men had enrolled.

Accommodation had been secured at Tilly's restaurant on Blackett Street, which was used as a billet for half of the first raised battalion. They could accommodate and feed 500 men per day at a cost of 2/3d. The remainder of the battalion were billeted at Simpson's Hotel in Wallsend.

Also supplying 100 mattresses at £1/101/2d. 100 blankets were procured from Messrs Lowes at a cost of 6/9d each. Training premises were being sought and local printer Andrew Reid and Co printed local recruitment posters. Clothiers Adelman and Thompson of Newcastle were contracted to supply uniform for the men, promising to make 600 suits per week from 24 Nov 1914 at a cost of £2-5s-0d for 2 serge jackets and two pairs of serge trousers. The contract to make the Greatcoat went to Messrs Herbert Nisbet, who said they could produce 200 coats per week at a cost of 27/9d each. From the first idea of raising the battalion the case had been put forward for the men to wear kilts, the idea being turned down at every request. It was though agreed the men could wear the 'Glengarry cap.'

Parade and drill took place at either Newcastle United football ground or at Wallsend Cricket club – depending whether you were billeted at Tilley's or Simpsons.

By the end of October 1914 recruitment drives for men to join the Tyneside Irish were taking place. The battalion paraded at Eldon Square at 9a.m. each morning and would march to the Town Moor to begin a day's training.

Headquarters were established at 10 Osborne Villas, Osborne Avenue, Jesmond. £5000 was allocated to the battalion to secure accommodation at Dunn's buildings, in Low Friar Street, Newcastle. Raby Street School in Byker was also used to billet men.

Again, as with the Scottish battalions, contracts for clothing and other equipment was placed with local businesses.

Recruitment died down in December but picked up again in the New Year and the War Office agreed to a fourth battalion being raised.

On 9th January 1915, the battalion Rugby Fifteen met with the Second Tyneside Scottish. The Irish won 35-0.

Let us move forward in time now to Saturday 1st July 1916, probably the most infamous day in the whole of the Great War. 18,767 men died on that one day; 1,644 of them were Northumberland Fusiliers. The 34th Division as a whole, lost 6,380 men that day.

Of those from Walker, the number of men injured was many times that of those killed, unfortunately no records exist that record the true number of men injured that day.

The lead up to July 1st had begun in mid-June, when British guns constantly bombarded the German lines in readiness for the 'Big Push.' The thinking was that by the time 1st July arrived, when the British planned to explode their mines ahead of the 'Big Push' the German front line would be pretty much decimated and the Allied troops would easily be able to make their way through the now broken barbed wire defences and take the empty trenches.

Several mines were exploded under the German front line positions on the Somme on 1st July 1916. A charge of 60,000 lbs (26.8 tons) of Ammonal explosive was blown at 7.28am resulting in crater 90 feet deep and 300 feet across - Lochnagar Crater, named after the trench from where the main tunnel was started. Units of the 34th Division attacked this area and the nearby village of La Boisselle. The formation contained two whole brigades of 'Pals' battalions – the Tyneside Irish and the Tyneside Scottish. Cecil Lewis, then an officer in the Royal Flying Corps, witnessed the explosion of the mine on 1st July from his aircraft high above La Boisselle: *"The whole earth heaved and flared, a tremendous and magnificent column rose up into the sky. There was an ear-splitting roar, drowning all the guns, flinging the machine sideways in the repercussing air. The earth column rose higher and higher to almost 4,000 feet."*

In eight successive waves, the infantrymen of the 34th Division stood up from their trenches, and in straight lines – with the officers in front, set off at a walk to attack the German front line trenches. One mile behind, the four battalions of the Tyneside Irish Brigade climbed from their trenches, on the Usna and Tara ridges, and started off down the hillside. In a matter of minutes this Brigade had sustained heavy casualties from enfilading machine gun fire.

Each man carried with him; Rifle, bayonet and equipment. Two extra bandoliers of ammunition. 2 Mills grenades.1 iron ration and rations enough to last the day of the assault. Haversack and waterproof cape. Four sand bags (empty.) 2 Gas helmets. Pick/shovel. Full water bottle. Mess tins were to be carried in their haversack. Bomb buckets, bomb waistcoats and wire cutters to be distributed under supervision of OC companies. Bombers to carry equipment ammunition only.

During the intensive bombardment of the previous days the Germans had sheltered deep in their bunkers, tormented by the incessant 'crumps and thuds' as they were battered by the British artillery fire…..They survived, as had most of their barbed wire. The silence of the barrage lifting was the signal for them to come up from their dugouts, hauling their machine guns with them. Taking position on their front line, through the hazy clouds of smoke the German's peered out onto an astounding sight - successive waves of British soldiers marching steadily toward them. The enemy were offering themselves as perfect targets.

The slaughter was immense, the machine guns cut down the British infantry like a scythe through hay. Within minutes German artillery was raining down on the attacking survivors, the regimental rows of British soldiers were quickly disappearing.

Small groups of survivors continued forward, occasionally taking cover in shell holes – others seeking sanctuary in Lochnagar Crater itself. By early evening, some were able to make contact with the men of the 21st and 22nd Northumberland Fusiliers, who held a position in the former German second line between Lochnagar Crater and the village of La Boisselle.

The men of Walker, known to have lost their lives on 1st July 1916.

Private **MATTHEW CARROLL**   Service No 24/143
Tyneside Irish.
Matthew was 40 years old when he died. A former coal miner 'Hewer' born at Sacriston in County Durham. In 1911 he, his wife Emma and children Thomas, James, Matthew, Emma, Hannah and William were living at 15 Dormands Cottages, Lancheser, County Durham. The family were living at 983 Walker Road, St Anthony's, when he died.
He is remembered with honour on the Thiepval Memorial, Somme, France.

Private **FRANCIS CABLE** Service No 11189
10th Bn. Prince of Wales Own (West Yorkshire Regiment.)
Francis was single and aged 32 when he was killed on 1 Jul 1916. His next of kin was his sister Mrs. Abigaile Auchterlonie who was living at 66, Cuthbert St., Hebburn-on-Tyne.
Francis is buried at DANTZIG ALLEY CEMETERY on the Somme, France.

Private **JOHN THOMAS CHARLETON** Service No 24/302
Tyneside Irish.
John's father William (deceased) had been a butcher – at No 3 Walker Road in 1881
and in 1911 mother Elizabeth was living at number 1705 Walker Road with her niece Iris Allan. John Charleton address at the time of his death was recorded as being Church Street, Walker. He was 43 years old and likely single as no wife's name is recorded.
Remembered with honour on the Thiepval Memorial, Somme, France.

Piper **JOHN WILLIAM FELLOWS**   Service No 20/1585
Tyneside Scottish.
Piper John would proudly marched ahead of the troops
playing his bagpipes and bedecked in his Glengarry hat, kilt
and sporran (Pipers were the only members of the regiment
allowed to wear kilts.)
John William Elan Fellows was living at 789 Walker Road on
the 1911 census with his father William, a shipyard' Plater' his
mother Martha and his sister Nora who was a year younger.
John at this time was working as a Plumber at the shipyards.
He was 21 years old when he died and was residing at 29
Weardale Avenue, Walker.
Remembered with honour on the Thiepval Memorial, Somme,
France.

(*The following dialogues are taken from the 'Tyneside
Scottish' written by Graham Stewart and John Sheen –
published by Pen and Sword Ltd.)
*The war diary of the 23rd Battalion contains the following
excerpt regarding the part played by the Pipers during the
battle. *Each Company was played over into No Man's land by its
pipers who continued to play until killed or wounded.*

Piper Alex Boyd of the 22nd Battalion wrote to his mother from
hospital in Cambridge:
*The only thing the matter with me is I have a finger blown off. The
only thing disabled is the pipes, I got them blown away when
playing in the charge. You would see in the papers about the Piper
playing in No Man's land – that is between out trenches and those
of the German's, it was I. I was playing Tipperary and all the boys
were singing and shouting. I could see them falling all about me. It
was a lucky day for me that I was not blown away, I shall never
forget it as long as I live.*

An un-named officer of the 2/Middlesex regiment reported
the following tale;

The pluckiest thing I ever saw in my life was a piper of the Tyneside Scottish playing his company over the parapet in the attack on the German trenches near Albert. The Tynesiders were on our right, and as their officers gave the signal to advance I saw the piper – I think he was the Pipe Major (20/290 Pipe Major John Wilson) – jump out of the trench and march straight over No Man's land towards the German lines. The tremendous rattle of machine gun and rifle fire, which the enemy at once opened up with on us and completely drowned the sound of his pipes. But it was obvious he was playing as though he would burst the bag, and just faintly through the din we heard the mighty shout of his comrades gave as they swarmed after him. How he escaped death I can't understand for the ground was literally ploughed up by the hail of bullets. But he seemed to bear a charmed life and the last glimpse I had of him , as we too dashed out , showed him still marching erect, playing furiously, and quite regardless of the flying bullets and the men dropping around him.

Private Elliot of the 20th Bn. recounted this sight;
"I never heard the pipes but I did see poor 'Aggy Fife' (L/Cpl Piper Fife) He was riddled with bullets, writhing and screaming. Another lad was just kneeling, his head thrown right back. Bullets were just slapping into him knocking great chunks off his body...... It was hell on earth; that is the only name I can give it. We were the first over the trenches after the signal to advance and never a man faltered. It was like going to a picnic, the way the men marched on, but it was only a few yards, until the Hun got sight of us. Then every kind of shell they possess was dropped amongst us and their machine guns also got in on the act........ That was awful, hearing men who were your mates pleading with you and pulling at your ankles for help but not being able to do anything. One lad alongside me was chanting 'Mother of God No! Mother of God No!' just like that. Others were effing and blinding. I don't know how I got through it."

Private **EDWARD HOPKINS** of Mrs Hopkins of 31, East Terrace, Walker. Service number 20/178 and who served with the 20th Bn. Tyneside Scottish. He was reported missing on July 1st, but his body was later found and he is buried Ovillers Military Cemetery, France. Previous to joining the army he worked at the Rising Sun Colliery, Wallsend.

Lance Corporal **GEORGE LAWSON** Service No 21/68 Tyneside Scottish.
I have no further information on George's former occupation nor address. He lived in Walker though when he attested to the Army. He is Remembered with honour on the Thiepval Memorial to the missing, Somme, France.

Private **DANIEL MCGEE** Service No 25/1164 Tyneside Irish.
Daniel was born Felling, to Daniel and Ellen McGee in 1890. In 1911, he was living at 15 Thames Street, Wallsend, with his parents and brothers William and Michael and sister Mary. Also living in the same house was his cousin Elizabeth Keife and her 7-year-old daughter Constance. Daniel Snr and Ellen had two other children who had died in infancy.
 Like his father and brothers Daniel was a miner; his father a 'Hewer' his brothers 'drivers (below)' and he himself a 'Putter.'
Daniel was 26 years old when he died and is remembered with honour on the Thiepval Memorial, Somme, France.

Private **JOSEPH PARKER**   Service No 23/755 Tyneside Scottish.
Joseph was born 1890 at 268 Church Street, Walker to Charles and Johanna Parker. Charles was originally from Islington in London and Johanna from Durham. Joseph had one older brother – Charles. Another brother Thomas, born in 1880 died aged five – before either of the surviving siblings were born.

By 1901 Charles was a widower and had moved with his children to Slag Row, Walker. He was working as a 'machine man' at the shipyards and employed a housekeeper, Margaret Place to look after the boys. I am unable to find Joseph on the 1911 census, nor his brother Charles.

Charles survived the Great War, having served with the Northumberland Fusiliers (Service No 2887) and the Yorkshire Regiment (Service No 266866.) He married Sarah Nash, also from Walker and moved to Ashington, Northumberland. Remembered with honour on the Thiepval Memorial, Somme, France.

Private **WILLIAM EGERTON**   Service No 27/1527 Tyneside Scottish.

There is little or no information on William Egerton, He apparently, he was a resident of Walker at the time of his enlistment to the Northumberland Fusiliers Tyneside Scottish.

Private **JOSEPH ROBSON**   Service No 23/254 Tyneside Scottish.

Joseph was aged 15 during the 1911 census and living at John Clay Street, South Shields, having been born Durham. His father Thomas was a 'coal mine hewer'. His elder brother William was a 'driver down pit' and Joseph is described as being a 'trapper down pit.' His Thomas and Hannah had been married 19 years and produced 9 children – 6 of whom were still alive. The family them moved to 963 Walker Road, Walker and this is where they were residing when Joseph was killed in 1916. Remembered with honour on the Thiepval Memorial, Somme, France.

Private **JOSEPH GILCHRIST** Service No 20/1433 Tyneside Scottish.

Joseph was 33 years old when he was killed alongside his Tyneside Scottish comrades in 1916. He had married Jenny Fairgrieves in 1909 and on the 1911 census they had no children' though possibly they had started a family by the outbreak of war. They were then living at McAdams buildings and Joseph was a 'hand putter' in the coal mines. He was the son of the late Anthony and Elizabeth Gilchrist. His wife Jenny was living at 12, Heworth View, St. Anthony's, Newcastle-on-Tyne at the time of his death. He is remembered with honour on the Thiepval Memorial, Somme, France.

Private **THOMAS NESBIT WHITE** Service No 23/1312 Tyneside Scottish.
Thomas was born in South Shields in 1879 and later moved north of the Tyne to Walker, where he worked as an 'engineman' at a local Colliery. He lived at 1353 Walker Road, with his wife Elizabeth and children Isabella and Thomas. He was 37 when he died in 1916.
Remembered with honour on the Thiepval Memorial, Somme, France.

Private **JAMES WHELAN** Service No 11134 10th Bn. Prince of Wales Own (West Yorkshire Regiment.
There is also very little information available regarding James Whelan, but we do know that he lived in Walker at the time of attestation to the 10th Bn. Prince of Wales Own (West Yorkshire Regiment.) He was 29 years old when he died on 1 Jul 1916 and the son of Patrick and Catherine Whelan. He is the only one of our men killed that day who was not in the Northumberland Fusiliers. He is buried with honour at FRICOURT NEW MILITARY CEMETERY, France.

Sergeant **HENRY YEATS** Service Number 23/792 Tyneside Scottish.
Henry was born Walker, in 1873 and at the age of 9 in 1881 was living at 29 Fisher Street with his father Alex a 'cabinet maker' mother Christina and siblings Alex, James, Walter, Christina, Margaret and twin brother Charles.

On the 1911 census he is aged 37, single and boarding at 11 Sedley Road, Wallsend, with his widowed sister Christina Armitage, her two children and his mother Christina who is now 83.

Henry was working as a 'labourer' at a Sodium Works.

Remembered with honour on the Thiepval Memorial, Somme, France.

George Nugent:

Hundreds of British soldiers were killed in the vicinity of Lochnagar Crater on the morning of 1st July. Four battalions of the Tyneside Scottish (21st, 22nd, 23rd and 24th Northumberland Fusiliers), some 2,400 men, advanced to the crater after it was exploded, passed around the crater and made for the German positions at the rear. George, along with many of our Walker men from the Tyneside Scottish and Irish battalions was posted as 'missing in action' that day and is commemorated on the Thiepval Memorial to the Missing. However, eighty-two years after he was killed, his remains were found in ground at the south side of the crater on 31st October 1998. Identification was made possible due to the engravings he had made of his name and service number on some of his personal items.

Private George James Nugent, No. 22/1306 aged 28 was serving with the 22nd Bn. Northumberland Fusiliers (Tyneside Scottish) on 1st July 1916. He was the son of William and Emma Nugent and husband of Nora Nugent and lived at 34 Frankling Street, Shieldfield, Newcastle-upon-Tyne.

George's remains were reburied at the nearby Ovillers Military Cemetery in grave reference Plot I, Row A, grave 26A. A wooden cross marks the spot on the south side of the Lochnagar Crater where he was found.

The belongings that eventually identified him are held at the 'Discovery Museum' Blandford Square, Newcastle upon Tyne.

First of July 1916 by Helen Charlesworth

At 7.30am precisely, on 1st. July 1916,
Whistles blew in unison,
The length of the British front line.
Slowly the leading masses appeared,
Steadily walking forth, rifles at the ready.
Rank upon rank, line after line.
The counter barrage crashed down,
Machine guns blaze away excitedly.
Wave after wave of khaki, simply
Withered away…
Merrily the shells rained overhead,
Obliterating those who followed,
Almost before they began.
The cries for help, drowned in a sea of death.
The open wound of no-man's land,
A hell for the living,
A slaughter yard for the dead.
As dusk settled,
Survivors crawled back to the remaining trenches.
Making their way 'home' through wire,
Shell holes and broken bodies.
A motionless battlefield of khaki and grey.
The distant cries for help were heard,
As the stretcher bearers searched for signs of life
In the fields of death.
As the sun went down, on the first day of the battle of the Somme

2nd Lieut. ARTHUR COULSON, recipient of the Military Medal. Arthur was killed on 27th March 1918, aged twenty-two.

Official photograph of the 'Fighting Fifth' Northumberland Fusiliers. Taken April 1916, after the battle of St Eloi.

Men of the 5th Battalion queuing up for a haircut from the battalion barber.

Officers of the 5th Battalion Northumberland Fusiliers.

TILL THE BOYS COME HOME (2).

Keep the home-fires burning, while your hearts are yearning,
Though your lads are far away they dream of home ;
There's a silver lining through the dark cloud shining :
Turn the dark cloud inside out, till the boys come home.

Official WW1 Postcard.

Photograph taken by my Grandfather John Robert (Bob) Edwards in May 1918.

Written on the back:
Chemin des Dames (France) Front, beginning of May 1918. 149th Northumbrian Infantry Signal Section.
Taking over from the French. A French soldier (left front.) Three of our lads with French helmets on. Second on the left, Peter Crawley, used to box at St James Hall. This photo taken prior to "Jerry's" last offensive; 27th May 1918, when he got to within 15 miles of Paris. On this part of the Front, three divisions (21st, 24th and 50th) were in a quiet sector, after being smashed up and replaced later (July) by three battalions – 1st Leinsters, 1st Dublin Fusiliers and 1st Northumberland Fusiliers.

Other Walker men who served with the Tyneside Scottish/ Irish and survived the 1st July 1916.

Private **GEORGE CARMICHAEL**   Service No 27/140
Northumberland Fusiliers. Tyneside Irish. Moved to 22nd Bn.
Tyneside Scottish after being wounded in January 1917.
Moved to reserve and rated up to Lance Corporal

Private **PETER FOLEY**   Service No 27/225
Forty-three years old Peter - at the outbreak of war, enlisted
on 4 Jan 1915 to the Northumberland Fusiliers, Tyneside Irish.
He was moved numerous times between the 19th, 14th, 12/13th
Bn.'s. He did not serve overseas with the Tyneside Irish. He
was discharged on 16 Oct 1918.
 Peter of 15 Rhodes Street, Walker worked as a 'Miner' and
was married to Elizabeth and had three children, Mary
Thomas and Robert.

Private **JAMES GRAHAM**   Service No 27/256
James Graham, of 11 Hill's Yard, Walker road, Walker enlisted
at the age of 50 on 4 Dec 1914 and was discharged on 4 Apr
1916. He was transferred to the 30th (reserve) Bn. during his
service and did not serve overseas. A 'Boilermaker' James
was married to Mary Ann and three grown up children,
Thomas, Charlotte and Florrie.
James died due to complications of his war service on 27 Dec
1920 aged 56 and is buried at All Saints Churchyard,
Newcastle upon Tyne.

 Private **ISAAC CALVERT**   Service No 26/131
Thirty-one ear old Isaac attested to the Northumberland
Fusiliers, Tyneside Irish on 3 Dec 1914. He was discharged
from the service on 16 Nov 1917 suffering from the effects of
gunshot wounds.

Isaac was married to Elizabeth according to the 1911 census and living at 18 Wilson Street, North Shields. They had three children – Elizabeth, Margaret and Wilfred. The family later moved to Walker.

Private **JOHN MCGEE**   Service No 27/468
John McGee attested on 11 Nov 1914 to the Northumberland Fusiliers, Tyneside Irish.
He lived at 58 Mitchell Street, Walker.

Private **GEORGE BILTON**   Service No 23/332
George, a 'Platers Helper' at the Shipyards, attested on 24 Nov 1914 and was discharged 15 Oct 1917 after having suffered gunshot wounds in July 1916. Born Kent, George was married to Helen. The 1911 census states they were then living at 1604 New Road, Walker with their four surviving children – one having died in infancy, though five children were named - Josephine, Susan, George, Allison and Henry.

Lance Corporal **JOHN JENKINSON** Service No 23/206
291825
John resided Walker, but I cannot find any address for him. During his Military service, he was reported as having gone AWOL 6/10/1915 – no record of punishment. He was then injured in August 1917 and transferred to the 8th and 1/7th Bn. Northumberland Fusiliers before being discharged.

Lance Corporal **JOHN WILLIAM BREESE**   Service No
22/1085
In 1911 John was living at 12 Mitchell Street, Walker, with his step father Frederick Stoker, his mother Mary and seven half siblings. John was 21 years old at the outbreak of war and was working at the Shipyards as a 'Ship's plater's marker.'

The last picture of John and Archie

*Browsing through an old photograph album, one particular picture
stands out. Bessie with her fathers' camera, taking pictures for the
Parish magazine.*

*The bright eyes that squint against the sun. Cheery smiles captured
in their un-aching pose. Taken near the Mill on a warm July Sunday
afternoon. Time did not spare the others in the group
photograph. Ernie who ended up blind and in a wheelchair, after a
gas attack in '17. Sisters Elsie and Lily who never married, and until
a few years ago regularly tended the graves of their family; both now
in a nursing home. The graves no longer lovingly tended, but lichen
stained and partially hidden by overgrown weeds.*

*Giles and Clarry… They came out of it unscathed. Having raised
their families and lived their lives as close to the good book as they
could, they now lie in the village cemetery (The church spire visible
in the photograph.)*

*Unlike John and Archie - forever young, their image encapsulated in
a carefree pose. Only the tingeing of the sepia, showing any signs of
age. John and Archie killed in their prime - forever nineteen. Their
youthfulness hidden beneath the covers of an old photograph album;
under the heading 'Picture at the Mill 4th July 1915.'*

*A few pages further on - if the viewer cares to look there is a
photograph of John in uniform looking much older than his nineteen
years. In faded pencil is scrawled 'To Mother with love, John xx'*
There are no more pictures of Archie.

Helen Charlesworth

Men of Walker whose Military records survived
The WWII bombing raids of 1940 on London.
(Also, information from other sources.)

From the 'Burnt Records' collection at the National Archives at Kew, I have discovered more men from Walker who enlisted during the First World War. Unfortunately, more than half of the service records were destroyed in September 1940, when a German bombing raid struck the War Office repository in Arnside Street, London. An estimated 2.8 million service records survived the bombing. This means that there is a roughly 40% chance of finding the service record of a soldier who was discharged at some time between 1914 and 1920. The papers that survived are varying in their degree of completeness.

You will notice that a number of men are with a Battalion and then get transferred to the 'Labour Corps' – this was a unit manned by officers and other ranks who had been medically rated below the "A1" condition needed for front line service. Many were returned wounded. Labour Corps units were often deployed for work within range of the enemy guns, sometimes for lengthy periods.

No1*** and No2*** Field Punishments – the starred icons are to refer you to the separate section I have written describing what these punishments actually involved.

Here are small snippets of information I have been able to gather and research through using the 1901/1911 census, Medal card index, surviving service records and other lines of interest to put together a picture of the men from Walker, of whom many of their service records, survived the 1940 bombings.

Private **JOHN THOMAS ANDERSON**
Residing 4 Cambrian Row, a former miner and son of Frances (and Henry deceased) Anderson, he joined the 1/5th Bn. Northumberland Fusiliers. John was transferred numerous times to different battalions and ended up with the 2nd Bn. Sherwood Foresters (Notts and Derby Regt.)
Taken prisoner on 21 March 1918, John sadly died in Germany as a Prisoner of War on 16 July 1918 and is buried in Cologne Southern cemetery, Germany.

Private **HENRY ARMSTRONG**
 Aged 22 'apparently' of 5 Baker Street, Walker (none existent address) was working as a shop assistant when he attested at Darlington on 26 Oct 1915 to join the 151 (Darlington) Heavy Battery Royal Garrison Artillery, and took up his training on 29 Oct 1915. He deserted 1 Nov 1915, having served for 3 days. He had previously served for 10 months as a Territorial in the Durham Light Infantry. There is no record as to whether Henry re-enlisted at a later date. I did find him though on the 1911 census aged 18 working as a drapery assistant and living in lodging at 28 Ellison Place, Newcastle and in 1901 living Gosforth, the son of a Horse Dealer. What his connection is to Walker we shall probably never find out.

Private ROBERT ATKINSON   30/118   101650
Robert Atkinson lived at 119 Middle Street, Walker with his sister Mary Ann Anderson (Cpl Thomas Craggs was also at the abode when he attested in 1915.) Robert was a single 34-year-old 'painter' when he attested to the 30th Bn. Tyneside Irish on 18 Nov 1915. He was posted to Scotton Camp on 22 Nov 1915. His service is as follows:
Home 11 Nov 1915 – 19 May 1916
France 20 May 1916 – 14 Sept 1917
Home 16 Sept 1917 – 2 Jul 1918
Transferred to the Durham Light Infantry April 1918.
France 3 Jul 1918 – 28 Nov 1919

Home 29 Jan 1919 – 27 Feb 1919

Robert received a contusion to his left knee and a gunshot wound to his right thigh while in France. He was awarded a 30% pension in 1919. He wrote to the war office in 1921 to say he had not as yet received his medals and was now residing at 81, Middle Street, Walker.

Corporal **WALTER BAIN** 301519

Living at 60, Foster St, Low Walker, Walter, the son of Adam Henderson Bain and his wife Prudence. Walter, born 1899 joined up aged 17 years and 5 months. An apprentice motor mechanic for Murray & Charlton in Newcastle, he joined the Army Service Corps as a motor mechanic in Oct 1916 and was posted March 1917.

Private **JACOB BARKER** 341276

Jacob was 17 years and 360 days old when he enlisted and was described at his medical as being 5 feet 2½ inches in height. He was living with his mother Margaret at 846 Walker Road, Walker and joined the 36th Bn. Northumberland Fusiliers, attesting to service on 13 April 1917 and posted May, later being transferred to the Yorkshire Regt. Demobbed in 1919.

Private **ROBERT BARTON** 19878/44476

Robert, of 46 River View, Low Walker, enlisted into the Labour Corps at Manchester in June 1915. He was first sent to join the 20th (Service) Lancashire Fusiliers, later 12th Bn. North Staffordshire Regiment.

A former farm labourer Bob joined up aged 24 and was described as being only 5 foot ¼ inch tall. His mother Jane Ann was deceased – having passed away in Tynemouth Workhouse. He enlisted on 1 May 1915 and was later transferred to 12th Bn. North Staffordshire regiments. Robert was killed on the 11th Sept 1918 and is remembered on the Ploegsteert Memorial, Belgium. His belongings were to be sent to Mrs Jane Wait of 52 White Street, Low Walker. Likely a sister.

Private **WALTER WILLIAM BARTON** 4716
Walter lived at 46 Fisher Street, Walker when he attested on 10 Dec 1915 aged 34 and was sent to France 16 June 1917, having spent a year serving in the UK, He was originally attached to the Northumberland Fusiliers but in July 1917 was transferred to the Durham Light Infantry. Served in both France and Italy and was described as having an 'under developed' chest on his demobilisation medical in Sept 1919. William is the older brother of Robert Barton (above.)

Private **THOMAS BELL**   213131
Of 39, White Street, Walker, a married father of five, to Florence Margaret, Marie, Catherine, Thomas and William. Thomas had been working as a joiner prior to his enlistment under the Derby scheme, aged 38 years and 6 months to the Royal Engineers on 10th Dec 1915. He was mobilised 11 months later, on 10th Nov 1916 working as a skilled carpenter on home shores (likely in the shipyards) and in April 1918 he was transferred to what looks like working at a Glass Works supplying the Armstrong Whitworth engineering works at Elswick. He was discharged as being surplus to requirements on 14 Dec 1918.

Private **THOMAS WILLIAM BELL**   1637
Aged 27 in 1914 (born 1887) a Clerk for the Tyne Improvement Commission (Docks and Tyne Police) and living with his parents at 6 Kings Drive, Whitley Bay (born Walker.) Taller than many of his compatriots Thomas was 5 feet 10 inches tall and with a 36 inch chest. He joined Royal Army Medical Corps (R.A.M.C) as part of the Northumberland Field

Ambulance on 10th Sept 1914, though wasn't posted overseas until September 1916. In 1918 he was transferred to the Cameron Highlanders 2nd Bn. He was discharged from service on 31 March 1920.

Private **ROBERT STEELE BELL** 59585
A 'fitter' of 956 Walker Road, was born 1st Dec 1899. He joined the Northumberland Fusiliers but served with the South Staffordshire Regiment during the Great War. After demobilisation in Nov 1919 he chose to re-enlist in the 6th Bn. Northumberland Fusiliers Territorial force for a term of 8 years.

Gunner **HERBERT BELL**   2073
Of 25 Westbourne Gardens, Herbert joined the 1st Northumbrian Brigade Royal Field Artillery in May 1915. He was immediately embodied into service and embarked at Southampton 3 Jul 1916 arriving Le Harve on the 4 Jul 1916. In 1917 he was transferred (doesn't say where to) and in early 1918 – due to receiving a bomb wound in his left arm, was sent to a British hospital then after a month there he was sent home on a week's leave. He was posted to High Wycombe mid-1918 and discharged at Ripon on 31 Jan 1919
An interesting note on his documents was that he was awarded 7 days Field Punishment ***No 2's by his C.O on 14 Aug 1917 for baring a light in his billet at 11.15pm on 12 Aug 1917 also absent from 6a.m parade on 13 Aug 1917.

***Rules for Field Punishment under Section 44 of the Army Act.

1/. A court-martial, or a commanding officer, may award field punishment for any offence committed on active service, and may sentence an offender for a period not exceeding, in the case of a court-martial three months, and in the case of a commanding officer twenty-eight days, to one of the following field punishments, namely: –

Field Punishment No. 1
Field Punishment No. 2.

2/. Where an offender is sentenced to field punishment No. 1, he may, during the continuance of his sentence, unless the court-martial or the commanding officer otherwise directs, be punished as follows: –
A/. He may be kept in irons, i.e., in fetters or handcuffs, or both fetters and handcuffs; and may be secured so as to prevent his escape.
B/. When in irons he may be attached for a period or periods not exceeding two hours in any one day to a fixed object, but he must not be so attached during more than three out of any four consecutive days, nor during more than twenty-one days in all.
C/. Straps or ropes may be used for the purpose of these rules in lieu of irons.
D/. He may be subjected to the like labour, employment, and restraint, and dealt with in like manner as if he were under a sentence of imprisonment with hard labour.
3/. Where an offender is sentenced to field punishment No. 2, the foregoing rule with respect to field punishment No. 1 shall apply to him, except that he shall not be liable to be attached to a fixed object as provided by paragraph of Rule 2.
4/. Every portion of a field punishment shall be inflicted in such a manner as is calculated not to cause injury or to leave

any permanent mark on the offender; and a portion of a field punishment must be discontinued upon a report by a responsible medical officer that the continuance of that portion would be prejudicial to the offender's health.

5/. Field punishment will be carried out regimentally when the unit to which the offender belongs or is attached is actually on the move, but when the unit is halted at any place where there is a provost marshal, or an assistant provost marshal, the punishment will be carried out under that officer.

6/. When the unit to which the offender belongs, or is attached is actually on the move, an offender awarded field punishment No. 1 shall be exempt from the operation of Rule (2), but all offenders awarded field punishment shall march with their unit, carry their arms and accoutrements, perform all their military duties as well as extra fatigue duties, and be treated as defaulters.

Private **ALFRED BENN**   1588

Alfred of 40, Neptune Road, Low Walker, was a plumber at the shipyards, married to Annie and with three children, Isabella, George and Lilly.

George is described as 5feet 9½ inches tall, with dark brown hair, grey eyes, fresh complexion and medium build and had a scar on his right wrist. He joined the 1st Northumbrian Field Ambulance (R.A.M.C) and was attached to the 50th Northumbrian Division after attesting at Newcastle on 31 Aug 1914. He later became a Lance Corporal but forfeited that badge on 9th July 1917. He had been granted home leave and overstayed by one day, returning on the 8th July rather than the 7th.

On 31st Dec 1917 while on a training exercise in Blackpool he was tried and charged with the following....

1. *'When on active service using threatening language to his superior officer, in that he at Blackpool on the 15.12.17 after having been warned that he was on parade, said to Cpl F Rawling "I will have my own back on some of you b….s before I finish."* Or words to that effect.

2. *When on active service using insubordinate language to his superior officer, in that he at Blackpool on 15.12.17 after having been detailed for his duties said to Sgt Bewley R.A.M.C "I am waiting for my discharge and did not come here to work, and I will not be b…d about."* Or words to that effect.

He pleaded guilty to the 1st and 2nd charges and was sentenced to undergo detention for 14 days. Signed at Blackpool on 27th Dec 1917 W.G Williams Major.

Alfred was discharged as permanently unfit for service on 14th Jan 1918

Gunner **WILLIAM BESFORD**   149013/37488
Born Walker in 1887, 18-year-old Stable Groom William who stood at 5 feet 8½ inches in height and weighing 126 lbs, attested in Newcastle upon Tyne on 11th July 1905 to the 1st Bn. Northumberland Fusiliers (Territorial Force). He served in South Africa from April 1906 till March 1907 as well as within the United Kingdom. In the meantime, William had moved to Hexham and began working as a 'plate layer' on the Railways. He married Sarah Stokoe in 1910. At the outbreak of war, was mobilised at Athlone (in Ireland) on 6th August 1914. Over the next few years he had postings to Mesopotamia, India and Basra. He was discharged on 16th May 1919 and returned to his home address in Hexham.

Private **BENJAMIN BLAKE**   T/4/124307
Forty-six-year-old Benjamin, was married but had no children, he lived at 1 Byker Street, Walker, with his wife Jane, who he had married on Christmas Day 1891. He was now a miner but had previously served 10 years with the Durham Light

Infantry Militia and now, although much older than most men trying to enlist, he was accepted into the Army on 25th June 1915, at Aldershot. He was described by the medical officer as being 5 feet 5 inches tall, weighing 133 lbs and having a chest measurement of 37½ inches with a further expansion of 3 inches. He was stout and strong. He joined the Army Service Corps as a 'Packer/Loader.'

Benjamin was killed in action on 1 June 1917 and is buried at Dainville Communal Cemetery, France.

His wife Jane moved to 69, Cannon St., Elswick, Newcastle upon Tyne after his death.

Private **JAMES BONE**   7741/168892

James was born in Walker and at the age of 19 attested at Newcastle upon Tyne on 31 Jan 1908 to complete 6 years 'Special Reserve' service. He then on 2nd June of the same year joined the Northumberland Fusiliers as a full-time soldier.

His parents and brothers live at Stotts House Farm, Wallsend. A letter sent to his foreman in 1908 at 'William Dobson's & Sons' asks about his disposition and character. He describes James as a 'rivet heater' by occupation. He states that he has known James for 15 years and that he is of sober, honest and good character. A Sergeant of Police at Wallsend, George Cameron, is also sent a letter asking the same questions. He states that James, an apprentice riveter is a 'very capable young man, I have known him since boyhood.'

When James initially joined up in 1908 he was described as having his initials J.B and an anchor tattooed on his right forearm, 1 small (tattoo?) on left forearm and 3 small scars the back of his neck. He was 5 feet 3¼ inches height with a chest measurement of 34½ inches. He had brown eyes and dark brown hair.

At the time of the 1911 census Private Bone was stationed in India, working as a Cook with the 1st Bn. Northumberland Fusiliers.

At the outbreak of war in 1914 Bone is a L/Cpl and stationed in Amritsar, India. He made a request to reverted back to a being a Private. His request was granted….

Amritsar 14-8-1916

From   *2219 L/Cpl J Bone*
G Company
2nd Bn North'lnd Fusiliers.

To
The Officer Commanding
'G' Company
2nd Bn North'lnd Fusiliers
Sir,
I most respectfully beg to make application to revert to Private at my own request.
Reason's being necessary, I beg to state that I am fully convinced I am able to soldier more creditably as a Private than as a Non-commissioned Officer. Should this request meet with your esteemed recommendation I beg to ask that I may be transferred to H Company.
Hoping this application will be transferred to my Commanding Officer for his favourable approval.
I beg to remain
 Sir,
Your obedient servant.
J Bone L/Cpl
'G' Company detachment 2nd Bn North'lnd Fusiliers.

Bone had been promoted to L/Cpl (unpaid) on 8 Nov 1913 and on 26 Aug 1914 was reverted back to being a Private. He was discharged on 26 Feb 1919 as 'Being surplus to Military requirement (having suffered impairments since entry into service i.e. wounds.)

Private **CYRIL BOX**   135405

Enlisted at Alnwick, though resided at 122 Church Street, Walker. Cyril had been working as a 'Footman' possibly at Alnwick Castle. On 29th Oct 1915, he signed his attestation papers and became a member of the Army Service Corps. He passed his Motor Learners test in Jan 1916 (assume this to be a driving proficiency test?) He spent time with the Mediterranean expeditionary Force as well as in the UK and with the British Expeditionary Force in France. He served his time with the 31st Field Ambulance Unit.

Cyril got himself in to trouble on a couple of occasions and had his pay deducted.

On 13 Sept 1918, he absented himself by 24 hours after missing the leave train when returning to his unit: Forfeit 3 days' pay.

On 3 Aug 1919, He failed to comply with orders to proceed to H.Q and instead went to Bethune where he stayed the night and did not report until 10.30am the following day. Forfeit: 10 days' pay.

Gunner / Sapper **JOHN BRADLEY**   95894

John Bradley attested to the Royal Artillery aged 18, when working as a labourer in 1893. He was 5 feet 7 inches tall and weighed 135 pounds, and had a chest measurement of 35 inches which he could expand to 37. He had brown eyes, brown hair and a fair complexion.

His career took him to places such as St Lucia and Gibraltar and along the way he incurred a few battle scars including a fractured finger, sprained wrist and a head wound. His charge sheet was as long as your arm; drunkenness, breaking out of barracks, missing tattoo, drunkenness, missing roll call, more drunkenness…. He certainly spent a lot of time confined to barracks!

On the 28th June 1905, he married Susannah Main. By 1909 he had grown another inch in height and his resting chest measured an extra 4 inches. He was living at 183 Walker Road with his wife and children. His mother Margaret, not far away at number 142. His father had been in Morpeth Asylum for a great many years and there was no contact between them. After having served 16 years with the Royal Garrison Artillery John's service was terminated at this point and he transferred to the Army reserve.

Now living in Darlington and working as a boilermaker, John was recalled to the colours and attested - again to the Royal Artillery, on 28th Aug 1914. He was posted on the 4th September to Sheerness in Kent. In January 1917, aged 40 he was transferred to the Royal Engineers, with whom he served from the 26th March 1917 until demobilisation on 26th Feb 1919.

Sapper **CHARLES BRADWELL** 146231

Residing 71, Mitchell Buildings, Walker, Charles was a 'Platers helper' (shipbuilding) at Armstrong Whitworth's. He attested at Gateshead on 27th Nov 1915. He joined the Royal Engineer's as a 'Tunellers Mate' in the 185th Tunnelling Coy and was made up to L/Cpl in May 1917 but requested to return to the role of Tunnellers Mate in September of the same year. On 13 Jun 1918, he relinquished the right to the 6/- a day pay rate for a Tunnellers Mate, though his service record doesn't explain why. Charles was gassed on 26 Sept 1918 and was de-mobilized in Jan 1919.

Private **JOHN BRAIDFORD**   38888/66133

John had a deformed left ear - according to his medical notes. He was posted to the 4th Bn. Durham Light Infantry, later the 14th and then the 18th Durham Light Infantry. Later again he was transferred to the 17th Bn. Royal Defence Corps

(Employment Coy.) and was sent home to England in 1917 suffering from 'Trench Foot,' spending some time in Gloucester General Hospital.

Twice he forfeited 3 days' pay, once for overstaying his leave by 8 hours and once for being absent from his work station.

Sapper **JAMES BRANNAN**   50351/260893

James joined up aged 21 in June 1915 at Newcastle upon Tyne, whilst in employment as a 'Locomotive Fireman' with the railways. James was born in Walker but now residing Whitley Bay. He joined the Royal Engineers and was posted to the Railway Operating Division Royal Naval Unit at Deal in Kent and later posted to France. James lived with his parents and six siblings in a 3-roomed house at 332, Whitley Road, Whitley Bay. On leaving school he had joined the railways as a locomotive cleaner.

Corporal **JOHN BRITT**   306028/7335273

John had been a member of the 5th Bn. Northumberland Fusiliers Territorial unit since 1910 and when war was declared he was enlisted into the 1st Bn. Northumberland Fusiliers. He was unemployed at that time so he was likely very grateful for the opportunity to make some money. He then transferred to the Northumberland Field Ambulance Service (Royal Army Medical Corps.) When the war ended he was sent to Armstrong Whitworth's to continue de-mobilisation work until 31 Aug 1920.

*Lt/QM **RICHARD BROCKETT BROWN**   386022
     M.M M.I.D

Richard was born in 1882 and served with the 1st Northumbrian Divisional Field Ambulance. He was awarded the Territorial Force efficiency medal on 1st Jul 1912, when he was a Staff Sergeant. He lived with his family at 25 Byker Terrace, Walker – a nine roomed property. His father John owned a pharmacy at No's 2/4, Byker Terrace, where they both worked as Chemist's. Richard continued working at the pharmacy after the war. He married Dorothy Oubridge in 1919 and had three children.

He died at Newcastle upon Tyne in 1941 at the age of 59.

Private **WILLIAM BROWN**   240064/235985

William was aged 23, and in the employ of Armstrong Whitworth's at Walker and living at 68, River View, in 1912 when he signed up to the Northumberland Fusiliers, Territorial Battalion. He embarked to France in 1916 and was transferred to the York and Lancaster Regiment in August 1918. He was demobilised in January 1919 to 32, Mitchell Street, Walker, with A1 health.

Private **DAVID BRUCE**   3089/478071

 David, a former Blacksmith's striker at the shipyards was a member of the 2/5th Bn. Northumberland Fusiliers (Territorial Force). He attested in Nov 1914. He had been made up to Lance Corporal in early 1916 but was later demoted back to Private. Late in the year he was again promoted to Lance Corporal, but again appears to have been demoted shortly afterwards. On 9th May 1917 he was wounded in action (slight contusion) and less than a month later on 5th June, wounded again, suffering gunshot wounds to the 'lower extremities' (Right knee crossed out.) On Wednesday 13th June 1917 – Mrs (Lizzie) Bruce, Fisher Street, Low Walker has received information that her husband, Corporal Bruce, has been wounded.

In December of the same year, on recovery he was transferred to the labour Corps. On 27th Nov 1918, he went 'absent without leave' until apprehended by the civil Police on 11 Jan 1919. He was found guilty and sentenced to 42 days Field Punishments number 1.

David died from Influenza and bronchial pneumonia on 7th April 1919. Likely at Walkergate Hospital. I do wonder if his punishment was a major contributor to his death?

Private **ALEX BRUMWELL**   5/1456 345693 1297
Alex of 43, Ropery Walk, St Anthony's, a former shipyard worker, served with the 5th Bn. Northumberland Fusiliers. He was moved to the Labour Corps after being wounded in May 1915 and later returned to the 5th Bn. He survived the war.

Private **MONTGOMERY BRYDON**   16404
Aged 29 in 1914 Montgomery resided at 219, Back Welbeck Road, Walker and was a married to Annie Clegg and the father to her four children; Ann born 1905, Thomas born 1907, Margaret born 1908 and Robert born 1910.
Monty attested at Wallsend on 26 Aug 1914 and joined the East Yorkshire Regiment. He was subsequently posted, but like James Bradley he didn't particularly like Military life. He went absent 6 Oct 1914 until 11 Nov 1914, a period of 10 days. For this offence, he was forfeited 6 days loss of pay. He then disappeared from the 12 Jan 1915 until the 21 Jan 1915 and was fined 9 days' pay. He again went absent 17 Jul 1915 until 22 July 1915 and forfeited 6 days' pay.
Montgomery was killed in action on 26 September 1916 and is buried at Pozieres British Cemetery, Ovillers – La Boiselle, France. His wife and children later moved to 49, Grasmere Avenue, Walker Estate, Newcastle-on-Tyne.

Private **CHARLES BUGGY**   312925
Aged 18 and living at 148 Byker Street, Walker, Charles attested on 24 Feb 1916 and was called up straight away. The former miner was enlisted into the Royal Field Artillery 20th Bn. Tank Corps as a driver. He was UK based for the duration of his service and was demobilised 28 Dec 1918.

Private **WILLIAM BURNS**

William enlisted on 4 September 1914, likely looking for an escape from his job as a 'Holder up' in the coal mines. Charles lived with his wife Catherine and baby daughter Bella, at 11, Slag Row, Walker. Baby Nicholas was born in 1915.

William was attached for duty on 23 Sept 1914 within the UK and posted to do 'war work' at Armstrong Whitworth's at Wallsend in Sept 1916.

He was discharged no longer physically fit for war service on 30 Jan 1919 and de-mobilized.

Private **THOMAS BUTCHER**   13031

Born in Walker, 33-year-old Thomas is working as a labourer. He's keen to join and attested on the 11 Sept 1914. He passes his medical as 'fit' to serve. Something goes wrong somewhere though as he has 'DISCHARGED' 21/10/14 scrawled against his papers.

Captain **HUME SMITH CAMERON**

Hume, of the 3rd Bn. Norfolk Regiment, was killed in action on the Somme, on 4th September 1916.

Hume was the son of Duncan and Margaret Cameron, of the Old Mill House, Walker Gate, Newcastle upon Tyne. He had a brother, David, and a sister, Jane. He was educated at Hebburn Quay School and in 1909 attended Armstrong College in Newcastle, gaining a BSc and went in to teaching. He returned to Hebburn Quay School and was a member of staff there when war broke out.

Prior to his war service, Hume had attended the University's Officer Training Corps whilst at Armstrong College. He was commissioned into the Norfolk Regiment, 3rd Battalion, as a Second Lieutenant on 15th August 1914. Wounded in 1916. Hume was later that year to be killed in action at Guillemont, during the battle of the Somme, on 4th September 1916, aged 26. He is buried at Delville Wood cemetery, France.

Private **JAMES CAMPBELL**   8535
James, born in Walker, was a regular soldier with the 2nd Bn. Durham Light Infantry. He joined up in 1903 at the age of 19, having previously worked as a riveter in the shipyards.
In his early years of Army life, when stationed in India, he got himself in to trouble on a number of occasions due to being drunk in camp and at the 'Sudden Bazaar' in Lucknow. He also was forfeited pay on a number of occasions for being late for parade and once for allowing gambling in his billet.
James was one of the first soldiers to be sent to France at the outbreak of the Great War; arriving 8 Sept 1914. He appeared to be in the thick of it a lot of the time and was admitted to hospital on a number of occasions in 1915 – rib injury (x2) diarrhoea, and rheumatoid. On 26th Sept 1916, he was posted missing (believed killed next to it scribbled out.)
On 28 May 1917, a pension of 26/3 was awarded to his wife and children, who resided in Hebburn. He is commemorated on the Thiepval Memorial, France.

Sergeant **ROBERT WILLIAM CAMPBELL**   5/2520/ 263064   **D.C.M**
Residing 49 Lamb Street, Walker, a married man with three children and a fourth on the way, Robert joined the 5th Bn. Northumberland Fusiliers in September 1914. He was then transferred to the Kings Own Yorkshire Light Infantry in 1915. Robert was injured with a bullet wound to the thigh on 24th April 1915 but soon resumed his duties in the field. In 1925, he wrote to the British Red Cross relief fund asking for financial help. He had obviously struggled to find work after the war; like many returning heroes. I think he applied for a disablement pension, though likely it was a very small sum of money.

Extract from the London Gazette 30 Oct 1918
D.C.M awarded to 263064 Sgt. R.W Campbell K.O.Y.L.I
For conspicuous gallantry and devotion to duty. He was in charge of a platoon which he led with great success during an attack. He forestalled a heavy enemy attack on his flank and routed them completely, taking 16 prisoners. Throughout the operation he displayed fine qualities of initiative and leadership, and set a fine example of courage to all under his leadership.

Gunner **WILLIAM PARADINE CANDLISH**   185208
William was a 19-year-old Grocer's Assistant living at 1332, Walker Road when he attested in Oct 1916. He lived there with his Grandparents and two siblings – I assume his parents had both died.
 He served with the Royal Garrison Artillery (Royal Horse and Royal Field Artillery) in Egypt and Palestine, being posted there in 1917 and de-mobbed in March 1919. He is described in his entry medical as being 5 feet 7½ inches tall, weighing 104 pounds and having a 32½ inch chest with an expansion of a further 2 inches. His physique is described as being 'moderate.' On de-mobilisation William gave his address as being 19 North Parade, Whitley Bay.

Private **ARCHIE CARRADISE**   173574
Archie of 777 Walker Road, was born in Yorkshire. He joined the Army in 1918, having been conscripted for service in 1917 but not called until just before his 19th birthday in May 1918. An electrician and fitter, Archie was sent to join the 20th Training Bn. Machine Gun Corps in Nottingham. In 1919, he embarked to Egypt with the Corps and further continued his Military service until demobilisation. Archie died aged 73 in 1972 at Colchester in Essex.

Private **JOHN CARTY**   5811130
A labourer aged 27, John joined the Durham Light Infantry
(likely the 14th or 15th Bn.) in August 1914. He was then posted
to join his unit in Ireland and travelled with them to France.
He received a gunshot wound to the leg on 25 Sept 1915, at the
Battle of Loos. In 1918, he was transferred to the Labour
Corps from where he was discharged in Jan 1919. He claimed
a 20% disablement pension for having bronchitis, aggravated
by serving in the field. His de-mobilisation address looks like
42, Glasgow Street, Newcastle upon Tyne.

Private **JOSEPH CHAMBERS**   282638
Joined the Royal Engineers, Labour Corps in Sept1914 and
embarked to France Nov 1915 and was there until April 1917.
He then re-deployed to France in November of the same year.
In 1917, he was awarded a wage increase from 1/8- a day to
2/- due to a superior piece of work that he made/carried out.

Pte **GEORGE CLAYTON** 14073
George was born in Low Walker and later moved to
Gateshead with his family. He signed up to join the 9th Border
Regiment on 4 Sept 1914 and joined his unit at Carlisle the
following day. He was later (Oct 1915) transferred to the 3rd
Border Regiment, after having broken his left leg while based
in Eastbourne. He was confined to Barracks on 3 occasions for
being late for parade and once for causing a disturbance
outside of the medical room.

Private **JOHN CONVERY** (Alias **CONWERY**) 8/11219
Son of the late John Convery; born Essington in Staffordshire
16th Nov 1884. The family moved to the North East when John
was a child and he was educated at Hebburn Catholic School.
On finishing his education, he worked at a Colliery there and
then soon transferred to Walker Colliery. Whilst living in

Walker he met and married Jane Reid in 1907 and they subsequently had two sons William in 1910 and James in 1912. John enlisted on 10th Sept 1914 and subsequently fought in the Dardanelles with the 10th (Service Bn.) The Duke of Wellington's (West Riding Regt) where he met his fate on 11th Aug 1915.
(De Ruvigny's Roll of Honour)

Sapper **WILLIAM COOPER**   31051
William of 44 Rochester Street, Walker, joined the 10th Field Coy Royal Engineers attached to the Durham Light Infantry in 1915. He was posted to South Shields then Ripon – no further records exist. He did incur a number of minor offences including being later for parade, guard duty and being absent without leave overnight. These misdemeanours cost him a number of days pay each time they occurred. After leaving the Army (I'm assuming before the end of the war) he returned home to 13, King William Street, Gateshead.

Private **THOMAS HENRY CORNER**   46144
Thomas aged 18 lived 808 Walker Road with his mother and was an apprentice at a wire works when he joined up in 1917. He was sent to the West Yorkshire Regiment and later transferred to the York and Lancaster Regiment. He was sent out to France in early 1918 after completing his training. In October 1919, while still in France, he was admitted to hospital with gonorrhoea and was fined 33 days stoppage of pay. On 10 Nov 1919, he was posted back to England.

Sergeant **PATRICK COWMAN**   13540/27635

Formerly of 146 Byker Street, Walker, Patrick attested on the 13 Oct 1914 at Beverley in Yorkshire to the 7th East Yorkshire Regiment. He quickly moved up the ranks being made a lance Corporal in 1914, a full Corporal in 1915 and a Sergeant in 1916. It all started to go wrong though in June 1916. He began to miss parades, stay out overnight, etc. He went missing for 2 days in August 1916 and was reduced to the rank of Corporal as punishment. Further to this he had a severe reprimand for over sleeping by two and a half hours. Luckily, he got himself sorted out and got rated back up to being a Sergeant. Patrick was killed on the Somme 8 Feb 1917 and is remembered on the Thiepval Memorial.

Private **WILLIAM COX**   59422
A member of the Royal Garrison Artillery, thirty-one-year-old 'Coachman' William of 158, Middle Street, Walker was married to Ellen and had an 8-year-old daughter Hilda, when he enlisted in 1915. He was posted on 30th Oct 1915 (UK) but discharged on 8 March 1917 on account of his deafness.

Staff Sergeant **WALTER COX**   A2999
A watchmaker living 90 Church Street, Walker, formerly of 2 Eastbourne Gardens, twenty-five-year-old Walter was called up in Dec 1915 – the month of his marriage to Robertina Train, to the Royal Army Ordnance Corps. Walter is described as being 5feet 7 inches in height, weighing 155 lb and having false upper teeth. He returned to watch making after the war.

Gunner **COLIN COX**   42961
Colin was called up in 1915 to join the Royal Garrison Artillery. Married to Sophia and with a son also called Colin, born 1915 Colin Snr of 137 Middle Street, Walker, was not called in to service until 1917. He was posted to France in 1918 and stayed there till de-mobilisation in 1919.

Unknown soldier (Authors own collection.)

T2 Cpl **THOMAS CRAGGS**   288274

Thomas enlisted in to the Army on 8 Dec 1915 but was not mobilised until 6 Nov 1917. Thomas of Middle Street, Walker was working for the North-Eastern Railways as a signalman. On enlistment, he was posted to the Railway section of the Royal Engineers and on 1 Jan 1918 sailed to Alexandria in Egypt. He was de-mobilized 20 Jan 1912.

Private **MATTHEW CRAIG**   39235

Matthew of 60 Bernard Street, Walker, did his bit during the war in both the Northumberland Fusiliers from 27 Feb 1916 and then the Lancashire Fusiliers Aug 1917 till de-mob in Jan 1919. He re-joined the Northumberland Fusiliers in 1925.

Private **HENRY CROOKS**   58649

Henry, a fitter of 172 Byker Street, Walker, must be congratulated for the shortest time in the service. He attested on 17 Sept 1915 and deserted the same day.

Private **WILLIAM LOWERY CROWE**   879

Shields Daily News 12 July 1915: NORTH SHIELDS MAN KILLED AT THE FRONT. News has reached North Shields of the death on the battlefield of Pte. W. Crowe, 5th Northumberland Fusiliers, the eighteen-year-old son of Mr and Mrs John Crowe of 1,706 Walker Road (formerly of Wellington Street, North Shields). The young fusilier was in the special reserve prior to the war, and had been in France about four months. He was wounded on June 16th and succumbed to his injuries two days later. In peace times, he worked as a locomotive fireman at Percy Main.

Shields Daily News 15 July 1915

PRIVATE W. CROWE of the 5th Batt. Northumberland Fusiliers, formerly of Wellington Street, North Shields, died of wounds on June 18.

Shields Daily News July 13 1915: DEATHS. CROWE - Died of wounds received in action, in France, on June 18th, aged 18 years, William Lowery, eldest and beloved son of John and Martha Crowe of 1703 Walker Road, Walker, late of Wellington Street, North Shields.

Private **JAMES HARROW CURRY**   8068
Near neighbour of our Henry Crooks the deserter, James attested on 25 March 1916 in Newcastle upon Tyne. James lived at 188 Byker Street, Walker, with wife Sophia and daughter Eleanor. James aged 28 at attestation served from 1916 onwards and was allocated a small pension after the war.

Sapper **MICHAEL CULLEN**   3235/461121
Twenty-one-year-old Michael who lived 43 Mitchell Street, Walker, enlisted to the Royal Engineers in December 1915. Formerly a skilled joiner at William Dobson's shipbuilders Michael was employed in to the same trade in the Army. He was hospitalised twice in 1917 in France – the first time for 45 days having been wounded and the second time for 32 days having caught gonorrhoea. In 1918 he sailed to Basra, Baghdad and Ramadi (Iraq) where he stayed with the Royal Engineers until at least 1920.

Private **WILLIAM CUMMINS**   137502
William was 38 years old and married with 4 children when he attested in 1914. He was drafted the Royal Army Medical Corps attached to the Northumberland Fusiliers and posted to France. In 1917, he spent 3 weeks in a Military hospital in Cardiff suffering from Trench Foot.

Sapper **WILLIAM DAVIES**   4364
William, a Wharfinger (a person who is responsible for the delivery of goods, tide tables etc at a Wharf or Dockside) attested on 7TH Sept 1917 to the Northumberland Fusiliers

(and attached to the Royal Engineers) on 7th Sept 1914. His medical describes him as being 19 years and 7 months. He was 5 feet 7½ tall and weighed 125 pounds. His chest measured with 35 inches with a huge expansion of a further 4 inches. He had a fresh complexion, blue eyes and dark brown hair.
He was wounded by a gunshot wound to the left thigh (possibly 1917) and was then transferred to the 1st Suffolk Regiment and then transferred to a reserve Bn. He returned home to his mother's house at 23 Ripponden St, Byker, Newcastle upon Tyne.

Private **JOHN DEVLIN**   3/8472
John formerly of 4 East Terrace, Low Walker, a 'plater's helper' at the shipyards - enlisted into the 3rd (Reserve) Bn. Northumberland Fusiliers on the 8th August 1914. He was then transferred to the 9th (Service) Bn, Northumberland Fusiliers and it was with them that he was wounded on the 5th July 1916, on the Somme. The wound was later announced in the regimental journal, but not until September 1916; this was mainly due to the masses of Somme casualties and delays in reporting.
On recovery he moved to the 12th (Service) Bn, Northumberland Fusiliers and was either wounded again or taken ill as he was then posted to 'A' Company, 23rd (Service) Bn. Northumberland Fusiliers (4th Tyneside Scottish) He was killed in action on 17 Apr 1917 and is buried BEAURAINS ROAD CEMETERY, BEAURAINS, France.
When he died he was married so possibly had moved to another address in Low Walker.

Private **ERNEST DIXON**   102506
 A labourer aged 18 living at 65 Lamb Street, Walker, Ernest was called up to attest on 14 Aug 1918 and was drafted into the 5th Reserve Bn. Durham Light Infantry. No other papers are discernible but it is likely he served home service and de-mobilized early 1919.

Private **ALEXANDER DOCHERTY**   410

Working as an apprentice fitter and living at 104 Fisher Street, Walker, in 1908. Alexander, born 1889 joined the 1st Northumberland Field Ambulance (Royal Army Medical Corps) as a reservist. I don't know what he did or where he served during the Great War but he was awarded the 14-15 Star and the British and Victory medals so he must have served in at least one theatre of war prior to 31 Dec 1915 (only participants prior to this date got awarded the 14-15 Star.)

Private **JOHN DUMMINGHAM** 324731

John was a Private with the Royal Engineers Tunnelling Coy, previously with the 2nd Bn. West Yorkshire Regiment, service number 8574. John of 40 Fisher Hill, Low Walker was 33 years old when he re-joined the Army after having previously been discharged in 1916 after suffering a severe fracture to the metacarpus (a finger.) John is a 'hewer' in the coal mines and has voluntarily offered to re-join as long as it is with the Tunnelling Coy as he has special skills in this area. He is re-enlisted on 13 Apr 1918 and is posted on 22 April 1918 to the B.E.F in France. He is then discharged again in October 1918. Life isn't easy for John after leaving the Army, it looks as though he suffered badly, possibly neurasthenia (shell shock.) It appears his marriage breaks down soon after and he is living in possible lodgings in Newgate Street Newcastle upon Tyne. He loses his discharge certificate and writes to ask for a copy (1919) as it needs it to get employment, he writes to say that "When I came home from… *(paper very fragmented and burnt and only some words visible)* … I was a bit wild and it took a lot of….."

In another letter, he states "…lot of trouble when I left and put papers in the fire." He also states that the certificate was accidentally destroyed.

In 1924 money appears to be a problem and he is desperately trying to get some help from the army. He asks about a pension having been discharged in 1916 through wounds. The army refuse to pay a pension as he was re-enlisted fit for service in 1918. They refer him to a Royal Engineers charitable fund.

I really hope they helped John.

Private **ROBERT PERCIVAL ELLISON**   33425
Robert joined the 2nd Bn. York and Lancaster Regiment in 1915 and was posted to France in 1917. He was married with three sons. He was killed in action on the 20 Nov 1917 and is buried at Villers-Plouich Communal Cemetery, France. His family who were living at 124 Fisher Street, Walker, were awarded a pension of 29/7 a week in compensation for his loss.
Items returned to his wife after his internment included; a religious medallion, a religious book, cigarette cases and cigarettes, rosary.

Private **JAMES ELLIOTT**   34069 / 26548
     MM.
James Elliott, born 18 April 1898 was a junior clerk by occupation, attested on 25 May 1916 and was called up to serve with the Durham Light Infantry on 3rd Mar 1917. He was the son of James and Sarah Elliott – his father a former 'brass finisher' was now working as an insurance agent. Along with his five siblings the family lived at 1420 Walker Road. James was transferred to the Yorkshire Regiment in Oct 1917 and was admitted to hospital on two occasions in 1918 suffering from Trench feet. He was de-mobilised on 10 Oct 1919 and presented with his Military Medal on 14 Feb 1921 by the Lord Mayor of Newcastle.
James, now a 24-year-old Customs & Excise clerk, married Jemima Muir (a shop assistant) of 830 Walker Road, St Anthony's on 10 Jun 1922 and died aged 73 in March 1972.
I have unfortunately been unable to trace the action that led to James being awarded the Military Medal.

Sapper **JAMES ENGLISH**   51603

James, formerly of 41 Mitchell Street, Walker attested on 5th Sept 1914 at Redcar. He was now living at 38 Princess Street, South Bank, Middlesbrough with his wife Agnes and three children; John, James and Evelyn. Sadly, daughter Evelyn passed away in March 1915 aged 11 months.

James was attached to the 84th Field Coy, Royal Engineers and was posted to France on 15 Jul 1915. A sister living in America, got her employers brother, based in London to contact the Army and check on the whereabouts/wellbeing of James in Oct 1915 a she had not heard from him for some time. The Army chased up the request and apparently letters had again passed between the pair.

On 12 April 1916 his second born child, also called James passed away aged three. Before the news could reach the battlefield, James senior was already dead - he was killed in action on 14th Sept 1916. Wife Agnes and surviving son John had now moved to 49 Princess St, South Bank. The army awarded them a pension of 14/- per week.

James is buried at Bard Cottage Cemetery, Belgium.

Five months later James' younger brother John, died of wounds aged 21, on 15 Sept 1916 whilst serving with the 5th Bn. Northumberland Fusiliers. They left behind five sisters and a brother, both parents already having died.

So sad. (Authors own comment).

L/Cpl **GEORGE FAIRCLOUGH** 5/2583 240495

George Fairclough of the 5th Northumberland Fusiliers was wounded in May 1915. His parents, Mr and Mrs Fairclough, of 114, Byker Street, Walker, received information that their son, Private George Fairclough, No 2586, 5th N.F, had been wounded and was in hospital. He later was transferred to the 9th Bn. Northumberland Hussars and was killed in action on 24 Oct 1918. He now lies in Bermerain Communal Cemetery in France.

Sapper **JOHN FALLON**   173962

John a miner of 36 Berry Street, Walker, was called up just after the end of the war, though had attested in 1917. His service ran from 29 Apr 1919 until 10 Aug 1919 when he deserted. John was found to have fraudulently enlisted in to the R.A.F (using the name L. Martin – impersonating his step brothers' identity) and given the R.A.F number 334724 A.C2. Tried and convicted he was given 14 days imprisonment with hard labour for larceny. Discharged from the Royal Air Force under Para 392 (10) King's regulations as from 22.2.20

The sadness behind this young man's tale is that his father is (the late) Driver **Owen Fallon** of the Army Service Corps who is buried in Walker Church yard. Owen died at home 18 April 1918 aged 47, last known address Berry Street, Walker, Newcastle upon Tyne.

Owen, a former coal hewer, was born in Ireland; though likely came to England at a young age as all his children were born here. Owen didn't need to join the Army, as he was older than the 41 years old upper age limit when war broke out.

He left behind wife Elizabeth (formerly Martin) whom he married in 1905 after the deaths of their first spouses. Children from these unions are as follows: James Martin, Isabella Martin, **John Fallon***, Thomas Fallon*, Lowery Martin, Maggie Martin, William Fallon and Elizabeth Fallon. *children born to first wife Mary Ann Gilligan who died 1902.

Sgt **JAMES FARRELL**   478560

James Farrell, a 24-year-old grocer's assistant of 24 Rochester Street, Walker attested on 8 Dec 1915 to the Northumberland Fusiliers.

In 1919, he wrote a letter to the Army:

Dear Sir,   *May 20th 1919*

I should like to mention to you when I joined the Army for duty and was sent to France, I was attached to the 23rd N.F, better known as the Tyneside Scottish, and the Captain got me sent to the hospital with my ears, at the Hospital I was examined and marked for P.B at base, two days later I was sent down to the Base and put in front of a Medical Board and marked B.2., and then placed in to the 167 Labour Company, from there I was sent to join the 307 Prisoner of war company until I was demobilised. Now sir, I filled out one of the forms at the Orderly Room before I left my company and when the medical

officer came to examine us, he asked me if I wanted to make a claim, and I told him no, but I asked him about my teeth I had drawn, and he got me to give him my particulars, as to where I got them drawn, so I have heard no more about them.

I remain yours

Sgt. J Farrell.

On 17 Aug 1917 his musketry, squad, rifle, drill exercises etc were all described as 'fair' but overall, he was described as being too slack. Maybe this particular chap didn't like him as he was promoted through the rank to Serjeant.

James married Mary Nattrass on 17 April 1917.

His service was as follows:

Reserve 9 Dec 1915 to 10 Feb 1916

Home 11 Feb 1916 to 9 Sept 1917

France 10 Sept 1917 to 4 Nov 1918

UK leave 4-18 Nov 1918.

James left the Army to 96 Spencer Street, Heaton.

Private **WALTER WILLIAM FIDDES**   366856

Walter was a 30-year-old labourer residing at 1615, Walker Road, Walker, joined his unit the 1/4th Bn. Yorkshire Regiment on 12 Nov 1917 and was posted on the 12 Nov 1917 later being transferred to the 4th Manchester Regiment. He went out to France on 18 May 1918. What happens next is quite unbelievable.

On 12 Nov 1918 (The day after the armistice) Walter was in confinement after having returned to his unit that day having deserted on 15 Oct 1918. He stood trial for desertion, was found guilty and sentenced to **7** years imprisonment, commuted to **2.** On 7 July 1919, he was released from No5 Military prison; the rest of his sentence being remitted.

Private **THOMAS FINN**   845593
Thomas was an 18-year-old apprentice fitter at the shipyards and living at 615 Welbeck Road, Walker, when he attested on 17 Jan 1916 and was then enlisted into the 3 Bn. Northumberland Fusiliers Labour Corps. I can't make out where he was posted to
(likely abroad) but in 1919 was transferred to the Royal Army Medical Corps who later discharged him as no longer fir for Military service as he was suffering from a kidney problem which incurred recurrent bouts of cystitis leaving him with what they classed as a 30%   disability. He was awarded a pension of 8/3- a week as from 24 Jul 1919.

Sapper **EDWARD FINCHER**
Edward Fincher of Ivy House, Philipson Street, Walker was an 18-year-old clerk when he attested on 29 May 1916, he was called up on 16 Feb 1917 and was transferred on numerous occasion. His papers are hard to make out but I assume he joined the Northumberland Fusiliers as he was transferred to the Royal Engineers on 20 April 1916 'for the benefit of the service' – but appears to be held in reserve. He later moved to the London Regiment and then in Dec 1918 compulsory, temporarily transferred to the 837 area Employment Coy Edward was admitted to hospital twice with Trench Feet – in Nov 1917 and again in Feb 1918.
Previously to living at Philipson Street, Edward and his family has lived at 13 Watson Street, a 4-roomed property. His father,

also called Edward – was a co-operative store Clerk. Mother Mary was at home looking after their seven surviving children of the nine born alive.

Private **NORMAN FOGGON**   185011

Norman attested to the Army on 20 May 1916. He was living at 1399 Walker Road, Walker, described his employment as that of a 'shell inspector' (probably at a munitions factory.) He was attached to the Durham Light Infantry but later moved to the Labour Corps – 209 Divisional Employment Company on account of suffering bouts of bronchitis. He was dismissed from the service in Oct 1919 on account of having a 20% disability due to his chest.

Cpl **JOHN HENRY FORBES**   111490

Known as Henry, a warehouse man, he served with the Royal Regiment of Artillery in the later part of the war, only being awarded the Victory medal. Born in 1893 and living at 8 Birch Terrace in the early 1920's he re-joined the Royal Artillery and served until 1930.

Pte **PETER FOREMAN**   11106

Peter a 29-year-old shipyard labourer was called forward to join the West Yorkshire Regiment at York on 24 Aug 1916 and sailed with the Mediterranean Force. Formerly of 16, Foster Street, Walker, Peter was now living at 237, Benson Road, Byker with his mother.

Peter had pay deducted on numerous occasions – though it doesn't state why, although he does go AWOL 17 Dec 1916 only to return on 8 Jan 1917.

Wounded by a bullet to the right foot while in the Dardanelles, Peter's military service includes service with the Mediterranean for and the British Expeditionary Force in France.

L/Cpl **WILLIAM GATHERAR**   16738/10738
Formerly with the 6th Bn. East Yorkshire Regiment and latterly
with the Royal Engineers, William a Locomotive Fireman
lived at 11 Caledonia Street, Walker. He attested on 14 Aug
1915 and was enlisted into service on the 26 Aug 1914. He was
charged 6 days stoppage of pay in Jan 1915 when he went
absent from the 13th to the 18th. He was soon posted tot the
Dardanelles where he was wounded on 22 Aug 1915. In April
1916, he transferred to the Royal Engineers, becoming a Lance
Corporal in July 1918.

Private **WILLIAM GIBSON**   6/24396
William of the 52nd Bn. Leicester Regiment resided 1366,
Walker Road, Walker with his mother Mary Ann Gibson.
Nothing really of his papers survived other than that of very
basic information. He attested in 1917 and survived his time in
the theatre of war as in 1920 he joined the 5th Bn.
Northumberland Fusiliers Territorial unit. From the 1911
census I can see he was 31 when he attested to the Army and
had been a 'boiler plater' at the shipyards. At that time, he
was living with his mother and 6 of his 7 siblings at 28 Buxton
Street,

Sergeant **EDWARD GEORGE GILLESPIE**   1076/ 484244
Edward enlisted to Tyneside Scottish Bn. Northumberland
Fusiliers. A former 'Labourer' and territorial soldier he
attested on 13 Nov 1914 and promoted to Corporal on 23 Nov
1914. He was given 3 severe reprimands during his time with
the unit – once for staying out overnight and twice for missing
parade. He transferred to the Kings Own Scottish Borderers
Agricultural Coy, Labour Corps in September 1917 at the age
of 41.

Private **JOHN HENRY GODFREY**   061896
The consecutive name and number with our chap below (both
men had joined up together) leads me to understand these

men to be brothers. John, aged 24 is living at 289, Church Street, Walker. He joined the Royal Army Service Corps as a Horseman/ Driver, being a former cartman. He was sent overseas to join the expeditionary force in France on 12 April 1915 and was demobilised 13 June 1919 suffering from Dermatitis.

Private **THOMAS GODFREY**   061897
A former 'cartman' of 103, Lamb Street, Walker, Thomas, who was slightly deaf in his left ear, was married to Sarah and had 4 children, Margaret, Sarah, Elizabeth and Thomas; another daughter Doris having died in infancy.
 Thomas joined the Royal Army Service Corps as a 'Horseman/ Driver' at the age of 36 in 1915 deployed to France and was there until 21 May 1918 when he was sent home on 10 days leave, returning on 31 May 1918. His daughter Elizabeth aged 5 had died on the 18th May 1918 of tuberculosis meningitis.

Private **MAURICE GLASGOW**   14/166
Age 23 Maurice of 23, Eastbourne Avenue, Walker, attested on 11 Nov 1914 as a Sapper to the Royal Engineers. He was super-nummary to work at Armstrong Whitworth's (Elswick) and in April 1915 was compulsory transferred to the Royal Army Service Corps as a Driver in the Motor Transport Coy. He was de-mobilized Feb 1919 to 7 Sandringham Road, South Gosforth.

CSM **WILLIAM HENRY GRAHAM**   350025
Nineteen-year-old William attested to the 8th Bn. Durham Light Infantry in November 1913, while a student at Bede College, Durham University. The son of a ships plater and formerly of 23 Westbourne Gardens, William had done well for himself – a pupil teacher by the age of 16.
Transferred to the 26th Bn. DLI, he was promoted through the ranks to Company Serjeant Major. He was admitted to Hill

House military hospital in Ramsgate, Kent on 9 Dec 1918 to undergo a double hernia operation and the removal of an undescended testes. On 1 Feb 1919, he was transferred to Sunderland war hospital, where he was discharged from on 4 Feb 1919 and returned to his family home at 61 Cambridge Ave, Whitley Bay.

Private **ALFRED GRANDISON** 9045

Alfred had served with the Royal Army Medical Corps (Territorials) since 1910, his service expiring in 1913. Aged 21 at the outbreak of war, he worked for Swan, Hunter & Wigham Richardson Ltd shipbuilders as an apprentice 'fitter' formerly having been a blacksmith at the 'yards. Alfred of 89 West Middle Street, Walker, attested on 10 Sept 1914 - again to the Royal Army Medical Corps and was attached to the 50th Northumbrian Division. His entry medical describes him as being 5ft 8½ inches tall with a 34½ inch chest with an expansion of 2 inches. Vision and physical development described as 'good'. Alfred served in France from April 1915 until mid-1916 when he was returned to the UK and where he was based until de-mobilisation on 31 Mar 1920.

Private **JAMES GUSTARD**   481757

No records appear to survive other than his medal index card; but I'm assuming him to be Private L Gustarel, who was recorded as being injured in May 1915 in the Newcastle Journal. There was a Gustard family living at Back White Street on the 1911 census. Could this be their eldest son James who would now be 20? I think most likely and the error was down to poor writing!

L/ Cpl **THOMAS BELL HARDY** 1363

Thomas Hardy, a former coal miner, had been born in Jarrow, Durham, to Robert and Mary Hardy. He was the third son and fourth of eleven children born to the couple. By the time of the

1911 census his mother Mary had been widowed and was living in a tiny cramped two roomed flat at 19 Lamb Street, Walker, along with ten of her children and a 36-year-old boarder named Michael Campbell, a labourer. (*1911 census)

Private **SWINTON HARWOOD** 38767
Swinton of the Lancashire Fusiliers was transferred numerous times and with a host of service numbers including 29915 / 4573 / 57013 and was for a period of time with the Northumberland Fusiliers and then the Durham Light Infantry. Swinton was a 33-year-old Chemical worker when he attested in 1915 and was living at 920 Walker Road, Walker. He was mobilized on 16 Jun 1916 and posted to the Northumberland Fusiliers. His transfers are not fully legible because of the damage to the documents but he was sent to France and admitted to hospital suffering from 'neurosthenia' after being in a shell explosion. He was discharged at Preston, Lancs, on 6 May 1918 no longer fit for Military service and awarded a full pension of 27/6 from 7 May 1918 being reduced to 22/- and to be reviewed in 13 weeks' time.

Gunner **WILLIAM HAYES** 30532
  Twenty-one-year-old coal miner William of 3 Lamb Street, Walker, joined the Northumberland Fusiliers on 9 Oct 1915 at Bardon Moor Camp. His medical examination describes him as being 5 feet 5 inches tall with a 34½ chest and with a pale complexion, grey eyes and light brown hair. In early 1916, he gets in to bother on a few occasions; overstaying leave by 13 hours, disobeying a brigade gardener by driving over a field and then again for overstaying his leave; this time by 24 hours. Punishments of loss of pay etc push him into asking for a transfer which was granted and he joined the Machine Gun Corps with immediate effect.
In 1917 it is discovered he is suffering from a *'disorderly action of the heart'* that he was unaware of until he had been in the Army for some time. He was sent back to the UK to return to

work in the colliery but kept in 'reserve' until his discharge in Nov 1918.

Private **THOMAS HEATHCOTE**   11105
29-year-old Thomas, was born in Walker but living in Wallsend when he attested in August 1914. He was previously working at Swan, Hunter & Wigham Richardson Ltd shipyards as a labourer. He served with the 9th Bn. West Yorkshire Regiment – while in the UK he was regularly punished for being late/absenteeism. On 1 Jul 1915, he arrived in the Dardanelles and was injured when blown up by a landmine on 9 Aug 1915, suffering a fractured ankle, bruised leg, and an injury to his back. On the 15 Aug 1915, he was taken out of the war zone on a hospital ship. By Feb 1916 he had recovered from his injuries and was posted to France with his unit. Here he suffered from rhumation and gas exposure while in the trenches.
On 10 Jan 1919, he was discharged from the Army surplus to Military requirements having (it states) not suffered any impairment since joining the service. Thomas died in the Royal Infirmary, Newcastle on 11 Aug 1920.

Private **WILLIAM HELLENS**   20012
A single man residing at 50 Riverview, Low Walker, William joined the Army Service Corps in October 1915 at the age of 42. He is described as 5 feet 4 inches tall with a chest measurement of 37 inches with an expansion of a further 2 inches. William was in France form 30 Oct 1915 until 14 July 1918, transferring to the Labour Corps 30 Oct 1917. On 23 Mar 1917, he was awaiting trial and was later convicted by the C.S.M of while on war service of drunkenness (illegible) resulting in 70 days (illegible.) It is likely due to this misdemeanour that he was transferred to the Labour Corps. William was discharged to his fathers' address; 33 Ropley Rd, Deptford, Sunderland after his discharge on 7 Jan 1919 as he is

no longer fit for war service having *"chronic rheumatism and defective vision."*

In 1933, he asks the Army for a copy of his discharge papers, the original having been stolen when his father's house was 'broken up' after his death and William being away. He states he did not report the theft to the Police.

Sapper **GEORGE WILLIAM HEWITT** 545299
The 21-year-old son of Jane Hewitt of 62, Church Street, Walker (formerly 1 Staiths St, Walker) attests into the Royal Engineers on 10th Dec 1915. George is described as being employed as an 'Engine man' standing 5ft 8½ inches tall and with a 36½ chest with an expansion of 3 inches. He begins his service as an Engine driver on 12 June 1916 with the 90th Field Coy R.E. In 1917 is transferred to the 7bn York and Lancaster Regiment but soon transferred back in to the Royal Engineers 'for the benefit of the service' at a base depot. In October 18, he re-joins his unit from hospital (no record of injury or illness) and is sent on 14 days home leave 2-16th October 1918. His de-mobilisation medical is held in Stockheim, Germany on 8 Sept 1918.

Gunner **RICHARD HICKS** 143016
Richard lived at 23, Lamb Street, Walker, attested on 11 Dec 1915 and joined the Army reserve the following day and was mobilized in the Royal Garrison Artillery on 6 March 1917. Richard was a 20-year-old assistant 'Banksman' at a local colliery when he got his call up. He joined at South Ripon Camp from where he joined his unit the 254th Siege Battery Artillery.
Richard's first few months in the Army didn't go too well; on 5 July 1917, he was charged with *"hesitating to obey an order and insolence towards an officer."* For this offence, he received 21 days Field Punishments No1***

On 1 Oct 1917, He was charged with not complying with an order and received 7 days Field Punishments No 1***.
On 11 Oct 1917, he fractures his ankle when slipping on muddy ground as he unloaded ammunition boxes from a limber.
After de-mobilisation in 1919 Richard re-enlisted into the Army, this time to the 5th Bn. Northumberland Fusiliers (Territorial's.)

Private **WILLIAM HOGG**   19/1412
William, a labourer attested on 3 Jul 1915 to the 12th Bn. Durham Light Infantry. He was killed in action aged 20 on 18 July 1916 on the Somme. He left behind a mother Christina, who he had resided with at 21, Fells Street, Walker, along with his 4 of his sisters. He is remembered with honour on the THIEPVAL MEMORIAL France.

Sergeant **JOHN JOSEPH HOLLAND**   171345
John of 6, Evistone Gardens, Walker Road – the former soldier, aged 37 is now a Clerk/Time keeper attests to the Northumberland Fusiliers in Newcastle on 2 Feb 1915 and is posted 6 Nov 1916. He originally got the rank of Sergeant in 1902 so was automatically made a sergeant on re-entering the service. He was based on UK soil serving with the Labour Corps and Employment Corps at base depot. He deployed to France on 24 May 1919 until 2 Sep 1919. This would have been to help with the 'Battlefield clearances.'

A/L/Cpl **ROBERT WOODS HUTCHINSON** 127547
 Thirty-one-year-old General Post Office employee Robert of 1 Airey Terrace, Walker and later 535, Welbeck Road, embodied into service 11 Dec 1915. He was posted to France with the British expeditionary force as a Sapper with the Royal Engineers, employed as a 'linesman' in the Signal Coy.

Men of the 50th Northumbria Division; wanting to go home.

A/L/Cpl Gunner **JOHN JOICEY** 204688

Former 'Machine man' at Walker Colliery. John attested at Elswick, Newcastle upon Tyne on 12 Dec 1915 and was mobilised on 2 Feb 1917 aged 21. He joined the Royal Horse and Royal Field Artillery and was posted to a number of Batteries and Brigades when fighting in France. John was fined 10 days loss of pay in August 1917 when he overstayed home leave by 5 days. In October 1918, he was admitted to hospital in Newcastle upon Tyne with cellulitis of the neck and was there until early December when he was returned to duty overseas. In May 1919, he was posted overseas to the Black Sea and Constantinople.

John lived at 8 Diamond Row, Walker, with his father and three sisters. Another sister lived at number 12 and brother Robert lived on Mitchell Street (see below) and James on Berry Street. Only brother Edward had moved away – to Hebburn.

Private **ROBERT JOICEY**   610362

Married to Annie Isabella Edwards on 25th May 1906 they had children Lilian born 1908, Gladys 1910 and Robert 1912. Robert senior was a Driver with the 4th Northumbrian Howitzer Brigade, Royal Horse and Royal Field Artillery (also Leicestershire Royal Horse Artillery.) He attested on 30 Sept 14 and was posted to France 3 July 1916. Reported missing and having been taken a prisoner of war on 24 March 1918 he was later released on 11 December 1918 to Ripon Camp - a month after the signing of the Armistice. His wife Annie had received a card from him explaining his predicament, which she duly sent to the Army as proof he had been captured. She then a few weeks later wrote asking for the card to be returned to her.

Dear Sir,
Would you kindly return card I sent to you a few weeks ago. It stated that my husband Driver R Joicey 610,362 RFA was a prisoner of war in Germany. It is urgently required by me. Any further word

regarding my husband will be greatly esteemed by me.
  Yours truly.
                    Annie Joicey.

He was returned to his unit and was discharged from the service *'having suffered impairment since entry to service'* including gunshot wounds to the right arm.
Robert was awarded a pension of 8/3 a week with an extra 3/- for his wife and children. He was 35 years old.

Private **JOHN WILLIAM JOHNSON**   4625
Private John (William) Johnson lived at 117 Middle Street, Walker, with his wife Letitia. He died on 7th July 1916 and is remembered on the Thiepval memorial. His death was not confirmed until late September 1916. He left behind a father Thomas who lived in Ashington. Letitia re-married (Turnbull) in 1917 and was living at Vera Caravan Showground, Byker in 1920.

Private **JOHN LAMB**   63195
Nineteen-year-old 'ships plater' John of 1259 Walker Road, Walker, he enlisted on 28 Oct 1916 but was not called for until 30 Jun 1918 when he was posted to the 4th Yorkshire Regiment later 5th Bn. Yorkshire Regiment Princess of Wales Own and was released for reserve service on 3 March 1919.
He made an application for a copy of his discharge papers in July 1933 as the original had been lost. He was now living in Salford near Manchester.

Corporal **THOMAS LANG**   9/15854
Twenty-four-year old Thomas formerly of Chapel Street, Walker was a coal miner in Thornley, Cleveland when he enlisted on 9 Nov 1914. He was employed by Weardale Steel, Coal & Coke in Thornley. He joined the East Yorkshire, York and Lancaster Regiment and achieved the rank of Lance

Corporal. He was wounded in May 1917 and shipped back to England aboard the 'Aberdonian.' He stayed in England for some time afterwards, based in Ripon, Pontefract and Sunderland. While in Sunderland he was dis-rated back to a Corporal on 14 Feb 1917 for 'misconduct' when in charge of an escort he allowed the soldier in close arrest to escape.

In August 1917 (44 days) and again in November of the same year (94 days), Thomas was admitted to hospital suffering the effects of having been gassed. In March 1917, he admitted to hospital for 90 days suffering from Trench Feet.

Thomas married Rose Hannah Firmstone on 19 Dec 1909 at Easington, Durham and they had a son Thomas born 1910 and daughter Nora in 1913.

Private **GEORGE SINCLAIR LAURIE** 46029

George of 76 Fisher Hill, Low Walker, joined the 21st Bn. Tyneside Scottish Regiment at Gosforth on 5 March 1915, aged 20. He was posted to France Jan 1916 but later admitted to hospital in Etaples, France with Pleurisy. He was sent back to England in April to recover and during this time married his sweetheart Annie Isabella Appleby at Walker Parish Church on the 25 Apr 1916. He was posted to Hornsea in Essex and from here returned to his unit in France of 15 Jun 1916. From here he was later attached to the 13th Bn. Durham Light Infantry (due to the decimation of the Tyneside Scottish on 1 Jul 1916 on the Somme) to which he was given a full transfer on 13 Sept 1916. In November, he was sent by hospital ship to England suffering from pleurisy once again.

George got himself confined to barracks or had stoppages of pay on a few occasions. Three times in 1915 when the battalion were stationed in the North East of England when he was late back from leave, by up to 5 days – having been arrested and returned to his unit by the civil Police. Again, when at Hornsea in 1916 he was twice deducted 3 days' pay – once for being dirty on Parade and once for overstaying his leave by two days.

A son David James Laurie was born in July 1917.
For an incident on 4 Oct 1917, George was told on the 7 Oct
1917 that he was to be deducted 3 days' pay (no mention of
said incident.) On 8 Oct 1917 George was dead, aged only 22
killed in action near Le Sars, Somme France. Items returned to
his wife included; Disc, 4 cards, 4 letters, photo's, pipe, cap
comforter, razor, watch case, cigarette case, 2 discs *(identity.)*
Widow Annie and son David were now living *at (or soon after
George's death they moved to)* 77 Fisher Street, Low Walker, to
live with George's family; brother Thomas age 21, Willie 20
(away in India) Jimmie age 16 and John aged 14 (away at
Murton Colliery.) Also, Private David Bruce's wife Lizzie
Bruce aged 33 and her children; David aged 10, Murdoch aged
9, Willie aged 7, Mary Lizzie aged 6, George aged 4 and Bruce
aged 2.
On 7th April 1919 at 77 Fisher Street, Low Walker, aged 22
months, David Laurie, son of George, died. He was suffering
from acute influenza and pneumonia.
Annie Isabella Laurie re-married in 1921 – Thomas Laurie,
brother of George, a year younger than herself. They had three
children a girl and two boys. Their first-born David, died in
1923 at a year old.

Gunner **WILLIAM THOMAS LAWSON**   133897
A 20-year-old grocer, William of 19 Byker Terrace, Walker,
attested on 1 Dec 1915 at Walker. The medical officer
described him as being 5 feet 7 inches tall with a 33½ inch
chest, being under weight and of poor physique. Also noted
was that he had poor vision and wore spectacles and a *'slight
defect but not to cause rejection'* (from Military service) and also
suffered from constipation. He was held in reserve until 5 Jan
1917 when he was mobilised and posted to the Royal Garrison
Artillery. On 16 Feb 1917, he was transferred from 2/2 to 2/1
Coy Royal Garrison Artillery. William was admitted to
hospital on the 19 Apr 1917 where he stayed until 29 Jun 1917
having suffered acute appendicitis and had to have it

removed. While in hospital he was transferred to the 4th Coy R.G.A. and in March 1918 posted to the 2nd Siege battery reserve at Catterick. William was posted back to France on 27 April 1918 and was returned to England 18 Sept 1919 for de-mobilisation.

Private **HAROLD LEEMAN**   58337

Harold was a chemist assistant living at 32 Woodside Avenue, Walker, when he was posted to the 91st Training reserve Ban at Horton Camp on 7 Feb 1917 and was later permanently transferred to the York and Lancaster Regiment as a 'Rifle Bomber'. On 2 Oct 1917, he was charged with missing 6.30a.m. Parade and had to forfeit 3 days' pay. On 8 March 1918, he arrived at the Etaples training base in France. He was demobilised on 10 Nov 1919.

Private **JOHN LEIGH**   18144

John, born in 1895 was one of eighteen children born to William and Mary Jane Leigh, of Cambrian Row, Walker. His father William was a coal miner (hewer.) The family moved to the Durham area in the later 1910's and the 1911 census shows John, now aged 16, also working in the mines as 'coal trimmer.' He is living with his parents and 16-month-old sister Mary Jane, at Barmston boat landing, Washington, County Durham. The family are lodging in a four-roomed property alongside a family named Dale; the husband also being a coal miner. (1901 -1911 census)
John Leigh joined the 8th Bn. Northumberland Fusiliers and was killed in action on the 26th September 1916.

Private **JAMES LEIGHTON**   48190

Eighteen-year-old James attested in 1912 to 5th Bn. Northumberland Fusiliers and was later transferred to the West Yorkshire Regiment. He was working as an apprentice riveter at Armstrong Whitworth's and residing at 15

Hibernian Road, Walker. James received gunshot wounds to the face and neck and due to this disability, he received 11/- a week. He was discharged on 25 May 1917 and awarded the King's certificate (number 6203) and silver badge. Wounds being cited as the reason for discharge.

He took up employment with Leeds Tramway Company but was released by them and he was taken back on by Armstrong, Whitworth & co (Naval Yard) doing 'light work' in his former employment, though instead of riveting they gave him work as a plater's helper. He was discharged fully from the military on 13 Nov 1918 aged 24.

On April 18the 1921 James again signed on for 90 days Emergency service to the 5th Bn. Northumberland Fusiliers, service number NF/220. He states that he is married to Grace Frizel and they have 3 children – Isabella born 9 Nov 1914, James 12 Jan 1917 and Grace born 4 April 1919.

During his 90 days 'Emergency service' he was on 3 occasions late/absent, including being drunk and improperly dressed and spent a total of 6 days confined to barracks.

Cpl **WILLIAM ROBERT LOCKING**   2067

Residing 21 Station Road, Walker, William was embodied into the Royal Army Medical Corps (1st Northumberland Field Ambulance) Sept 1915 and was made up to Corporal in October of the same year. He was posted on 9 Jan 1917 and de-mobilized 29 Aug 1919. No records of his actual service appear to have survived.

Private **WILLIAM LEWIS**   43292

Working as a 'holder up' for Armstrong Whitworth and Co ltd, forty-four-year-old William of 70 Rochester Street, Walker, a single man he attests in Sept 1914. He is described as being foot 5 inches in height with grey/brown hair, tattoos on both arms. His records state that in 1915 he is sentenced to 19 days imprisonment by the civil Police for 1, being drunk 2, assault and 3, wilful damage. Formerly a member of the 3rd Bn. Royal

Scottish Militia William enlists into the Tyneside Scottish Bn. but is transferred to the 250 Protection Company of the Royal Defence Corps.
On 19 Apr 1916, he is appointed L/Cpl but this is later reverted back to Private. His address is now 88 Church Street, Walker. On 5 Mar 1918, he is transferred to munitions work with Wright Anderson and Co Ltd, Gateshead.

Private **JOHN JAMES LOUGH**   4641
Residing 17 White Street, Walker, John served with the 69th Bn. 723 Labour Company during the war. His service records didn't survive but his re-enlistment papers in to the 5th Bn. Northumberland Fusiliers Territorial Bn, in 1920. He was de-mobilized from the labour Coy on 20 Apr 1912 and joined the Northumberland Fusiliers (Territorials) on 20 June 1920 to serve for 1 year. He is described as being 20 years and 10 months old with a fresh complexion, blue eyes and brown hair. He is 5 feet 1¼ inches tall and with a chest measurement of 24 inches with an expansion of 2 inches. He joined the labour Corps in May 1919 which was after the end of the war, but troops were still being sent out to France to help with the aftermath of the battles. He was actually in France from 1 Jul 1919 until 11 Apr 1920.

Private **JOHN ROBERT LOWERY**   399690
John was a 20-year-old 'brake hand printer' born in Belfast and now living 1405 Walker Road, Walker, when he enlisted in to the Army in December 1914. He was mobilised May 1915 in to the 30th Res Bn. Northumberland Fusiliers. In June 1916, he was transferred to the 34th Bn. Northumberland Fusiliers. On 31st Dec 1916, he overstayed his leave by 24 hours (*probably thinking it could be the last New Year he would ever see?*) and was deprived 3 days' pay as forfeit.
On 11 January 1917, he was transferred to the Kings Own Yorkshire Light Infantry. He was hospitalised on 28 April 1917 at Boulogne (*possibly with shell shock?*) and returned to his

Battalion on the 30th, from there he was transferred to the Employment Company of the Labour Corps. He was returned to the UK on 1st Feb 1919 and dismissed from the service as he was 'no longer fit to serve' and the reason cited was 'dementia.'

Gunner **WILLIAM LUCAS**   143319

William was a 27-year-old 'newspaper dispatcher' married to Annie and living at 239 Church Road, Walker, attested on 7 Dec 1914 – his first wedding anniversary. William wasn't called for until March 1917 when he was allocated to the Royal Garrison Artillery and posted to Bexhill, in Sussex. His only recorded misdemeanour appears to be when he overstayed his fist leave home. He was due back at his barracks on 4 May 1917 (a few weeks in to his service) and overstayed by 2 days and 19 hours. He was confined to barracks for 7 days and made to forfeit 6 days' pay. He didn't do it again.

On 10 June 1917 William landed in France and was straight away sent to join his new unit- the 113 Siege Battery. He spent 7 days sick in hospital in Sept 1918. He served in France until Sept 1919 with a couple of leave periods slotted in.

Private **WILLIAM MCGINN**

William was 19 years old when he sailed to France - he survived the battlefield a mere three weeks.

The McGinn family had moved from Limerick, in Ireland, to 12 Airey Terrace, Walker, Newcastle upon Tyne. The move was to enable his father, also called William, to get employment at the Swan, Hunter & Wigham Richardson Ltd Shipyard. William, had been a very bright lad and had passed his civil service exams to get him a prized job with the civil service. At the age of 18 he returned to Ireland to work for the Post Office in Dublin as a clerk. This was when the IRA were preparing for the Easter Uprising against British rule in Ireland. Even though William was Irish, the fact his family was now living in England made his compatriots see him as a traitor and he received threats that the IRA would kill him. He wrote home and his parents who sent him the money to return to Newcastle.

(Picture taken just prior to going to France.)

 Soon after his return to Walker, he joined the Civil Service Rifles Regiment and in early 1918 partook in a period of training at the army rifle training ground on Wimbledon Common. From there he was shipped over to France, thus making up the numbers of his regiment on the Somme who were waiting for the final German push. On the 1st of April 1918, he was killed when the Germans shelled Aveluy Woods south of Arras in which his regiment was encamped.

Driver **FREDERICK MADDISON**   469
Frederick Maddison was born in 1886 at Gateshead and married Mary Ethel Ridley on 2nd May 1914, although on the 1911 census it states that he has been married to Mary

for three years (at that time they had a 2-year-old son also called Frederick.) His Army papers are a little more honest and name the real date of marriage. A second son Norman was born in 1915. The family were now living at 62 Church Street, Walker.

There is a 'visitors report' made after Frederick's death regarding his son Frederick Jr – stating that the child is the illegitimate son of Mrs Maddison and Frederick Maddison. Up to the date of their marriage Frederick Snr paid 5/- a week towards his son's upkeep.

Frederick, prior to the outbreak of war was working as a porter/carter for AER Railways. His medical notes describe him as being 5 feet 6 inches, being of good physical development and having a tattoo on the back of his right forearm displaying clasped hands and a cross with the words 'IN MEMORY OF MY MOTHER,'

Fred got himself in to bother on 2 occasions – both times with harsh penalties. 0n 13 Jan 1916 he neglected to obey and order and left horses un-attended. The penalty was loss of ten days pay. On 4 Jul 1916, he went absent without leave from 5pm and didn't return until 6.15am on 6 Jul 1916. Penalty 15 days Field punishments No1***

The Army Service Corps (ASC) was responsible for the dispatch and supply of food, water, fuel, and general domestic stores such as clothing, furniture and stationery. "Lines of communication" was an army term used to describe what today we might call the army's logistics: the supply lines from port to front line, and the camps, stores, dumps, workshops of the rear areas. It is difficult to comprehend just what supply to an army that in France alone built up to more than 2 million men actually means. Goods were taken via sea Ports, rail, horse and man to the front lines. Pte. W. Rae of 2 Coy 50th Div, Train ASC was also injured in the same incident and also died of wounds on the same day.

Mary died in 1969 aged 81. Their son Frederick Jr emigrated to Coupar, NSW Australia and died aged 67 in 1976. Frederick is buried in DERNANCOURT COMMUNAL CEMETERY EXTENSION France.

Gunner **GEORGE MAGEEAN** 84644

George, of 13 Caledonia Street, Walker was a 33-year-old 'Plater's helper' at Armstrong Whitworth Naval Yard, when he attested to the Army on 11 Dec 1915. He was freed under the 'Munitions of War act 1915-1916' to leave the yards and go to war. He was posted to the Royal Garrison Artillery on 26 May 1916.

Unlike poor Frederick above, whose officers handed out very stiff penalties for misdemeanors, George's were a little more lenient. He twice returned drunk and was punished with being confined to barracks for a number of days. He once went absent without leave from 10am until 9.30pm and was given 14 days confined to barracks and 2 days loss of pay. In Sept 1917, he was absent from duty once again, this time during an Air Raid but only got punished with a 4-day confined to barracks order. George appears to have been stationed in Kent for much of his service. In 1918, he was transferred to Reserve Corps and allowed to go back to his civilian post at Armstrong Whitworth's.

Private **GEORGE MASON** 18222

George was the son of George and Margaret Mason of 73 Mitchell Street. In 1911 the family were living at 42 Bath Street, Walker, and unlike many larger families who were often crammed into two rooms, the Mason's had three. George had siblings John and Margaret – 4 others not having outlived childhood. George and his brother were both 'helper ups' in the local coal mine. His father was a coal hewer. In 101 the Regiment (Prince of Wales Own.) He died at home on 15 Jan 1918 and is buried in Christ Church churchyard, Walker, Newcastle upon Tyne.

Sapper **MICHAEL MAHON**   1063

You will read many sad stories here, very sad stories – men being killed needlessly thousands of miles from home, children dying of influenza while daddy fights on the battlefront. This story is equally as sad……

Michael Mahon born 1889 was the son of Patrick and Mary Mahon, raised at Wincomblee Hill, Walker, Michael became a skilled 'Boiler maker.' He joined the 2nd Northumberland Field Coy (T.F) in June 1909 and on 11 June 1910 he is passed as a 'skilled boilermaker' aged 21. Michael went on the 2-week summer camp every June, to places such as Ripon, Rothbury and Hornsea; until 1913 when his term of engagement came to an end.

 Michael was a tall strong chap – standing 5 feet 9½ inches tall and with a 38-inch chest with a further expansion of 3 inches. A powerfully young built man. On 6 Aug 1914 Michael was called up and was posted 'home' until 16 April 1915 when he set sail for France, arriving Le Havre the following day.

What happened next only Michael knows. On the 18 April 1915, after having been in France less than 24 hours Michael died of wounds – he chose to take his own life by slitting his throat with a sharp blade. He left behind at 259, Benson Road, Byker, a wife Catherine and children Joseph, aged 7, Mary aged 4 and James aged 2.

Catherine would not have received a widow's pension as Michael was not killed as an act of war. She would have had to depend on her family and the parish to support her. In 1924 Catherine re-married to a chap called William Graham. Michael is buried at Ste. Marie Cemetery. Le Havre, France.

Driver **THOMAS MARTIN**   15992

This story is equally as depressing as the last……Thomas Martin born 1889 spent his early years living at 108 Fisher Street, Walker – later residing Edward Terrace, Wallsend.

On the 1901 census Thomas is spending time at the North Eastern Reformatory School at Netherton, Stannington. Northumberland. This was a penal school for young boys who had got themselves into trouble with the law. It was here Thomas learned farrier and farming skills.

Thomas joined the Royal Engineers (Reserves) aged 17 in 1906 described as being 5 feet 3½ inches tall and having a scar in the centre of his neck, a scar inside right leg, tattoo marks on left forearm 'various' vowels and numbers. The following year aged 18 he had grown another two inches in height. Thomas worked as a shoe-smith and in 1913 he applied to the Army to allow he and his family to go to live and work in Canada, returning if needed for Military service. Thomas had married Mary Ann Dugdale on 5 Feb 1910 at Tynemouth Registry office, when their first child was 2 years old. The family came back to England from Canada when Thomas was re-called to serve with the 3rd Division, Signal Coy.

The children born to Thomas and Mary appear to be:
John born 1908 (appears to have died before they sailed to Canada.) Thomas Ambrose Martin born 1912. (Charlotte born 11 Apr 1915 Canada - I'm sure this is Edna May or a twin.) Elizabeth Alice born 14 Sept 1917 - died 8 Nov 1918 aged 13 months old of bronchial pneumonia and influenza, at 5 Headlam Street, Wallsend. Edna, born 1915 died 10 Nov 1918 aged 3 years old, of bronchial pneumonia and influenza, at 5 Headlam Street, Wallsend. Informant to the coroner of both deaths was Mrs. D. Dugdale, grandmother; who was present at both deaths and a resident of 7 Headlam Street, Willington Quay (next door.) As the rest of the country was celebrating the end of the war and looking forward to their brothers, sons and husbands returning, poor Mary was preparing to bury her two beautiful little girls.

Further heartache was to follow;
Driver Martin was de-mobilised in March 1919 but rather than returning to his family he stayed at 'School House' Bachelor Gardens, Bilton, Harrogate, while he waited for the army to

arrange and pay for his passage back to Welland, Ontario Canada. Meanwhile his wife and child were waiting at 5, Headlam Street, Willington Quay, Wallsend, for his return. Thomas wrote to the Army asking for repatriation to Canada…. *"Would (torn paper) special favour if you would give (torn paper) an early date, some idea as to when (torn paper) be repatriated to CANADA. (torn paper).. sider my claim worthy of early (torn paper).. ation since I have four years and (torn paper) en months active service to my credit. Hoping you will favour me with an early (torn paper)..ly. I beg to remain your obedient servant. T Martin"*

His wife had expected them to return to Canada as a family and wrote to the army asking for help with her and her son's passage back to Ontario. She had been informed her husband had returned to Canada of his own accord and she had not heard from him at all since de-mobilisation. (His parents were also apparently in Ontario.) Thomas had sailed from Glasgow on 7 June 1919 aboard the S.S Hesperian.

"…..I am writing to let you know that I am going out to Canada to see if my husband will keep me, as he deserted me and a little boy here in April and I only have 18 shillings parish money. I was up at the American council and he gave me the address of the Chief of Police in Welland, so if he does not keep us I will have to take proceedings again him. I was to come here on ship called Missanibie but was very ill but luggage came on that…."

Another letter from Mary states…" *would you be so kind as to send me another form to fill in for my pass as I have been very ill and it has got mislaid somewhere and would you let me know if your fare is paid right to destination for you see I have not had a cent off my husband since he was demobilised in March…"*

Neighbours Mrs. Cassidy and Mrs. Donnell, both of number 7, Headlam Street, bore witness to the fact Mary had been abandoned by her husband.

 Mary and son Thomas finally sailed to Canada on 20 Feb 1920.

Unbelievably Thomas and Mary were re-united and on the 1921 voters census of Welland, Ontario, Canada (taken on 1 June 1921) they were living at Broadway, Welland, Ontario, where Thomas was working as a labourer. Son Thomas was now aged 9 and baby Duncan, conceived not long after their re-union was aged 3 months.

Maybe Thomas could just not cope with having spent so long at war seeing comrades fall around him and the loss of three of his children. Who knows, but I'm so glad there was something of a happy ending for Mary.

Mary Ann Died 1934 in Welland, Ontario aged 45.

Private **SAMUEL MAUGHAN**   11069

Samuel Maughan, aged 29 of 23 Mitchell Street, Walker, attested and joined the 9th Bn. West Yorkshire Regiment in August 1914. On the 1911 census Samuel was lodging at South Bank, Middleborough, where he was working as a labourer.

 He along with three of his seven brothers served on the battle front – he was the only one to survive – brother Archibald was the first to be killed on 11 March 1916, a month later, Andrew aged 25 lost his life on 4 Apr 1916 and William, aged 27 fell on 25 May of the same year (**See Families at war for more on this story.**)

Samuel was wounded (slightly) in 1915 while serving with his regiment as part of the Mediterranean force in the Dardanelles.

Samuel reached the rank of Lance Corporal but was deprived of his stripe in Jan 1916 for being 'absent' whilst based at Whitley Bay. His service was as follows;

Home 28 Aug 14 to 1 Jul 15

Mediterranean 2 Jul 15 to 9 Sept 15

Home 10 Sept 15 to 27 Jan 1916

France 28 Jan 1916 to 5 Oct 1916

Home 6 Oct 1916 to 10 Jan 1919 This being when he was released for vital 'munitions' work at Armstrong Whitworth's.

Samuel died in 1965 aged 80, I have not found any records of him having married or had children.

Private **THOMAS MATTHEW McCLELLAND** 10/2510
Born Hetton-le-Hole, Durham, Thomas' family later moved to Newcastle and were now residing 1378 Walker Road, and he was now working as a 'Moulder' (making castings.) His father William was a Riveter at the shipyards and his two brothers were Labourers'. Thomas attested to the Durham Light Infantry on 14 Aug 1915 – his 21st birthday. He was then posted to his unit and was released from service on 21 Oct 1919. Very little information regarding him or his service exists.

Private **RICHARD McCLENN** 300311
Richard who was born in to a mining family in Walker, was one off the 11 surviving children of 12, born to Matthew and Ann McClenn. All their sons went in to the mines and the family moved together from Durham to Walker, then back to Durham and finally Ashington in Northumberland – looking for work in the mines. When war broke out Richard and his family were living at 84 Maple Street, Ashington. At his medical Richard is described as being 5 feet 6 inches tall, weighing 136 lb and with a 34-inch chest with a further expansion of 1 inch. He had a fair complexion, grey eyes and brown hair.
Richard joined the West Yorkshire Regiment on 20 Aug 1914 and was transferred to the 1st Bn. Lancashire Regiment in April 1916. This was after he deserted his unit and after being found, more than 2 months later, was imprisoned awaiting trial. His sentence was 112 days detention and stoppages of pay. This was on the 28 Mar 1916 – he joined his new unit on 4 Apr 1916. Richard's service is as follows:
Home 20 Aug 1914 to 1 Jul 1915
Mediterranean Force 2 Jul 1915 to 15 Nov 1916
Home 1 Nov 1916 to 5 May 1916

India 6 May 15 Oct 1918
Richard died on 15 Oct 1818 at Station Military Hospital
Quetta, India of pneumonia. He was 24 years old. He is buried
Quetta Government Cemetery and remembered on the Delhi
Memorial, India Gate. India.

Private **JOHN McDONALD**   18043
Twenty-nine-year-old John, a labourer, joined the West
Yorkshire Regiment in 1914 (previously served a year as a
volunteer in the South African war.) He was born in Walker,
but now living at 4 Railway Terrace, Wallsend, with his wife
Jane (nee Harwood) who he married in 19112 – they had no
children. John was discharged from the Army on 21 May 1915.
I can't see any reason given for his discharge, but to be honest
they were probably keen to see the back of him! John was
constantly in trouble for his sloppiness….. charges include;
being improperly dressed for parade, losing puttees by
neglect, neglecting to obey an order, not completing an order,
quitting parade, reporting sick without a cause, quitting his
billet during prohibition – the list goes on. I'm assuming he
was discharged as unlikely to make an efficient soldier.
John obviously wanted to do something for the war effort, as
soon   after his discharge he joins the R.N.R (T) Royal Naval
Reserve, Territorial unit. On 29th of November of the same
year his vessel, the H.M paddle minesweeper DUCHESS OF
HAMILTON owned by the Caledonian Steam Packet Co, was
sunk by a mine laid possibly by UC.3 near the Galloper
Lightship, Thames. 9 Persons were lost. John survived but his
'Discharge Certificate' was lost with the ship. He applied to
the Army for a new one and once proof of the fact that he did
lose it in this way, by letter of recommendation from the
Captain of the ship, a new one was hastily supplied.

Private **ARTHUR MCELWEE**   606018
Arthur was born at Bill Point Terraces, Walker in 1880 to
Arthur, an 'Engineman' born Ireland and Margaret – also born

in Ireland.

On attestation Arthur says he was born 1986; it appears he lied about his age to sign up. Possibly he was worried they may say he was too old at 34. He joined the Durham light Infantry whilst living at 14 Charlton Street, Hebburn, in 1914 and was sent out to France with the British Expeditionary Force in June 1916. He served in France until March 1916 when he received a gunshot wound to the head. He was transferred to the RAMC and discharged from Z class (unfit) on 12 May 1919 as being no longer suitable to serve.

Private **ROBERT McLACHLAN** R/65 formerly 1165

Robert, the son of a shipyard Joiner, was born in Walker in 1892. On the 1901 census, he was living in a two-bedroomed flat at 16, Middle Street with his parents and nine siblings. In 1911, aged 19 and working as an apprentice carpenter for Swan Hunter and Wigham Richardson, shipbuilders; he attested to a 5-year enlistment to the 5th Bn. Territorials. Robert of 3, Pontoon Road, Wallsend served with the 5th Battalion Northumberland Fusiliers from 1911 until 1916, when his time with the unit (5 years) was terminated as a completion of engagement. This seems strange as it was I have always assumed that a man had to serve till hostilities ended. Robert originally was contracted to 4 years' service; it expiring 1915 and being extended until 14th Feb 1916.

 Robert only appears to have spent four months overseas with the expeditionary force, April to August 1915. He was admitted to hospital at Armentieres on 14th May 1915 and immediately transferred to No 5 General Hospital at Rouen and from here returned to England on the SS St Andrew, the following day.

I can't find any record of re-engagement, though it is possible. Did R/65 mean reserve/retired (due to ongoing medical problems?) Possibly Robert went back to his former occupation at the shipyards. Though not medically discharged

, the fact is there that something that happened during his time in the Military was the cause of his death – 24 hours after the Armistice was called. He died 12th November 1918 aged 26.

Sergeant **EDWARD MEARMAN** 171046
Edward attested at the age of 37 in March 1915. A married man living at 1602 Walker Road, Walker, he found himself drafted to the Durham Light Infantry (to whom he had previously served with) and was made an acting Lance Corporal on 8 May 1915, and a paid Lance Corporal on 21 Aug 1915. Downgraded through injury or accident Edward was transferred to the Employment Coy of the Labour Corps and was discharged from the service on 28 April 1917 as no physically longer fit for Military Service due to age and chronic *(unreadable.)*.

Gunner **MATTHEW MEDCALF**   204992
 The son of a coal miner, Matthew, of 6 Diamond Row, Walker, was working as a 'Apprentice Plater' when he attested on 10 Dec 1915, aged 18. Standing 5 foot 7½ inches tall and weighing 140lb with a chest measurement of 36 inches and with an expansion of another 2 inches. He was posted to the 30th Bn. Royal Field Artillery on 1 Feb 1917 and was then sent out to join the British Expeditionary Force in France where he was wounded with a 'Blighty' a gun-shot wound to the thigh on 31 March 1918. He then spent 18 days in a Military Hospital in Newhaven, East Sussex. Luckily the damage was only to the muscle and no further complications arose so he was sent away with instructions to carry out leg exercises. In Oct 1918, he was posted to Catterick in North Yorkshire and to Reserve Brigade in Dec 1918. He was then sent to a dispersal centre in Feb 1919 from where he was de-mobilized on 19 Mar 1919.

On home leave (Author's own collection.)

Gunner **EDWARD MELDRUM**   285721
Un-married Edward aged 35 was living with his brother
Charles at 1387 Walker Road, Walker. He is described as being
a Labourer, 5 feet 8¼ inches tall and with a 38½ inch chest
with an expansion of 3 inches. He had tattoos on both arms of
a flower and a cross. Edward was sent to Reserve battalion in
December 1915 and mobilized in May 1917, serving with the
Royal Regiment of Artillery (Royal Garrison Artillery.) He
was gassed in 1918 and sent to the 55th General Hospital in
Boulogne and from there to a hospital in Edgbaston,
Birmingham. He was discharged Sept 1918 as no longer fit for
Military Service due to having been gassed and was allocated
a 11/- s week pension to be reviewed in 12 months' time.

Private **WILLIAM MIDCALF**   7999/28706
William of Diamond Row, Walker (now where the lower
numbers of Fairhaven Avenue are,) was first posted to the 12
Bn. Northumberland Fusiliers on 2 Oct 1915 and then
transferred to the Lincolnshire Regt on a full transfer. In 1916,
he was moved to a 'Reserve' battalion and kept there 'for as
long as necessary to retain him in his civil employment.' He
was discharged as no longer physically fit for Military service
on 21 Sept 1917 having been wounded in October 1915.
William attested on 7 Sept 1914 at Wallsend, aged 20.

Gunner **JOHN MIDDLEMOST**   200481/109993
John, who was born in South Shields was a 27-year-old
married father of four living at 4 Cecil Street, Walker, when he
attested to the Military in Dec 1915, and working as a
hairdresser. John was first posted to the Northumberland
Fusiliers and then to No 5 Reserve Bn. Royal Field Artillery
and from there he was transferred to the Tank Corps in 1917.
On 8 Aug 1918, he was charged with overstaying his leave by

14 hours and 15 minutes and forfeited 2 day's pay as a consequence. He was de-mobilized at Ripon in Feb 1919 and returned to his civilian occupation. John died 1949 aged 61.

Private **WILLIAM MITCHELL**   2600 / 384482
William Mitchell of 1623 Walker Road, Walker, was a 23-year-old Plater's helper, working at Armstrong Whitworth's, when he attested to the 5th Bn. Northumberland Fusiliers on 7 Sept 1914. In September 1915, he went AWOL for a week while his unit were based in Redcar. He then had to forfeit 8 days' pay for this misdemeanour. He served in France with the British Expeditionary Force between 30 Apr 1915 until 30 May 1915 (possibly home after this date through injury) and then again from 13 Nov 1916 until 1918 when he is transferred to the Labour Corps and in November of that year called to report to the Discharge centre for discharge to the Army Reserve for coal mining purposes. He was now living at 27 Pottery Bank, Walker.

Private **JOHN GEORGE MURRAY**   1627/386212
John originally joined the 1st Northumberland Field Ambulance Corps in 1908 as a 17-year-old, when residing at 42 White Street, Walker. Time served after a year was he keen to join up again at the outbreak of war and attested on the 4th Aug 1914, hours before it was officially declared in the media that Britain was at war with Germany. John was now 23 years old and working as a Boiler Maker for Swan, Hunter and Wigham Richardson Ltd. He had moved address to 2 Cecil Street, Walker (next door to John Middlemost above.) He again joined the 1st Northumberland Field Ambulance   (Royal Army Medical Corps) and sailed to France, disembarking at Harve on 18 Apr 1915. He was admitted to No1 Field Hospital on 13 May 1915 with Scabies and discharged on the 29th.

In Feb 1916, he was returned home as was *'needed in England to carry out munitions work'* with his former employer Swan, Hunter &Wigham Richardson Ltd. John was de-mobilized 16 Jan 1919 aged 27.

Gunner **JOSEPH NICHOLSON**   142640

Joseph was a 37-year-old married with three sons and working as a Cartman when he answered the call for fit men to serve their country in 1915. He was then living at 1432 Walker Road, Walker (later Neptune Road, Wallsend.) In 1917, he was called forward and posted to the Clyde in Scotland to join his unit of the Royal Garrison Artillery, Anti-Aircraft detachment and from there on to Heath Abbey Wood. In September of the same year he sailed to India and then on to Basra with the 61st Coy R.G.A. A few days after the armistice had been signed, while he was serving in Salonika with the 92nd Anti- Aircraft detachment, and it looked like troops would soon be heading home, Joseph came down with a fever. He was admitted to hospital on the 16th of November and died at 2.30a.m. local time on the 17th, without having gained consciousness.

The report in to his death states the following;

Patient died at 2.30a.m. without speaking or developing any other signs. Post-mortem. Nothing abnormal found except a large engorged pulpy spleen. Cultures taken from the spleen. Cerebro-spinal fluid examined Post mortem – nothing found. Cultures from spleen, sterile.

In my opinion, this man died of a fever of un-certain origin contracted while on active service.

(Buqabah 1918)   Signed B.E.A Batt Capt R.A.M.C

In my opinion Gunner Nicholson died of a disease attributed to Military Service.

Signed. J Doran Lt Col R.A.M.C

Returned to his wife in 1919 was a package containing a disc, 2 canvas belts, pair of spectacles (with case), silver chain with medal attached, 3 coins and a bundle of letters.
Gunner Joseph Nicholson is buried at Baghdad (North Gate) War Cemetery, India.

L/Cpl **EDMUND NIXON** 137518
Edmund was a 22-year-old Hairdresser living at 49 Rochester Street, Walker, when he attested in Dec 1915. Edmund was 5 feet 5½ inches tall and had a chest measurement of 36 inches with an expansion of 2. He was held in the Army Reserve until Aug 1916 when he was mobilised into the Yorkshire Infantry (Territorial Force.) He served with various battalions and was made up to Lance Corporal on 4 May 1915. He served 'at home' (UK Based, mainly Margate) and was demobilised early 1919.
Edmund lived until 1987. He died Newcastle upon Tyne aged 93.

Private **JOSEPH O'BRIEN**   38061/71070
Joseph was a Barman before enlisting into the Army, probably having served a good few names on this list with a pint or few. Joseph lived at 72 Byker Street, Walker and was a single man aged 31 when he attested in Dec 1915. He was at first attached to the Northumberland Fusiliers but later transferred (and given a new service number) to the machine Gun Corps and was posted to France with the British Expeditionary Force in late July 1916. He had a spell in hospital with Bronchitis and later on, possibly around August 1917 (hard to decipher writing) he was injured in an explosion. His condition was worsening by the day and on 9 Sept 1917 the decision was taken to amputate his left leg and forearm, as it was the only way to save his life. On the 3 Sept 1918, he was charged (*still in hospital over a year after his accident*) with the offence of taking alcohol while as a patient in hospital and being drunk and disruptive. Forfeited 6 days' pay.

Joseph was awarded a full pension of 27/6 for life.

Private **ALEXANDER O'HARROW**   23071
Alexander of 2 Weston Glower, Walker, was called up in April 1915 and was posted the East Yorkshire Regiment. He was later transferred to the Labour Corps and then to Class W Army Reserve (*Class W(T) was introduced in June 1916 by Army Order 203/16. They were 'for all those soldiers whose services are deemed to be more valuable to the country in civil rather than military employment'. These men did not wear uniform and were liable to be recalled at any time.*) Alexander was sent to the Armstrong Whitworth Naval Yard at Barrow-in Furness in May 1918. In 1922, he re-signed to the 5th Bn. Northumberland Fusiliers Territorial Force.

L/Cpl **PETER PATTERSON**   237842/35745
An apprentice shipwright (carpenter) of 176 Middle Street, Walker, Peter attested in Jan 1916 and was called up and mobilised in 3 Nov 1916, with the Buffs Regiment and sent to join his unit in Bristol. It's possible that Peter didn't serve overseas as I can't find any record of him having done so. In 1919, he was retained by the Army 'under order 14' and was posted to Ireland. In April, he was attached to a Command School. He was denied his well-earned Lance Corporal stripe in Aug 1919 after missing tattoo (evening roll call) by 30 minutes. He was seen by the Military Police in Patrick Street, Cork at about 10.30 p.m.
After de-mobilisation   L/Cpl Patterson enlisted on 4 March 1925 in to the Royal Engineers as a Sapper with the 232nd Field Coy for a 4-year engagement as a carpenter.

L/Cpl **IDRIS ARCHIBALD PHILLIPS** 35237
Idris joined the Army as part of the 28th Reserve Battalion in Feb 1916 but was soon transferred to the Machine Gun Corps in May of the same year. He was a 23-year-old shipwright

living at 11 Caledonia Street, Walker, when he joined the service. It seemed that throughout the duration of 1916 Idris was constantly taking long periods of 'leave' as he is recorded as forfeiting pay, 6 days here, 19 days there, another 7 days, then 14 and so on. He is based on 'home' soil for the duration of his service – mainly on the south coast.

Idris is made a L/Cpl in Oct 1917 after being transferred to the 98 Machine Gun Coy. He is then discharged in Dec 1918 due to having had a number of abdominal operations and no longer being fit for service (*this may account for his periods of absence.*). He is awarded a pension of 27/6 for 4 weeks and then 11/- thereafter.

Idris died 17 Feb 1919 aged age 26.

Private **EDWARD KNOX POAD**   83573

Edward Poad, a labourer, formerly of 18 Caledonia Street, Walker now 207 Welbeck Road, Byker, joined the West Yorkshire Regiment on 2 Sept 1919 and was posted the following day. He was discharged 'no longer physically fit for war service' on 25 Sept 1919 having suffered fits of hysteria. He was awarded a 20% disablement pension of 5/6 for 13 weeks. His age is said to be 19 but going by birth records and census he was actually only 17.

Private **JOHN WILLIAM POPE**   8281

John Pope, a general labourer, attested to the West Yorkshire Regiment on 8 Aug 1914 and was posted on 17 Aug 1914. He was transferred to the Notts and Derby Regiment in May 1917 and whilst serving with then received a wound to the abdomen. He was transferred to the Army Reserve on 10 June 1917 and dismissed from the service on 27 Oct 1917 to 63 Edmund Street, Hebburn. With a pension of 13/9 for 26 weeks reducing to 8/3. In 1901 John was living at 1 Pottery Square, Walker, with his mother and 3 siblings. On the 1911 census John is at the North Eastern Reformatory School at Netherton,

Stannington. Northumberland. This was a penal school for young boys who had got themselves into trouble with the law. His mother has since died and his now five siblings, are living with their father James at 135 William Street, Hebburn.

Sapper **WILLIAM PRESTON**   2485
A 49-year-old miner, William enlisted in 1917 and was posted to the Royal Engineers (Pioneers) to join the 303 Road Construction Company. William Lived at 256 Church Road, Walker, with his wife Alice Seaton whom he married in 1891 at Walker Parish Church, and their five daughters. Alice, Olive, Lily, Flora and Eleanor.
William was de-mobilized Jan 1919 at Clipstone, Nottinghamshire aged 51.

Private **ANDREW REID**   3030
Private Reid of the 2/4th Bn. Northumberland Fusiliers, is buried in Walker Churchyard. Andrew a Boiler Maker's Holder upper, at the shipyards enlisted at Wallsend. Married to Ellen, he was 38 years old when he was died on 12th May 1916. They had at least 4 children and were living at 26, East Terrace, Low Walker in 1911.

Sapper **MATTHEW GEORGE RENSHAW**   WR/178882
Matthew of 6 White Street, Walker, was a 20-year-old 'Riveter' at Armstrong Whitworth's when he attested in Feb 1914 and was called up immediately at the outbreak of war and posted to the to the 2nd Brigade, Royal Field Artillery. He was then moved to a number of other Northumberland Artillery units before being fully transferred to the Royal Engineers. He embarked with the British Expeditionary Force to France on 18 April 1917. He was hospitalized twice during his deployment – 2nd August 1917 until rejoining his unit on 14 Sept 1917 and another short stay in Sept 1918. Neither hospitalization is recorded as to why he was admitted.

While based at Quebec Barracks in Bordon, Hampshire on 1 April 1917, Matthew missed 8 a.m. church parade and was punished with 3 days confined to barracks.

Private **WILLIAM RIDLEY**   1771/388319
Colliery worker William, who lived at 12 Cambrain Row, High Walker, joined the 2nd Reserve Northumbrian Field Ambulance (Royal Army Medical Corps) in Jan 1915. He served in France from 19 Apr 1915 until 9 Oct 1916. Taller than many of his contemporaries William stood 5ft 10½ ins tall and had a 36 inch chest with an expansion of 2 inches. His vision and physique were described as 'good.' In 1918 William was awarded a pension of 27/6 for 4 weeks and then dropping to 8/- a week thereafter and to be reviewed 48 weeks later. I don't know what disability he received during his service but he was transferred to reserve and returned to his previous employment at the Rising Sun Colliery in Wallsend.

Private **GEORGE RIDLEY** 388318
Thirty-seven-year-old George, of 13 Ambrose Place, Walker, joined the Royal Army Medical Corps in 1915 as part of the 2nd Northumbrian Field Ambulance, attached to the Royal Field Artillery. He served in France from 19 Apr 1915 until 19 Oct 1918. In Dec 1918, he was transferred to Army Reserve and went back to his employment as a 'Coal Hewer' with the Walker Coal Co Ltd, who he had worked for, for the past 30 years. In 1922 George joined the 5th Bn Northumberland Fusiliers Territorial Battalion with whom he served 4 years.

Private **WILLIAM MARSH ROBSON**   23648
Twenty-seven-year-old William of 60 Bath Street, Walker, served with the Oxford and Buckinghamshire Light Infantry with the Mediterranean Expeditionary Force during the war. He was based in Italy from 9 Nov 1915 until 5 Jul 1918 and then moved to Italy from 6 Jul 1918 until 4 Jan 1919 when he sailed back to England. During William's service, he was

admitted to hospital on 3 occasions; firstly spending 3 weeks in hospital in Valetta, Malta, with a 'Hematoma' in 1917 and then two further admissions; once for hepatitis and another time for gastritis and headaches.

On return the England William went back to working in the coal mines and died in 1973 aged 85.

Private **JAMES ROBSON** 227356

James, a 27-year-old 'Cart man' who lived at 85 Church Street, Walker, joined the Labour Corps in June 1917 but was discharged in November of the same year as he was no longer physically fit to serve as he suffered from chronic bronchitis.

Sergeant **THOMAS ROBSON** 245238

Thomas originally served with the Northumberland Fusiliers, joining in Nov 1915 at the age of 23, but later transferred to the Durham Light Infantry. His Military service was cut short after an accident whilst carrying out salvage work in Jan 1919. He picked up a detonator which exploded and caused lacerations to his hand. He was discharged in May 1919, with a pension of 6/6 for 26 weeks when it would be reviewed. Thomas lived at 1665 Walker Road, Walker.

Private **ALFRED PERCY ROBSON** 63207

Alfred of 1354 Walker Road joined the Army one month before his 18th birthday in Aug 1917. He was posted to the 4th Bn. Yorkshire Regiment. He was discharged as physically unfit for Military service in Feb 1919 suffering from 'nephritis' – a kidney complaint. He was awarded a 40% disability pension on 11/- a week.

Private **JOSEPH ROONEY** 22469

Joseph, a miner, joined the 321 Road Construction Coy of the Royal Engineers in 1917 at the age of 43, and deployed to France until Jan 1918. He lived at 1574 Walker Road, Walker with his wife Elizabeth and 6 children Lizzie (Jane), Mary Ann, Ellen, Josephine, Margery and Joseph.

Private **CHARLES ROONEY**   11208

Twenty-nine-year-old Charles was born in Walker, though later moved to Wallsend. He attested to the West Yorkshire Regiment at Wallsend on 27 Aug 1914 whilst working as a riveter at Swan, Hunter, Wigham, Richardson's shipyard. He was posted to the Mediterranean in July 1915. In August 1917, he was released (aged 32) to temporarily continue munitions work with him former employer at Wallsend shipyards. His address at this time was 14 Maude Terrace, Wallsend. He was released surplus to military requirements in 1920 and moved to Birkenhead – likely to work in the shipbuilding industry there.

Gunner **JOSEPH SMITH ROUTLEDGE**   65550

Joseph was more eager than most when he joined up in Nov 1915. On his attestation papers, he states he is a 19-year-old farmhand and his medical back it up by describing him as 5ft 6½ins tall and with a stout and strong build. Joseph was born on 8 Oct 1898 and was actually only 17 years old – this fact wasn't found out though until he been posted to the French batteries and had been firing at the enemy for quite some time. His mother sent his birth certificate to the Army to prove he was underage and Joseph was sent back to England in August 1916 when still only 17 years old. He was kept with a reserve battalion in the UK and posted back to France in Nov 1917 – when he was officially old enough to serve overseas. Joseph was killed in action on 2 Sept 1918.

Items returned to his family at 55 Sunningdale Avenue, Walker; Letters, photo's, note book, religious book, wallet. His mother later wrote to the Army to ask if other items not returned, could be forwarded; 2 watches, note case, belt with pouches attached.

Air Mechanic 2nd Class **HARRY HERBERT AMOS SEABOURNE,** was born in Hereford, England in 1900. On the 1911 census he was living with his Grandmother Elizabeth Taylor and his brother George (who was born in the Tower of London) at 7 Bath Street, Walker. It appears that his mother, Margaret, was actually living in Armstrong Whitworth's shipyards at this time, with his elder sister, Maud. His mother was a cook/housekeeper at the 'dining club' there. In 1901, he was living in Heworth, again with his Grandmother, along with Grandfather and aunt Kate. (Assuming father was in the Military, hence brother born at the Tower of London.)

Harry was a member of the newly formed Royal Air Force, based at the Western Experimental Workshops (Cardiff). Whether he died there and his body brought home or he died at home as a result of his injury is unknown. He died aged19 on 17th Oct 1918. His mother, after the war, residing at of 4, Chilton St., Walker, Newcastle-on-Tyne. Remembered with honour WALKER (CHRIST CHURCH) CEMETERY, Newcastle upon Tyne Seaborne

Private **JOHN SHEAVILLS**   112593

A 'Shipyard Labourer' living at 12 Front Row Factory, High Walker and later on at 182 Byker Street, Walker, John attested to the Labour Corps in Nov 1915. He spent 12 days in France in Dec 1917 and then 3 months in 1918 from May to Aug, the rest of his service being served in the UK. He was de-mobilized in March 1920 and re-enlisted in to the 5th Bn. Northumberland Fusiliers (Territorial's) in July 1920 when living at 3 Back Welsh Row, Walker.

Private **WILLIAM MAIN SIM**   58156/43745

William, son of Police Constable William Main Sim of the River Tyne Police – lived at 46 Bath Street, Walker. He enlisted in June 1918 to the East Yorkshire Regiment and was then compulsory transferred to the Loyal North Lancashire Regiment.

Private **FRANK WILFRED SKINNER**   10250

Frank was the son of Herbert Skinner of 19 Woodside Avenue, Walker. Newcastle upon Tyne. He died of cholera (likely caught from a carrier) on 24th May 1915 aged 26 while serving with the 1st Bn. Durham Light Infantry in Nowshera, India. He is remembered on the DELHI MEMORIAL (INDIA GATE) India. His Territorial Force entry medical in 1908 describes Frank as being 19 years old, being 5 feet 4 inches in height and weighing 118lb. His chest measured 34½ and had an expansion of 2.5 inches. He was of fair complexion and had hazel eyes and dark brown hair.

When he attested in Dec 1914 he was working at Armstrong Whitworth's as a 'fitter and turner.'

After his death, his brother wrote to the Army the following letter:

2 Kitchener Street. Sunderland.
Dear Sirs,
It was my brothers wish before he died, to his comrade Private J Sandiland, in the Quarter master's store with him, that all his belongings should be sent to me, as well as telling me in his letters that if anything happened I had to have all as I was the only one he confided in. Now in regards to his bank book and other things that I had in my possession when he died. I divided equally out among my brothers and sisters. Now for (Unreadable) in commemoration to my brother. I would like (unreadable) and it would be taken every care of.
Yours sincerely
E Skinner.

Private **WILLIAM M SMART**   S/18432

William, a 19-year-old 'Pitman' lived at 11 Diamond Row, Walker. He joined the Cameron Highlanders part of the 44th Brigade in 15th (Scottish) Division in 1915 and was posted to

France in Oct of the same year. In July 1916, he was shot in the right thigh and sent back to Brighton in Sussex to convalesce after being treat at a Red Cross hospital in Etaples, France. He was back in France in March 1917 as part of an entrenching Bn. with the 7th Cameron Highlanders. He was later killed in action sometime between the 31 Jul and 3 Aug 1917. His name is remembered with honour on the YPRES (MENIN GATE) MEMORIAL, Belgium.

Corporal **ALEXANDER SMITH** 125407

A 41-year-old 'Labourer' living at 5 Western Glower, Walker, with his wife and young son Thomas, Alexander attested to the Army on 22 Oct 1915 in London and was in France with his Pioneer, Royal Engineer's unit by the 28th of the same month. Alexander died of wounds on 30 Dec 1915 and was interred at BAILLEUL COMMUNAL CEMETERY EXTENSION, France. He had lost his life after only 70 days in the Army.

His wife was awarded a weekly pension of 15/- for herself and their 2-year-old son.

Private **JONAS SMITH** 340514

Jonas, a miner in 1914 when he attested in Sept of that year. Lived at 3, Diamond Row, Walker. He suffered a gunshot wound to the right forearm at the battle of St. Julien on 26 Apr 1915, whilst serving with the 36th Bn. Northumberland Fusiliers. He was returned to England on the ship 'Brighton' and was discharged from the army 'No longer fit for Military service in Oct 1917.

Sergeant **JONAS SMITH** 2481

Serjeant Jonas Smith of the 6th Bn. Northumberland Fusiliers – a cousin of the above-named gentleman of the same name, was killed in action on 15th Sept 1916 and remembered with honour on the Thiepval Memorial, Somme, France. I can find a Jonas Smith living at 25, Diamond Row, walker, with his wife Elizabeth on the 1911 census. Jonas at that time was working as a coal miner 'shot firer.' He would have been 28/29 when he was killed. In 1911 the couple had one child Robert. Another having died in infancy.

Quarter Master Sergeant Major **ROBERT SMITH**   9
Robert joined the 1st Northumbrian Field Ambulance, Royal Army Medical Corps (Territorials) in 1908 at the age of 24, while working as a 'Plumber' for Arthur Scott of Byker and living at 190 Byker Street, Walker. He had previously been a member of the Northumberland Fusiliers (Territorial Bn.) since he was 17 in 1901, gradually working his way up the ranks from Private to Quarter Master Sergeant Major.
 Robert dies of accidental injuries on 1 Aug 1916. An enquiry in to his death states that he was found lying unconscious in a ditch near to H.Q with severe wounds about his head. He was taken to a casualty clearing station but died without regaining consciousness. No one saw the accident but the injuries were consistent with falling from a horse. His horse was later seen on its' own with cuts on its near fore leg above and below the knee. A slight scrape on its' near shoulder and flank and the left-hand side of the saddle was scraped. Smith had left at about 10 a.m. to go to 50th Div Depot, at Westoutre and the accident happened on his return journey to H.Q – he was 31 years old. He left a wife Margaret and three small children, Mary born 1911, Robert born 1913 and Percy born 1915. He was the youngest of eight siblings – two of whom (brothers) lived in Brisbane, Australia. Robert's body is interred at BAILLEUL COMMUNAL CEMETERY EXTENSION, France.

Private **THOMAS WILLIAM SNOWBALL**
Born 1888 in Newcastle upon Tyne, was a house painter by trade on the 1911 census and was living with his parents, George and Sarah, at 18 Tyne Terrace, St Anthony's estate, a 3

roomed property. Also at the address was his two older brothers – John and Robert. John, aged 35 was a night watchman in a factory and Robert, aged 32, was a house painter like Thomas. Also living there was Thomas's wife Frances (née Travis) of three years, and their two sons George aged 3 and Thomas 11 months.

By the time Thomas was conscripted, he and his wife and their now five sons; Robert, Francis and Edward arriving in 1912, '14 and '15 had moved to 11, Kirk Street, Byker. Newcastle upon Tyne.

Thomas died of wounds at a base hospital on 29th May 1918 and is buried at TERLINCTHUN BRITISH CEMETERY, France.

Private **GEORGE HERBERT STEPHENSON**
George was the son of George Henry and Annie Mary Stephenson of 6 Jackson Street, Walker, Newcastle upon Tyne. He was educated at Rutherford College, Newcastle. Prior to his regular military service, George attended the University's Officer Training Corps whilst at Armstrong College. He was a Private in the Coldstream Guards, 1st Battalion. He was killed in action at Pilkem Ridge on 31st July 1917 aged 22 and is commemorated on the Ypres (Menin Gate) Memorial, West-Vlaanderen, Belgium.

(Sourced from Universities at War. Digital memory book. Newcastle University.)

Private **ARTHUR (ALEXANDER) MAXWELL LANG STEWART**   2424889
This chap was living in Walker after at the war, I'm not sure where he originated from but likely Yorkshire. He served with the Durham Light Infantry and West Yorkshire Regiment from 1915 to 1919 and in 1920 whilst living at 119 Lamb Street, Walker, he joins the 5th Northumberland Fusiliers (territorials)

and states his next of kin as being a friend – Miss M. Moorhouse of 47 Rhodes Street, Walker. In 1921 'Alexander' marries Martha Moorhouse in Sunderland. They were now living at 1412 Walker Road, Walker.

In Feb1928 the Chief Constable of Bradford Police wrote to the West Yorkshire Regiment, asking for the service history of Arthur/Alexander Stewart, as he was to stand trial for Bigamy the following month. He states he joined the Durham Light Infantry in Jul 1915 and transferred to the 1/6th West Yorkshire Regt, being discharged at demobilization in 1919. This was a true account of his service and he did serve overseas in France. He returns to his home town of Paisley in Scotland and is working as a dairyman at Crosslight Dairy, Glasgow Road, Paisley.

Sapper **WILLIAM STOREY**   463194

William's Great War records did not survive but his re-embodiment in to the 5th Bn. Northumberland Fusiliers (Territorial's) state that he served with the Royal Corps of Signals (Royal Engineers) attached to the 5th Division. William lived at 13 Ambrose Place, Walker in 1920, formerly of 5 Western Glower, Walker.

L/Sgt **WILLIAM SUTHERLAND**   15725

William, a 24-year-old 'Labourer' living at 18 Foster St, Walker, attested in to the 8th Bn. Yorkshire Regiment on 3 Sept 1914, at Washington, County Durham. His medical examination describes him as a fine specimen of a man – 5ft 10ins tall, 169lb in weight and with a 40-inch chest - with an expansion of another 3 inches. With his fresh complexion, hazel eyes and dark brown hair, William was your ideal soldier. He made huge strides and promotions were handed out left right and centre. He was appointed Lance Corporal on 22 Sept 1914, he then became a full Corporal on 26 Oct 1914 and was made Lance Sergeant a month later on 4 Nov 1914.

Maybe William had been a little too keen…. maybe the Army had been a little too rash?
William was discharged on 21 Nov 1914 as 'not likely to become an efficient soldier.'

Acting Serjeant **FRED SUTTON** 325202

Fred was born in Walker, but by the time war broke out he was 31, single and living at 149 Hyde Park Road, Gateshead, working for the Gateshead Tramway Company. He served from Sept 1914 until 1919 when he was de-mobilised in Cologne, Germany. He continued to serve with the Durham Light Infantry (territorials) and attend summer camp up until 1931.

Private **THOMAS FREDERICK THOMPSON** 5091

Thomas, who was a 'Machine Hand Driller' in civilian life when he was mobilised by the Army in May 1916 was a skilled 'Boilermaker' by the time he left – obviously a trade he learned during the war. 23-year-old Thomas of 21 Bath Street, Walker was posted to the 5th Bn. Northumberland Fusiliers in 1916 but was quickly transferred to the North Staffordshire Regiment and a few months later in March 1917 he was posted to the South Staffordshire Regiment. Two weeks later he was attached to the Lincolnshire Labour Coy and in July 1918 attached to the Royal Engineers.
On 10 June 1917 Thomas was deprived 5 days' pay for 'making an improper imply to an N.C.O (Sgt Bull.)

Private **THOMAS WILLIAM THOMPSON** 80007

Thomas variously described himself as a' labourer', a 'stager' and a 'miner' prior to being mobilised by the Army. What we do know though is that he was employed at the Wigham Richardson Neptune Yard. I think his reference to 'miner' could be due to the fact he was released from the West Yorkshire Regiment aged 20 in Dec 1918 to work in the coal mines. Possibly he had spent some time in the mines before working in the shipyards - 18 Diamond Row, where he lived was right next to Ann Pit.

Private **JOHN IRVING TOBIAS** 63316
Nineteen-year-old John was an 'Apprentice Plumber' of 597 Welbeck Road, Walker, was mobilised in Jun 1918 and posted to the 4th Yorkshire Regiment, attached to the 5th Lancashire Fusiliers. Infantryman Tobias was penalised by having to serve 2 days confined to barracks for talking while on Parade, at Scarborough on 2 Aug 1918.

Private **JACK TODD**   101529
Jack Todd of 12 New Row, Walker, attested in Dec 1915 but due to his occupation as a miner, he was held in a reserve battalion and not called forward for Mobilization until 15 May 1918. The following day he was attached to the 5th and later the 13th Bn. Durham Light Infantry and soon found himself in France. Jack died aged 22 of wounds in the 53rd Casualty Clearing Station in France. His belongings which amounted to; Photo's, a card, a cigarette holder and a razor in a case, were returned to his father Fawcett Todd of 39 Hadrian Road, Wallsend.

Private **GEORGE TOLSON**   1599 / 386189
George was 23 years old when he attested to the RAMC on 31 Aug 1914. He had only married his sweetheart Annie Franks 3 weeks previously. George had been working as a shipwright Swan, Hunter's prior to his military service. He spent 18 months in France and Belgium and was then transferred to 'home' to work at Swan, Hunter& Wigham Richardson Ltd

Neptune Yard at Walker. George, as a child lived at 51 Mitchell Street with his mother and siblings. He then lodged at Davis Street, Wallsend. Once married to Annie they lived at 49 Eleanor Street, Cullercoats. Between 1915 and 1920 Annie bore three children. At his medical for the 1st Northumberland Field Ambulance, RAMC – George was described as being 5 feet 7 inches tall, with a 36-inch chest, a dark complexion, dark grey eyes and dark brown hair. He had a tattoo on his right forearm bearing his initials 'G.T' between a horses' head and crossed clasped hands over a read heart.

Instead of accepting a de-mob suit (all soldiers were given the option on demobilization, to have a suit and overcoat, supplied by the military – to take then into civilian life.) George chose to take the £2/12/6 cash value instead.

Private **MICHAEL JOSEPH TUCKER**   694724

Michael joined the 3rd Bn. Royal Inniskilling Fusiliers in 1915 and was posted to the Mediterranean on 20 July, but due to a shrapnel wound to his arm he was heading back to England from Mudros in late August on the Hospital Ship ESMERELDA.

In November, he was attached to Armstrong Whitworth's Naval Yard at Walker. Released from there in Dec 1915 and was transferred to Dalmuir on the Clyde, in Scotland in Jan 1916. A year later he was returned to the North East, to Messrs Palmer's in Hebburn. In Jun 1918, Michael was transferred again to Vickers Armstrong in Barrow in Furness. In 1919, he was posted to France and was with his Unit (Labour Company) in Ribecourt in Jul 1920 when he was returned to England for de-mobilization aged 35.

Michael was a labourer before joining the Military, but came out of it as a skilled 'Boilermaker.' He was married to Margaret and had 6 children: Mary Ann, Margaret, John,

Michael, Wilhelmina and Catherine. Michael born 1915 died as a baby. In 1919, he was described as being 5 feet 3¼ inches tall and weighing 126 lb. He had a 33½ inch chest with an expansion of 1½ inches.

2nd Cpl **JOHN TURNBULL**   463196   **MM**

John Turnbull was a 'Shipyard Labourer' for Armstrong Whitworth and living at 1640 Walker Road, Walker with his brother and a married sister when he attested on 10 August 1914. He was 5ft 7 ins tall, with good vision and physique. He was drafted in to the Royal Engineers, 50th Northumbrian Division, Signal Coy No 19 as a Telegraphist. In 1916, he was promoted to Lance Corporal (unpaid in March but paid in September.)   He was granted leave on 26 Dec 1916 until 5 Dec 1917, likely received at home even more of a hero than most, having recently been awarded the Military Cross on 9 Dec 1916. Unfortunately, I have been unable to find out what for what heroic feat.

In 1917, he was made a 2nd Corporal and in October admitted to hospital for two weeks – again on mention as to why.

John was killed in action on the 12 April 1918 and is remembered with honour on the PLOEGSTEERT MEMORIAL, Belgium. Items returned to his family after his death: 2 letters, 2 wallets, 2 pieces of medal ribbon, 3 photos, 2 pocket note books and miscellaneous papers.

A Signaller - somewhere on the Western Front. (Author's own collection.)

Driver **WILLIAM DIXON TURNER**   14/036560

William Turner was a martyr to Field Punishments No2*** I can find 5 occasions totaling 40 days he spent in such conditions, each occasion was drink related or causing a disturbance (while probably inebriated.)

Thirty-seven-year-old William of 103 Lamb Street, Walker attested in Dec 1914 and was sent to Ripon Camp and then on to the 189 Coy Royal Army Service Corps, where he took up position as a driver and embarked to France on the 'La Marguerite' on 3 Sept 1915. William was de-mobilized in Jun 1919 aged 41.

Private **FREDERICK TURNER**   3018

A 33-year-old 'Cartman' Fred lived at 18 Lowthian Street, Walker. He attested in to the South Staffordshire Regiment in Dec 1915 and was wounded in the left leg on 25 Jul 1918. He was awarded a 24/- a week pension for a 60% disablement of having his left leg amputated at the thigh.

Private **THOMAS WALSH**   11248

Twenty-nine-year-old Thomas of 39 White Street, Walker attested to the Army under the Derby scheme and was held in reserve and then discharged after 59 days (28 Aug 1914 to 22 Oct 1914) due to working in a 'protected trade.' He was a 'Furnace-man stoker' likely at Armstrong Whitworth's. Unbelievably he sounded an ideal specimen for a solider; 5 feet 11 inches tall and weighing 161lb and with a 40½ chest with a further expansion of 2½ - quite a big man. He was also described as having a dark complexion brown hair and brown eyes.

Corporal **PHILIP WARD**   12753

Philip Ward was born in Walker in 1894, an only child. This was a true account of his service and he did serve overseas in France. At the outbreak of war, he was living at 5 Furness

Street, West Hartlepool and married to Christina, with two children – Wilfred and Elizabeth. Philip was working as a labourer at a Zinc works.

On 1 Jan 1916, he was admitted to hospital with influenza and released back to his unit on 11 Jan 1916.

On 28 Aug 1916, Philip was killed in action on the Somme battlefield, aged 31. He is buried at Delville Wood Cemetery, Longueval, France.

Private **SAMUEL WATERS**   1590/393159
       MM

Samuel of 69 Byker Terrace, Walker attested in April 1915 to the 1st Northumbrian, Royal Army Medical Corps. He served in the UK until March 1916 where he was until Dec 1916 when he was transferred to the Mediterranean theatre of war. While in France he was awarded the Military Medal for operations on the field on either the 3rd or 8th Sept 1916.

Later on in the war he served for a second time in France and was in 1918 attached to the West Riding Regiment at the 1st Northern General Hospital in Newcastle upon Tyne. He was discharged from the service as no longer physically fit to serve due to a chronic inflammation of his left ear, caused by active service causing a 40% disablement. He was to receive 27/6 for 13 weeks and then 11/- thereafter for another 36 weeks and then to attend a medical review.

Private **JOSEPH WATSON**   132355

Joseph enlisted at the age of 49 in 1917 and was accepted in to the Royal Army Medical Corps in Aug 1917. The former miner who lived at 1679 Walker Road, Walker, was illiterate and signed his 'mark' with a cross. He was later transferred to the Labour Corps and given a £10 gratuity for his service.

Private **WILLIAM WATSON (DOTCHIN)**   120390

William, was born out of wedlock – his father's surname was Dotchin but he assumed his mother's surname. He enlisted in

1915 aged 46 to the Pioneer Labour Battalion and served in France from 1 Oct 1915 until 3 Sept 1916. While in France he was transferred to the 6th Bn. Labour Company Royal Engineers. William was also a miner, having previously worked at the Rising Sun Colliery at Wallsend for 2 years. He lived at 1617 Walker New Road, Walker. William was 5 feet 10 inches ins tall with a chest measurement of 35 inches with an expansion of 2 inches. He married Sarah Wood a widow in July 1914 (also his second marriage also) and father to Margaret and Joseph and step-father to George.

Gunner **WILLIAM COOPER WATSON** 167890
A barber by occupation, the married father of three, living at 3 Sunningdale Avenue, Walker, William joined the Royal Field Artillery in Aug 1916 aged 28 after attesting in Dec of the previous year. He was posted to France in 1917 but appeared to spend most of his service in England. He spent a good deal of time in Bexleyheath and Woolwich. He was appointed the Regimental Barber at Cambridge Barracks, Woolwich in 1918. Someone called E Choal (?) twice wrote to the army asking for the private address of William Watson giving their address as c/o Mrs. Wheatley, 29 Church Road, Bexleyheath, Kent. They didn't give a reason as to their enquiry. There is no note as to whether the Army passed on any details to either party.
The only recorded misdemeanor William committed was going absent without leave from 22.00 hrs. on 31 Dec 1918 until 21.30 hrs. on 1 Jan 1919 – charges levied against him were dropped.

Private **THOMAS WATSON** 113083
Thomas of 4 Cecil Street, Walker, enlisted on 19 June 1918 as soon as he turned 18. He was posted to the 4th Bn. (Res) East Yorkshire Regiment. He served in the UK until March 1818 when he deployed to France, though how long he was there is not noted, although I know he was still there (Boulogne) in May 1919. He was demobilized from the Army in 1920.

There are a number of misdemeanors recorded against Thomas – leaving his tent in a dirty condition, missing Parade, and going absent after his leave (forfeited 20 days' pay.)

Dear Sir,

In reply to your letter dated 8 June 19124 regarding your war medals, I have to inform you that as you did not serve overseas during the Great War i.e. between 4-8-1914 and 11-11-1918 you are not entitled to any medals.

I am to request that you will be good enough to return your Demobilization Certificate (A.F Z.21) to this office for the purpose of being amended as the entry stating that you are entitled to the award of the British War Medal has been inserted thereon in error.

Infantry Records Office. York.

I think it is rather sad that Thomas' service in the Military was not recognized with an award of some kind……..

L/Cpl **JOSEPH WEAR**   488682

Enlisted in September 1914 and was mobilized with the Duke of Cornwall Light Infantry at Bodmin, Cornwall, on 5 Sept 1914. Joseph who was 27 years old and lived at 11 Westbourne Avenue, Walker, was working as a 'Cinema Camera Operator' before he enlisted. He is described as being 5 feet 5 inches tall and weighing 126 pounds. He has a fresh complexion, brown eyes and black hair. He serves in the UK until Jan1916 when he sails for the Mediterranean and is in Salonika until May 1918. While serving there he comes down with Malaria and is hospitalized and posted back to the UK. Due to the implications of having had Malaria he is transferred to the Labour Corps and posted to France in Oct 1918 *'for anti-malaria treatment.'* He is posted to the 173rd and later 62nd Labour Companies. Joseph is demobilized at Ripon on 6 Apr 1919 and awarded a pension of 11/- being reduced to 8/3 and to be reviewed at a later date.

Driver **EDWIN WEAR**   224481

Younger brother of Joseph Wear, Edwin a 'Draughtsman' at Donkin & Co, Newcastle upon Tyne, attested on 2 Dec 1915 and was mobilized 10 months later in Sept 1916, being attached to the Royal Army Service Corps as a Driver with the 988 Motor Transport Coy. He passed his driving test on 21 Jan 1917 and by 12 Oct 1918 was assessed as a 'Driver 1st Class.' Edwin who was 19 in 1915, was 5 feet 5 inches tall and weighed 99 pounds. He had a 32½ inch chest with an expansion of a further 2½ inches. He was described by the doctor as being 'under developed.'

Edwin was posted to Egypt in May 1915 traveling via Southampton, Harve, and Marseilles, eventually arriving Alexandria. He was admitted to hospital of a number of occasions – diarrhea, styes to both eyes etc. On 30 Nov 1918 he is admitted again, this time with Flu – a week later he re-joins his unit but is re-admitted on 7 Jan 1919 with tonsillitis. Gradually his condition worsens and he develops pains in his back and legs, headaches etc. His sputum shows signs of blood in lungs and on 21 Jan 1919 Edwin dies of a combination of influenza and pneumonia.

Private **JOHN WILKINSON**   11212

John, a 'labourer' attested on 28 Aug 1918 at Wallsend to the 8th Bn. Duke of Wellington (West Yorkshire) Regiment. He is described as 5 feet 8½ inches tall weighting 136 pounds and with a fresh complexion, grey eyes and fair hair. He was discharged on 25 Oct 1914 to 16 Railway Terrace, Hebburn, as *'not being likely to become an efficient solider.'*

Private **JOHN WOOD**   58804 / M/417542

John of 1 Cowen Street, Walker, was an apprentice fitter when he attested to the 3rd Bn. Northumberland Fusiliers in July 1915, aged 18. He is later transferred to the Royal Army

Service Corps. His parents John and Annie, along with sister Annie and brother Tom, move to no 2 Cowen Street while John is at war. John wasn't mobilised until 12 Jul 1918 when he was attached to the Motor Transport Coy of the Royal Army Service Corps. On 7 Jul 1919, he proved himself *'as a suitable learner lorry driver.'* Soon after demobilization he moved to Canada to find work.

Private **GEORGE CONNOR WOODHEAD**   113503 / 3648
George was a 38-year-old married man with 4 children – Hannah born 1904, George born 1906, Lucy born 1908 and William born 1911, when he attested in Nov 1913. Working as a miner he and his family resided at 4 Pearson Street, Walker. Born in Barnsley in 1876, George likely moved to Walker for employment in the mines. He was first with the 16th (service Bn.) Cheshire Regiment and then transferred to the Labour Corps. He was discharged on 19 March 1919 aged 43.

In Walker churchyard there is grave to Bugler 1575 **REGINALD ARTHUR NANKERVIS**, who died 3rd March 1915. A member of the 5th Bn. Duke of Cornwall's Light Infantry. Reginald was only 15 years old, still a boy. He was from Newquay in Cornwall, pretty much as far away from Newcastle as you could get in England. He died at Walkergate hospital for infectious diseases. By 1911 his parents had eight children and likely could just not afford the expense of having their sons body repatriated nearly 500 miles to Cornwall.

Also buried in Walker cemetery is Private **WILLIAM EDWARD LAWS**, 1557, of the Royal Army Medical Corps, 1st Northumberland Field Ambulance. William died on the 16th January 1916. Prior to the outbreak of war William worked as a general labourer and was married to Elizabeth. In 1911, they were living at 7, Blagdon Street, Newcastle upon Tyne, with their two sons and two daughters. Their eldest daughter Isabella Lowery Laws, was born three years prior to their marriage. Three other children had died in infancy. I cannot find a Walker address for the family, but assume possibly they moved there after the 1911 census or more likely, he died at Walkergate Hospital.

Families at war.

There will have been many Walker families that sent a number of their members to war – sons and brothers, fathers and sons.

See the '**King's letter to a Walker woman'** Mrs Livingston, of 1, Colin Street, Walker, had five sons serving in the Cameron Highlanders, that a sixth son, James who served with the Coldstream Guards and was killed in action in 14th September 1914. She also had a seventh son who was engaged on war munitions work at Elswick arsenal.

I am sure I will have omitted a number of siblings/fathers/sons who lived in Walker and fought in the Great War. These are the families with more than one family member serving their country that I have been able to trace.

Private **FRANCIS ARTHUR NAPIER** of the 5th Bn. Northumberland Fusiliers was the son of Private **ARTHUR FRANCIS NAPIER** of the 6th (National Reserve) Bn. Northumberland Fusiliers.

Father Arthur died on 14th Dec 1914 aged 46 and is buried in Walker Churchyard (Old Portion West Plot. Row 5 from 3rd path to West from Tower. Grave 4 North from Central path.) Arthur had been a 'holder up' at the Shipyards prior to attesting to the Army. He had also previously served 16 years with 2nd Bn. Northumberland Fusiliers; and had served in the South African Campaign.

Arthur and Mary had 6 children, though only 5 surviving childhood – Two of them losing their lives during the Great War. Francis, died of wounds 8 months after the death of his father, on 25 July 1915 is buried at BOULOGNE EASTERN CEMETERY France, and brother Able Seaman (RNVR)

ROBERT NAPIER, HAWKE Bn. was killed on 13th November 1916 and is remembered on the Thiepval Memorial, Somme, France. Both sons are also remembered on their fathers CWGC headstone in Walker churchyard.

They were survived by siblings James, Arthur, Daniel and Rosemond. The family lived at 12, later 85, Byker Terrace, Walker.

Private **WILLIAM DAVIDSON** (Service No 8005 M/404338) a woodcutting machinist, also living at 155, Church Street, Walker, William attested to the Military on 28 June 1918 at the age of 20. He was first attached to the West Yorkshire Regiment then transferred to the Royal Army Service Corps, where he was employed in the motor transport section as a driver. In 1919, he sailed to Port Said in Egypt where he stayed until de-mobilization in April 1920. He stayed on as a territorial soldier with the Northumberland Fusiliers, service number 4260968. He was finally discharged from Military service at the age of 31 in 1929.

On the 1911 census William was living a few doors further along the road, at 159, Church Street; a two-roomed property. His father John was a ship's joiner and mother Janet a housewife. The couple had parented eight children, six of whom were still alive (a brother John having died on war service in 1914 and buried Walker). Five of those surviving children with ages ranging from six to twenty-three were still living at home. There is no mention of the occupations of the older siblings. Brother Private **JOHN DAVIDSON** (Service No:10868) died 11th Oct 1914, aged 26. A member of the West Yorkshire Regiment (Prince of Wales's Own). Husband of Margaret Davidson) of 141, Clifford St., Byker, Newcastle-on-Tyne. Likely died in the illness or injury sustained in training, he is buried at Christ Church cemetery, Walker.

Private **DAVID BRUCE** 3089/478071 and Private **GEORGE SINCLAIR LAURIE** 46029 were related, as were many other families in Walker, by marriage.

David was a member of the 2/5th Bn. Northumberland Fusiliers. He attested in Nov 1914. He lived with his wife Elizabeth (nee Laurie) at 44, Fisher Street, Low Walker.

George lived at 76 Fisher Hill, Low Walker, and joined the 21st Bn. Tyneside Scottish Regiment at Gosforth on 5 March 1915, aged 20. George was posted to France Jan 1916 but later admitted to hospital in Etaples, France with Pleurisy. He was sent back to England in April to recover and during this time married his sweetheart Annie Isabella Appleby at Walker Parish Church on the 25 Apr 1916. A son David James Laurie was born in July 1917.

George was later attached to the 13th Bn. Durham Light Infantry (due to the decimation of the Tyneside Scottish on 1 Jul 1916 on the Somme) to which he was given a full transfer on 13 Sept 1916. In November, he was sent by hospital ship to England, once again suffering from pleurisy.

George got himself confined to barracks or had stoppages of pay on a number of occasions. Three times in 1915 when the battalion were stationed in the North East of England when he was late back from leave, by up to 5 days – having been arrested and returned to his unit by the civil Police. Again, when at Hornsea in 1916 he was twice deducted 3 days' pay – once for being dirty on Parade and once for overstaying his leave by two days.

Brother-in-law David, was twice promoted to Lance Corporal and twice demoted back to being a Private. He also went 'absent without leave' on 27th Nov 1918 until apprehended by the civil Police on 11 Jan 1919. He was found guilty and sentenced to 42 days Field Punishments number 1.

George was the first to die – On the 7 Oct 1917 he was charged with an offence and informed he was to be deducted 3 days' pay (no mention of said incident.) On 8 Oct 1917 George was dead, aged only 22 killed in action near Le Sars, Somme France. Likely never having seen his baby son, who was only weeks old. Items returned to his wife included; Disc, 4 cards, 4 letters, photo's, pipe, cap comforter, razor, watch case, cigarette case, 2 discs *(identity.)*

Widow Annie and son David moved to 77 Fisher Street, Low Walker, to live with George's family; brother Thomas age 21, Willie 20 (away in India) Jimmie age 16 and John aged 14 (away at Murton Colliery.) Also, Private DAVID BRUCE'S wife Lizzie, the matriarch of the brood, aged 33, along with her children; David aged 10, Murdoch aged 9, Willie aged 7, Mary Lizzie aged 6, George aged 4 and Bruce aged 2.

(Annie Isabella Laurie re-married in 1921 – Thomas Laurie, brother of George and Lizzie. They had three children, a girl and two boys. Their first born David, died in 1923 at a year old.)

On the 7th April 1919, the Bruce/Laurie family suffered a double tragedy, little David Laurie, son of George, died at 77 Fisher Street, Low Walker, aged 22 months. He was suffering from acute influenza and pneumonia.

Private David Bruce died from Influenza and bronchial pneumonia, also on 7th April 1919, at the 1st Northern general Hospital, Newcastle upon Tyne.

I do wonder if David Bruce's 'Field Punishments Number 1' was a major contributor in the two deaths, or were they simply victims of the Spanish flu that ravaged Europe?

The name David unfortunately appeared to be cursed in the Laurie/Bruce families.

Driver **OWEN FALLON** of the Royal Army Service Corps is another man who died at home - on 18 April 1918 aged 47. He left behind wife Elizabeth (formerly Martin) whom he married in 1905 after the deaths of their first spouses and children: James Martin, Isabella Martin, John Fallon*, Thomas Fallon*, Lowery Martin, Maggie Martin, William Fallon and Elizabeth

Fallon. * children born to first wife Mary Ann Gilligan who died 1902.

Owen's son Sapper **JOHN FALLON** was called to the Colours a year after his father's death and just after the end of the war, though had attested in 1917. His service ran from 29 Apr 1919 until 10 Aug 1919 when he deserted. He was found to have then fraudulently enlisted in to the R.A.F (using the name L. Martin – impersonating his step brothers' identity) and given the R.A.F number 334724 A.C2. He was tried and convicted and given 14 days imprisonment with hard labour for larceny. Discharged from the Royal Air Force under Para 392 (10) King's regulations as from 22.2.20

Private's **THOMAS GODFREY** and **JOHN GODFREY** were brothers. Both were 'cartmen.' Thomas was living at 103 Lamb Street, Walker, with his wife Sarah and 4 children, Margaret, Sarah, Elizabeth and Thomas, another daughter Doris having died in infancy. He is described as being slightly deaf in his left ear.

He joined the Royal Army Service Corps as a 'Horseman/ Driver' at the age of 36 in 1915 deployed to France and was there until 21 May 1918 when he was sent home on 10 days leave, returning on 31 May 1918. His daughter Elizabeth aged 5 had died on the 18th May of tuberculosis meningitis.

JOHN GODFREY lived at 289 Church Street, Walker. He too joined the Royal Army Service Corps as a Horseman/ Driver. He joined the expeditionary force in France on 12 April 1915 and was demobilised 13 June 1919 suffering from Dermatitis.

Poor Isabella Scullion – she lost two sons Private **JAMES WALTON LOUGH** when he was 19 in May 1915, and Private **THOMAS LOUGH** when he was aged 23 in April 1918. James is buried at Hazebrouck Communal cemetery in France and Thomas is remembered on the Ploegsteert memorial in Belgium. Both men were in the 1/5th Bn. Northumberland Fusiliers.

Their father, the late John Lough had died in 1910 aged 40. The family had then been living on Lamb Street Walker and John had been employed as a steam Engine fitter.

Isabella finding it hard to cope with 4 children James, Thomas, Isabella and 2-year-old William (she and John had 10 children but 6 had died in infancy.) took in lodgers. She, the four children and 3 lodgers shared a 3-roomed property at 105 Lamb Street according to the 1911 census.

Thomas at the time was working as an apprentice carpenter and James as a driver in the coal mines.

Isabella re-married in 1912 to a chap called Francis Scullion – the only chap of that name I can find on the 1911 census was over 20 years her junior and was at that time living in Stockton on Tees.

After her marriage she moved to 78, Bath St., Walker, Newcastle-on-Tyne with her new husband and children. I don't know if she had any more children with her second husband; but of the 10 children she had to her first husband only 2 were still alive by late April 1918.

Here are four brothers, three of whom fought with the 1/5th B. Northumberland Fusiliers during the Great War. **ARCHIBALD, ANDREW and WILLIAM MAUGHAN**. Elder brother, **SAMUEL,** served with the 9th Bn. West Yorkshire Regiment. The boys had been brought up with their five other siblings – Jane, John, James, Septimus and Thomas. The family lived at 65 Mitchell Buildings when the 1901 census was carried out and had moved to 23 Mitchell Street by 1911, a two-roomed property where eight members of the Martin/Maughan family lived, along with Elizabeth Henzell aged 14, a servant.

Their parents were Samuel, a shipyard labourer, and Annie (née Kenny) Maughan. Samuel had passed away in 1894 aged only 36, due to heart disease. Annie at the time was pregnant with her 9th child, Thomas. In 1903 Annie re-married, her new husband – also a shipyard labourer; was ten years younger than Annie. He was a good man and happily took on her nine children and brought them up as his own, until his own early passing in 1913.

Samuel, the eldest of the four serving brothers, had previously been a member of the 5th Bn. Northumberland Fusiliers Territorial Force, prior to the outbreak of war. He was 29 years old when he attested in 1914 at Wallsend and served at home and abroad until Oct 1916 when he was recalled to Armstrong Whitworth's to carry out much needed munitions work.

His recall was possibly partially due to the fact that three of his siblings had been killed in action within weeks of each other earlier in the year. If not, it was surely a huge blessing to his mother as he was now back at home and relatively safe from harm's way. The shipyards were a dangerous place to work - but certainly not as dangerous as the battlefields of the Eastern and Western Fronts.

Archie, the youngest of the brothers, a bachelor, was the first to be killed, aged 23 on 11 March 1916 and is buried at Railway Dugouts Burial Ground (Transport Farm) Belgium. The following month Andrew, a former grocer's salesman was killed on 4 April 1916 aged 25. He left behind a wife Sarah Anna Green (Anna) who resided with her parents at 156, Dunns Terrace, Byker. Andrew and Anna had only been married a matter of months, having tied the knot on 1st June 1915. They had a few brief months together before he was landed in France on 1st Nov 1915. In his will he left £120 to his wife – quite a substantial sum of money in 1916. In March 1918 Anna went on to marry James Herbert Watts and she died aged 73 in 1966.

Andrew's body was never recovered and he is remembered with honour on the Ypres (Menin Gate) memorial in Belgium. A few weeks later the telegram every mother dreads, once again was delivered to 23 Mitchell Street. This time it was to tell Annie that yet another of her children had been taken from her. Private William Maughan aged 27, had been killed on the 25 May 1916. He is buried at Le Laiterie Military Cemetery, Belgium.

Margaret, his wife, whom he married on 28th June 1912 at St Anthony's Catholic Church in Walker and now residing 60 Mitchell Buildings; her parents address - would have received her telegram the same day. Their only child, Samuel, was just 5 months old and the likelihood is that his father had never seen him and now never would.

Margaret and William had known each other all their lives – near neighbours in Mitchell Street and Mitchell Buildings since childhood. They would have played together and attended school together. Margaret's father Nicholas Bowden, a former riveter at the shipyards, passed away months later in December 1916, aged 76.

One telegram bearing the terrible news a son has been lost must have been terrible – but to have received three and just weeks apart would break any mother.

Annie had to have been an incredibly strong woman, having suffered so many losses in her life, but she continued to fight on and was there for her surviving children and their children and for her great grandchildren. She died aged 93 in 1952

MARK MADDISON of 181 Back Church Street, Walker, a 4-roomed property; had previously served 6 years with the 3rd Bn. Durham Light Infantry Militia. He was a 47-year-old coal miner when he attested on 25 June 1915. He was posted 2 days later to a 'reserve' position so that he could retain his civilian employment and be available to be called up if needed. Mark and his wife Mary Clarabella Coulson (always known as Isabella) married in June 1894 and had eight children – Henry who died as a baby is 1895, Isaac who was killed in the Great

War, Hannah, Naomi; who died aged 13. Margaret, Elizabeth; who died aged 15 in 1920. Mary who died as a baby in 1909. Isabella and finally another Mary. Mary died in 1916 aged 39 leaving Mark him to bring up the family – his youngest child being 3 years old and his son Isaac having been killed in Gallipoli only months earlier in August 1915. Did Mary die of a broken heart?

ISAAC MADDISON (named after his maternal Grandfather) was born 18 Feb 1897 at Condercum Cottages, Benwell, Newcastle upon Tyne. In 1911 at the age of he was attending the Industrial School on Jubilee Road, Newcastle. It's likely he had been a 'bad lad' and was sent by the courts to the 'reformatory' school to try and straighten him out. Mark no doubt hoped to get called up so that he could avenge his sons' death. He was released 'surplus to requirement' on 14th Dec 1918. A member of the 9th Bn. West Yorkshire Regiment, Isaac is remembered on the Helles Memorial, Gallipoli, Turkey. Mark Maddison passed away on 23rd March 1938 aged 70.

A letter written to the Times of London in October of 1923 by Mr. John Still, adjutant in the 6th battalion describes the battle in which Isaac died;

Publish but please read it eliminating all self-praise, radically. As there was no self-praise, cutting out was not necessary. I am IAN HAMILTON, 1 Hyde Park Gardens W2
Dear General Hamilton, - You will not remember meeting me on the occasion of a dance held upstairs in this office about a dozen years ago. But I do not write as secretary of this association, but as an officer who served under you on Gallipoli. I have just read your Gallipoli Diary, and read it with an extraordinary interest; for rather an extraordinary reason for it so happens that I am perhaps the only person in the world who can throw light upon some of its greatest puzzles. In your map of the Suvla area, square 105 F/K, you give a position on Scimitar Hill occupied and withdrawn from, apparently without your knowledge for two years! I was there. I know exactly what happened, why, and when. For I was adjutant of the 6th East

Yorks Regiment on that hill after Estridge (the regular adjutant) had been wounded. I was also signalling officer. And if I may say so, I was the only officer on that hill who had spent years in jungle and with two officers of whom one was killed, and the other – Devenport [sic] – severely wounded. And this left us in the air. Your orders given to General Stopford at 6pm never reached us on Scimitar Hill. Why? They knew where we were, for I was in touch by day with Brigade H.Q. signallers on Hill 10 or close to it. By night I lost contact for both my lamps failed me. As you justly say, anyone with half an eye could see Tekke Tepe was the key to the whole position. Even I, a middle-aged amateur who had done a bit of big game shooting and knocking about saw it at once. We reconnoitered it, sent an officer and my signaller corporal to climb it, and got through to Brigade H.Q. the message giving our results. I sent it myself. The hill was then empty. Next morning you saw or heard that troops had actually reached the top of Tekke Tepe. Yes they had. A worn and weak company, D Company of my regiment together with my Colonel (Moore). Major Brunner, of the R.E., and myself started up that hill. About thirty got to the top: of them five got down again to the bottom, and of those three lived to the end of the war. I was one of them. You wonder why we did not dig in (pages 78 and 79 of your Volume II) as we had lots of time. There, Sir, is where that war was lost. You set a Brigade at that empty hill on the afternoon of the 8th. Actually, owing to staff work being so bad, a battalion received orders to attack and did not receive those orders until dawn on the 9th. I received them myself as adjutant. The order ran to this effect: "The C.-in-C. Considers this operation essential to the success of the whole campaign". The order was sent out on the late afternoon of the 8th, when we were on scimitar hill. It reached us at dawn on the 9th in a Turkish trench at Sulejik. In the meanwhile, for those hours more precious to the world than we even yet can judge, the Brigade major was lost! Good God why didn't they send a man who knew the country? He was lost, lost, lost and it drives one almost mad to think of it. Excuse Me. Next morning (from the order) at dawn on the 9th you saw some of our fellows climbing cattle tracks. You don't place theme exactly where I think you really saw them, but as I know there were none just precisely where you say you saw them, I am pretty certain it was us you saw from the ship, only we were half a mile north of where you describe. Then we climbed Tekke Tepe. Simultaneously the Turks attacked through the gap from Anafarta. Their attack cut in behind D Company and held back the rest of the battalion who fought in the trench, with the Duke of Wellington's on their left. We went on, and, as I said, not one of us got back again. A few were taken prisoner. I was slightly wounded, and stayed three years and three months as a prisoner. Later that morning we who survived were again taken up Tekke Tepe by its northern ravine on the west side. Turkish troops were simply pouring down it and the other ravines. On the top of Tekke Tepe were four field guns camouflaged with boughs of scrub oak, and a Brigade H.Q. was just behind the ridge. I had a few minutes conversation there with the Turkish Brigadier in French. But I am coming home on leave in March or April next. May I have the honour of meeting you and going over it on the map? I think much might be cleared up that was still obscure when you wrote your book. There are one or two things one prefers not to write. Please let me know your wishes in this matter. I loved your book and I want to do any small thing possible to complete your picture. Yours truly (Sd) JOHN STILL Victoria Commemoration Buildings, Nos 40 and 41 Ward Street, Kandy, Ceylon Sept 19.

Driver **EDWIN WEAR** was the younger brother of Joseph Wear, Edwin a 'Draughtsman' at Donkin & Co, Newcastle upon Tyne, attested on 2 Dec 1915 and was mobilized 10 months later in Sept 1916, being attached to the Royal Army Service Corps as a Driver with the 988 Motor Transport Coy. He passed his driving test on 21 Jan 1917 and by 12 Oct 1918 was assessed as a 'Driver 1st Class.'
 Edwin who was 19 in 1915, was 5 feet 5 inches tall and weighed 99 pounds. He had a 32½ inch chest with an expansion of a further 2½ inches. He was described by the doctor as being 'under developed.' He was posted to Egypt in May 1915 traveling via Southampton, Harve, and Marseilles,

eventually arriving Alexandria. He was admitted to hospital of a number of occasions – diarrhea, styes to both eyes etc. On 30 Nov 1918 he is admitted again, this time with Flu – a week later he re-joins his unit but is re-admitted on 7 Jan 1919 with tonsillitis. Gradually his condition worsens and he develops pains in his back and legs, headaches etc. His sputum shows signs of blood in lungs and on 21 Jan 1919 Edwin dies of a combination of influenza and pneumonia. His brother L/Cpl JOSEPH WEAR Enlisted in September 1914 and was mobilized with the Duke of Cornwall Light Infantry at Bodmin, Cornwall, on 5 Sept 1914. Joseph who was 27 years old and lived at 11 Westbourne Avenue, Walker, was working as a 'Cinema Camera Operator' before he enlisted. He is described as being 5 feet 5 inches tall and weighing 126 pounds. He has a fresh complexion, brown eyes and black hair. He serves in the UK until Jan1916 when he sails for the Mediterranean and is in Salonika until May 1918. While serving there he comes down with Malaria and is hospitalized and posted back to the UK. Due to the implications of having had Malaria he is transferred to the Labour Corps and posted to France in Oct 1918 *'for anti-malaria treatment.'* He is posted to the 173rd and later 62nd Labour Companies. Joseph is demobilized at Ripon on 6 Apr 1919 and awarded a pension of 11/- being reduced to 8/3 and to be reviewed at a later date.

Private **ROBERT BARTON** of 46 River View, Low Walker, enlisted into the Labour Corps at Manchester in June 1915. He was first sent to join the 20th (Service) Lancashire Fusiliers, later 12th Bn. North Staffordshire Regiment. He was the younger brother of Walter Barton of 46 Fisher Street. A former farm labourer Robert joined up aged 24 and was described as being only 5-foot ¼ inch tall. His mother Jane Ann was deceased – having passed away in Tynemouth Workhouse. He enlisted on 1 May 1915 and was later transferred to 12th Bn.

North Staffs. Robert was killed on the 11th Sept 1918 and is remembered on the PLOEGSTEERT MEMORIAL Belgium. His belongings were to be sent to Mrs Jane Wait of 52 White Street, Low Walker - his sister.

Private **WALTER WILLIAM BARTON** elder brother of Robert, a married man living at 46 Fisher Street, Walker when he attested on 10 Dec 1915 aged 34, was sent to France 16 June 1917, having spent a year serving in the UK. He was originally attached to the Northumberland Fusiliers but in July 1917 was transferred to the Durham Light Infantry. Served in both France and Italy and was described as having an 'under developed' chest on demobilisation in Sept 1919.

The **ROBBIE** brothers **RICHARD** and **FREDERICK** both served on the Western Front, and during interesting careers spread their talents across the three arms of the British Forces. After demobilisation, both left the Army; Frederick to join the Royal Marines and brother Robbie later on joining the Royal Air Force.

Fred, the younger of the two, by three years, was already married at the outbreak of war. He had married Mary Jane Ramsey in 1910, their son Reuben Walbank Ramsey having been a year earlier. Fred his wife and son were living in a two-roomed flat at 42 Mitchell Street on the 1911 census and he was employed as a hand driller at the shipyards. In 1913 another son, John, was born to the couple.

He attested to the 1/6th Northumberland Fusiliers (service no: 3471) and was then transferred to Royal Engineers (service no: 90251.) He is then again transferred to the Army Service Corps (service no: EMT/61214) the EMT denoting he was voluntarily posted to the Motor Transport section on re-enlistment after the war under Army Order 4/19. On 7th April 1919, he transfers to the Royal Marines Divisional Engineers in Kent. His family are now living at 25 Mitchell Street, Walker. Newcastle upon Tyne.

Brother **RICHARD ROBBIE** served with the Royal Army Medical Corps during the war. An apprentice engineer, he had been with the Army Medical Corps (Territorial Force) since 1911 and was called up immediately war was declared. Richard married Elizabeth Redhead on 31st December 1915 and they went on to have three children Nora, Richard and Ethel. In 1923 Richard joined the Royal Air Force as a hospital orderly, but was later discharged in 1925 on compassionate grounds. Richard was awarded the Military Medal, sometime prior to mid-1917. Almost certainly for bringing in wounded men, whilst under fire from the enemy.

Staff Sergeant **WALTER COX** along with two of his brother's William and Colin participated in the Great War overseas. All survived the war pretty much unscathed and were able to return home to their families after the war.
Walter's parents, William and Mary had both been born in Yorkshire but had moved north at an early age and their children were all born in Walker. John, William, Thomas. Joseph, Walter and Colin. Walter was a 'watchmaker' living at 90 Church Street, Walker, formerly of Byker Street, Walker. He 25-year-old enlisted on 10th Dec *1915 (the same month as his marriage to Robertina Train)* and was called up on 12th Dec 1916 to join the Royal Army Ordnance Corps. His wife had just given birth to their first child.
Walter is described as being 5 feet 7 inches in height, weighing 155 lb and having false upper teeth. He sailed for Salonika, Greece, in June 1917 and in 1918 was posted to Taranto in Southern Italy. He returned to watch making after the war and proved to be a successful businessman who ran a shop on Church Street for many more years. Walter died in 1972 aged 81. Robertina died in 1940 aged 48.

Elder brother Private **WILLIAM FAWCETT COX** 31, joined the Royal Garrison Artillery. He had worked as a 'Coachman' before the war and resided at 158 Middle Street, Walker. Married to Ellen and with an 8-year-old daughter, Hilda. William attested on 13th Oct 1915 and joined his unit at Dover in Kent on the 18th Oct 1915. He was then posted on 30th Oct 1915 (UK) but discharged on 8 March 1917 on account of his deafness.

Gunner **COLIN COX,** the youngest of the Cox brothers also attested on 7th Dec 1915 to join the Royal Garrison Artillery. His medical describes him as being 5 feet 9½ inches tall and having an appendectomy scar. His chest measured 38 inches with another 1½ inches expansion. Colin describes himself as being Church of England. Married to Sophia and with a son, also called Colin born in 1915. Colin Snr. of 137 Middle Street, Walker, was not called in to service until 1917. He was posted to France in 1918 and stayed there till de-mobilisation in 1919.

Private **WILLIAM RIDLEY** a Colliery worker who lived at 12 Cambrain Row, High Walker, joined the 2nd Reserve Northumbrian Field Ambulance (Royal Army Medical Corps) in Jan 1915. He served in France from 19 Apr 1915 until 9 Oct 1916. Taller than many of his contemporaries William stood 5ft 10½ ins tall and had a 36-inch chest with an expansion of 2 inches. His vision and physique were described as 'good.' In 1918 William was awarded a pension of 27/6 for 4 weeks and then dropping to 8/- a week thereafter and to be reviewed 48 weeks later. I don't know what disability he received during his service but he was transferred to reserve and returned to his previous employment at the Rising Sun Colliery in Wallsend.

Elder brother Private **GEORGE RIDLEY** aged 37, of 13 Ambrose Place, Walker, joined the Royal Army Medical Corps in 1915 as part of the 2nd Northumbrian Field Ambulance, attached to the Royal Field Artillery. He served in France from 19 Apr 1915 until 19 Oct 1918. In Dec 1918, he was transferred to Army Reserve and went back to his employment as a 'Coal Hewer' with the Walker Coal Co Ltd, who he had worked for, for the past 30 years (since the age of 7.) In 1922 George joined the 5th Bn. Northumberland Fusiliers Territorial Battalion with whom he served another 4 years.

Private's **JOSEPH PARKER** and **CHARLES PARKER**. Joseph was born 1890 at 268 Church Street, Walker to Charles and Johanna Parker. Charles was originally from Islington in London and Johanna from Durham. Joseph had one older brother – also called Charles. Another brother Thomas, born in 1880 died aged five; before either of the surviving siblings were born.
By 1901 Charles was a widower and had moved with his children to Slag Row, Walker. He was working as a 'machine man' at the shipyards and employed a housekeeper, Margaret Place to look after the boys. I am unable to find Joseph on the 1911 census, nor his brother Charles. Joseph, a member of the Tyneside Scottish was killed in action on 1st July 1916. Charles survived the Great War, having served with the Northumberland Fusiliers and the Yorkshire Regiment. He married Sarah Nash, also from Walker and moved to Ashington, Northumberland.

Private's **FRANCIS HENRY BRADLEY** and **JOHN THOMAS TERRY BRADLEY** were the sons of Dominic and Catherine Bradley, of 30 Mitchell Street Walker. Both men were to lose their lives in the Great War. John was the first to die – on 22 Aug 1915 whilst serving with the 9th Bn. Prince of Wales Own (West Yorkshire Regiment) in Gallipoli, he was 31 years old. Three years later and again at the age of 31 Francis was killed whilst serving with the 11th Bn. East Yorkshire Regiment. He left behind a wife of Sarah Jane Bradley (nee

Harvey), of 296, Church St., Walker, Newcastle-on-Tyne. He is buried at PONT-D'ACHELLES MILITARY CEMETERY, NIEPPE, France.

On 4 March 1916 -John Harvey (37) – brother of Sarah Bradley was killed in an accident at the Armstrong Whitworth Walker shipyard. Some men from Pearson's Works at Wallsend had been sub-contracted to fit a fan to a ship there. They raised the fan 15 feet on wire ropes which were strong enough to hold 2 tons (as had done with 2 previous fans safely.) When within 3 feet of the fixed position the rope was substituted for an independent rope which then snapped and the fan fell, crushing John and another man, who were working in the boiler room below. John was injured about the head, back and legs and he succumbed the following day, Thursday 2nd March 1916.

certainly was the right choice.

Robert had no previous Military experience when he joined the Australian Infantry Force – he was probably looking for another adventure. The battalion was raised within a fortnight of the declaration of war in August 1914 and embarked just two months later from Sydney harbour on 20 Oct 1914. His Unit the 4th Bn. Australian Infantry set sail aboard the Transporter A14 Euripides After a brief stop in Albany, Western Australia, the battalion proceeded to Egypt, arriving on 2 December. The battalion took part in the Anzac landing on 25 April 1915 as part of the second and third waves. Robert died on 29 May 1914 and is buried at the 4th Battalion Parade Ground Cemetery, Turkey.

Rifleman THOMAS McELHONE

Thirty-six-year-old Rifleman Thomas Stephen McElhone of the 4th Reinforcements 4th Bn. H Company Otago Regiment was living in Ugbrooke, Blenhein, New Zealand with his sister Annie and was working as a labourer when he signed up to serve with the ANZAC's.

Thomas had been born and brought up in Walker, his parents Hugh and Rose still lived on Walker Road. Thomas's sister Annie had sailed to Australia on 11 Nov 1911 on the Waipara, and from there she had travelled on to New Zealand. She must have been enjoying life on the other side of the world as three years late on 24 Jul 1914 Thomas boarded the Corinthic and began his journey across the oceans. Arriving likely early September.

Back in his native Newcastle Thomas had a variety of jobs, from Postman, to being a waiter at the Union Club on Westgate Road, to being a fitter. His father Hugh's occupation on the 1901 census is described as being a 'Corporation Scavenger!'

In New Zealand Thomas got himself a laboring job and was doing quite nicely. Whether he was called up or volunteered isn't clear, but I would think that due to his age and very likely patriotism towards his homeland – he would have volunteered.

Less than two years after arriving in New Zealand, Thomas boarded the 'Tofua' on 27 May 1916 and headed back to England with his unit – destination Plymouth. It is very unlikely that he would have had an opportunity to see his family as the likelihood his unit would have entrained along the coast and then straight across the channel to France from Southampton, Portsmouth or Dover. The 4th Otaga Regiment arrived in France just as the 'Big Push' of 1st July 1916 was in preparation.

Thomas survived the 'Big Push' – but was killed on 15th October 1916 and is buried at Warlencourt Cemetery on the edge of the Somme battlefield.

TILL THE BOYS COME HOME (3).

Over seas there came a pleading, "Help a nation in distress!"
And we gave our glorious laddies: honour bade us do no less;
For no gallant son of Britain to a foreign yoke shall bend,
And no Englishman is silent to the sacred call of friend.

WW1 postcard.

The Joicey boys Joseph and John. A/L/Cpl Gunner **JOHN JOICEY** a former 'Machine man' at Walker Colliery. John attested at Elswick, Newcastle upon Tyne on 12 Dec 1915 and was mobilised on 2 Feb 1917 aged 21. He joined the Royal Horse and Royal Field Artillery and was posted to a number of Batteries and Brigades when fighting in France. John was fined 10 days loss of pay in August 1917 when he overstayed home leave by 5 days. In October 1918, he was admitted to hospital in Newcastle upon Tyne with cellulitis of the neck and was there until early December when he was returned to duty overseas. In May 1919, he was posted overseas to the Black Sea and Constantinople.

John lived at 8 Diamond Row, Walker, with his father and three sisters. Another sister lived at number 12. Brother Private **JOSEPH JOICEY** of the 12th Bn. Northumberland Fusiliers
was killed on 13th July 1916 aged 22 and is remembered on the THIEPVAL MEMORIAL France.

Brothers **JOHN** and **JAMES ENGLISH**, formerly of 41 Mitchell Street, Walker. Died within months of each other. John died of wounds aged 21, on 15 Sept 1916 whilst serving with the 5th Bn. Northumberland Fusiliers. Elder brother James had been killed five months previously on 14 April 1916. They left behind five sisters and a brother, both parents already having died. One sister was living in America. James left behind a wife and son – two children having died in infancy – one, a son, also named James dying only 2 days prior to his fathers' death and before the news could reach the battlefront.

The **GOODWIN** brothers **GEORGE**, **THOMAS** and **LEVISON**, all lost their lives in the Great War. They were the sons of the late John and Sarah Goodwin, of 53, Mitchell St., Walker, Newcastle-on-Tyne. Thomas was the first to be killed, while serving with the West Yorkshire Regiment (Prince of Wales Own) in Gallipoli, Turkey, on 9 Ag 1915, aged 24.

On 31 Dec of the same year, elder brother Levison was killed whilst serving with the 5th Bn. Northumberland Fusiliers in Flanders. He left behind a wife, Margaret Goodwin of 16, Mitchell St., Walker-on-Tyne. He is buried at Railway Dugouts burial ground, Belgium.

In September 1916 the only brother left (other than for Hugh who wasn't old enough to fight) was killed. George, who was with the 1/6th Northumberland Fusiliers, joined his brothers on 15 Sept 1916 and is remembered on the Thiepval Memorial, France.

John and Sarah had 12 children, 3 dying of illness in childhood. Here another 3 were taken by a war.....

Private's **WILLIAM** and **ROBERT HELLENS** were brother, both living River View, Walker. Robert who lived at number 28, was killed in May 1915 aged 30, whilst serving with the 1/5th Northumberland Fusiliers. He left behind a wife Mary. He has no known grave and is remembered on the Ypres (Menin Gate) Memorial, Belgium.

 William was un-married and residing at 50 River View, joined the Army Service Corps in October 1915 at the age of 42. He is described as 5 feet 4 inches tall with a chest measurement of 37 inches with an expansion of a further 2 inches. William was in France form 30 Oct 1915 until 14 July 1918, transferring to the Labour Corps 30 Oct 1917. On 23 Mar 1917, he was awaiting trial and was later convicted by the C.S.M of while on war service of drunkenness (illegible) resulting in 70 days (illegible.) It is likely due to this misdemeanour that he was transferred to the Labour Corps.

William was discharged to his fathers' address; 33 Ropley Rd, Deptford, Sunderland after his discharge on 7 Jan 1919 as he is no longer fit for war service having "chronic *rheumatism and defective vision.*"

In 1933 he asks the Army for a copy of his discharge papers, the original having been stolen when his father's house was 'broken up' after his death and William being away. He states he did not report the theft to the Police.

The Visit (Long awaited.) Guillemont Road cemetery.

Well, here we are, all lined up neat and tidy, ready for our visitors –
if they come. We don't have many these days. Don't know why? We
used to get quite a few, but they've died off now.

When it happened they kept us out in the field for a while. It wasn't
safe to bring us in. They did finally get us here, cleaned us up and
gave us a decent place to rest.

We are looked after well, they're always brightening the place up
with plants and flowers – they are really for the benefit of the
visitors - it keeps them happy.

Harry's niece came to visit a while back. She brought some crocuses,
said they'd look nice in the spring. Cheered him up no end. Thought
they'd forgotten all about him! "Course not!" I said. "They'll not
forget us – will they?"

Turnpike's brother (forget his name now) used to come and visit.
We'd been in the same battalion, the same trench... Anyway,
stopped coming. His health wasn't what it used to be.

Once thought I heard a fellow mention my name – he looked
vaguely familiar around the eyes, but I couldn't place him. He
slowed as he walked past and gave a look as if to say "Poor chap,
never mind". Didn't see if he found who he was looking for. Shame,
it would've been nice to have had a visitor.

Wyndham and Asquith, they get plenty of visitors – and don't know
any of them! Rank and who you know counts for a lot. Hope I do
get a visitor. A relative would be nice, 'course they'll be busy I
suppose, with their families and things...

A soldier of the Great War
Known unto God

Helen Charlesworth

Unknown soldier and wife (Author's own collection.)

The young Subaltern.
We're off to fight in the war,
Gun-ho!
We're off to fight in the war.

We'll fight the Boche,
Take all his dosh.
Then send him off home to his Mum!

I'll rattle my gun
Have lots of fun,
And pot a few Hun before lunch.

These billets are stark,
It's not such a lark.
Hurry up: get us out to the front!

The bully is bland,
Please do lend a hand -
Send out some seed cake for tea?

It's cold and it's wet.
'Be over by Christmas' they bet.
So why still here March '17?

The skies are ablaze
With the sickening haze
Of gunfire cordite and Gas (Gas Gas!)

The noise overhead,
Fills me with dread;

My nerves are all tattered and torn.

My old pal Fred,
I fear is dead.
He bought it at half past three.

We're here to fight in this war.
 Gun-ho!
We're here to fight in this war.
Oh, give us a Blighty,
Lord Almighty.
And get us away from the Hun!

Helen Charlesworth

The Geordie Antipodeans.

Private **ROBERT MARTIN**

Bob Martin was a member of the 7th Bn. Australian Imperial Force (Raised in Victoria, Australia)

The 7th Battalion was among the first infantry units raised for the AIF during the First World War. It was recruited from across the state of. Victoria by Lieutenant Colonel H. E. "Pompey" Elliott within a fortnight of the declaration of war in August 1914 and embarked just two months later. After a brief stop in Albany, Western Australia, the battalion proceeded to Egypt, arriving on 2 December. Bob lost his life on 25th Feb 1915 due to complications of injuries sustained in an 'accident' the previous day.

Bob Martin wasn't a true Aussie – he had been born in Walker and raised in Elswick. He went to Armstrong Road school and was still living in Elswick when the 1911 census was taken – aged 25, sharing home with his parents Robert and Margaret and four of his seven surviving siblings (of the twelve children born to Robert and Margaret) and was working as a general labourer.

Bob had spent a number of years serving with the Northumberland Royal Engineers, volunteers, when living in Elswick.

At a time when people were looking to expanding their opportunities in life and make something of themselves, Bob and his sister Margeurite decided to 'up sticks' and emigrate to Australia. They had heard the stories of people having land and freedom and there being no shortage of work – it sounded ideal. Had they already decided to what part of Australia they planned to live? Did they already have relatives out there? Many Northumbrians had previously moved to New South Wales, where they had set up townships called Newcastle, Wallsend, Morpeth etc - named after where they had originated from in England.

I can't find a record of Bob emigrating to Australia between 1911 and 1914 – but I am assured by records he arrived there in 1911 and at the time of enlistment on 17 Aug 1914 he was living at 74 Windsor Street.

Footscray Victoria and working as a general labourer. His next of Kin was listed as Rita Martin (Marguerite – his sister) of Wingfield Street, Footscray. Victoria.

His unit embarked from Melbourne, Victoria on board Transport A20 Hororataon on 19th October 1914.

He was described by those who knew him as "interested in soldiering for his country. Also, he was an excellent marksman and one time and keenly interested in all branches of sport."

Private **ROBERT SOWERBY**

Robert Sowerby was living at 78 City Road, Sydney, New South Wales when he enlisted to the Australian Army on 24 Aug 1914. He was working locally as a groom. Robert had emigrated to Australia in 1912 aged 16. He had boarded the 'Themistocles' in London on 12 Sept 1912 and disembarked in Sydney, approximately 6 weeks later.

He is described as being a native of Allendale Victoria – did he live here previously to moving to Sydney? Robert was born in Cumberland but was brought up in Walker, living at 15 Byker Terrace, a house owned by and also occupied by his grandfather William, who was and Insurance Agent and building society worker. Robert's father Matthew, a school master and mother Margaret also lived there along with Robert and his siblings. By 1911 mother Margaret was a widow. His Grandfather was 84 and living by independent means. Brother William 21, was a Marine Engineer, sister Maggie 19, was helping out at home. Mary aged 17 was a student at Rutherford College and little sister Wilhelmina was still at school. Robert was a farm labourer – maybe he emigrated to Australia because he wasn't academic like the rest of the family. Possibly he preferred working with his hands and on the land. If that was the case then Australia

Articles reported in the Newcastle Journal 1914 - 1917 relating to Walker.

Friday 2nd October 1914 - A meeting of the Housing Committee of the Newcastle Corporation was held yesterday, when reports were adopted recommending the erection of workmen's dwellings at St. Lawrence and City Road; also on the Walker estate of the Corporation near Armstrong's Works. About 300 people will be accommodated by the St. Lawrence and City Road scheme, and about 1000 on the walker Estate. At the latter place the houses will be detached and semi-detached, and the rentals will vary according to the size of the houses which will be provided with gardens, and allotments will be near at hand. The rents will not be more than 7s 3d per week at the other places they will range from 4s upwards. The scheme, it has been estimated will cost about £66,000.

Tuesday 20th October 1914 - Mr Alfred Appleby, City Coroner, held an inquest at the Central Police Station in Newcastle last night concerning the death of John Thomas Graham, two years of age, son of John Graham, a painter of Walker Road, who is at present serving with Lord Kitchener's Army. The child was knocked down and killed by a tramcar in Walker Road on Saturday night.
Joseph Smith, a pit sinker, of Walker Road, said he was standing at his own front door when he saw the child cross the road. The car was going slowly, and the witness was of the opinion that the driver did not see the child, as he could have pulled up before the child was knocked down.
The jury returned a verdict of 'accidental death' and attached no blame to the motorman.

(November 1914) Information has been conveyed to Mrs Moody, of 37, Glue Terrace, Elswick, that her husband, Private John Robert Moody, has been killed in action in France. Private Moody, after serving in the ranks of the King's Own Yorkshire Light Infantry, stationed at Pontefract, was employed for several years at Armstrong Whitworth's shipyards at Elswick, and at the time he was called up with the reserves, he was engaged at the Walker shipyards. He was also chairman of No.2 branch of the Gas Works Society. He leaves a widow and five children, the eldest being 13 years and the youngest 2 years.

Thursday 17th December 1914 - Recruits for the Reserve Battalion of the 5th Battalion Northumberland Fusiliers have been coming in freely during the last few days. There are still vacancies for good men between the ages of 19 and 38, who are willing to go abroad, in the new companies being formed at Walker and Wallsend. Application should be made at the Depot on Church Street, Walker or at the Drill Hall, Wallsend, where full information can be obtained

Saturday 5th December 1914 – Fatal fall on a ship- An inquest was held at the Central Police Station, Newcastle, last night, before Alfred Appleby, City Coroner, touching the death of a plater's helper named Charles Buggie (49) who died at his residence, Byker Street, Walker, on Thursday night. The evidence showed that on Tuesday last, while Buggie was following his employment at the Neptune Yard of Messrs Swan, Hunter, and Wigham Richardson, he fell from a plank on to a tank top, a distance of about eight feet. Dr Appleby stated that he made a post mortem examination of the body of the deceased, and found that he had been suffering from a heart disease of long standing. He might have turned faint and fell from the plank, or he might have slipped. He found no marks of violence. The jury returned a verdict in accordance with the medical testimony.

On 4th December 1914 the Riveters and Holders-up at Sir W.G
Armstrong, Whitworth and Co Ltd donated £3 4s 2d for the
Belgian Refugee Fund

13th December 1914 - an inquest was held into the death of
George Little (15) of Monk Street, Gateshead, who met his
death on Sunday 12th Dec, whilst in employment at Walker
Naval Yard owned by Armstrong, Whitworth and Co Ltd.
John William Short, foreman riveter said of 84 Eighton Street,
Byker, said that on Sunday afternoon he was proceeding
along the jetty of a ship's berth when he saw Little going up a
ladder on to a staging of the ship. It was a 50ft ladder and was
standing on four planks about 2ft from the ground. The boy
was carrying two dozen bolts weighing about one stone. He
fell from the ladder and the witness found him lying face
downwards on the gantry below. His head was injured, and
witness was of the opinion that he had been killed
instantaneously.
Francis H.B. Spencer a holder-up said he saw Little, climbing
the ladder. He was holding a bag in his left hand, and was
grasping the outside of the ladder with his right hand. Little
was about 35ft. from the ground when he suddenly fell off the
ladder.
In answer to the coroner, Little's father said he had been
informed that his son had worked from Friday morning until
midday Saturday and then resumed work on Sunday
morning. The coroner remarked that the accident was
probably due to overwork, but in the present extraordinary
conditions they could not say anything. A verdict of
accidental death was returned.

Monday 22nd March 1915 – 5th BATT. NORTHUMBERLAND
FUSILIERS.
The 'Fifth of the Fifth' have been rewarded for their special
recruiting efforts made during the past few weeks. Men have
been coming in freely at Headquarters, Walker, Newcastle,

and for the detachments at Wallsend, Gosforth and West Moor. There are still several hundred needed for this old-established and highly efficient corps, and it is hoped that those who have 'looked on' during the past seven months will now come forward and fill the ranks so that the 1st Line Battalion, who are trained and ready, may be free to go to the front.

This battalion has been fortunate in having one of the latest Salano targets fitted up at Walker where they already have an excellent miniature range, in addition to one at Wallsend Drill Hall, whilst the 2nd Line Battalion based at Seaton Delaval, possess both an indoor and outdoor range, which are always fully employed in teaching recruit's musketry.

A large number of the N.C.O's have attended a course in musketry during the past month or two, and are fully qualified to teach musketry based on the experience of the present war.

Recruits can be fitted out in uniform and equipment, etc, on the day they join us.

Monday 3rd May 1915 – Mr Alfred Appleby, city coroner, held an inquest at Newcastle Infirmary on Saturday, on William Elliot Purvis (55) a plater, who resided in Foster Street, Low Walker and who died in the institution on Friday, as a result of injuries received whilst following his employment at Messrs Armstrong, Whitworth, and Company's works at Low Walker. The evidence showed that on Tuesday last, Purvis was standing on the stage of the main deck of a vessel guiding a plate which was being lowered into the hold. The wind caught the plate, swung it round, and it struck Purvis, knocking him in to the hold, a distance of about 20 feet. He was seriously injured about the head, and was removed to Newcastle Infirmary where he died from compression of the brain – the jury returned a verdict of "accidental death."

Thursday 6th May 1915 – 5th Northumberland Fusiliers. Wounded – Private John Mullroy, White Street, Walker. Private L Gustarel*, and Private McCarthy, both of Walker. Private Nicholas Atkinson 45, Park Road Wallsend. Private T. Barnes 31, Laurel Street, Wallsend. Private Joseph Pearson, Annitsford.

Royal Engineers, wounded – Sapper William Storey, Low Walker. Sapper R.R. White, Lemington.

*There was a Gustard family living at Back White Street on the 1911 census. Could this be their eldest son James who would now be 20? I think most likely and the error was down to poor writing!

Friday 7th May 1915 Wounded 5th Northumberland Fusiliers – Lieut H.T Richardson, Gosforth. Private John Purvis, Mitchell Street, Walker. Signaller Alex. Brumwell, St Anthony's.

Saturday 8th May 1915 BETTING PROSECUTION. Benjamin Irving (39) of Gateshead, was fined £5 by the Newcastle magistrates, yesterday, on a charge of having loitered in Welbeck Road, Walker on Thursday afternoon.

Wednesday 19th May 1915 - Mrs Woodman of 44 Back Church Street, Walker, has received word that her husband George Woodman, Royal Naval Division, has been wounded.

21 May 1915 - There was a large attendance of parents and friends of the scholars at the East Walker Council schools, Welbeck Road, yesterday, when Empire Day was celebrated. The programme included songs, hymns, part-songs etc. by the children. There was an address by Sir Walter Plummer and later in the afternoon the flags of the school, the city of Newcastle, Belgium, France, Russia and Great Britain were un-furled in the playground.

Saturday 22 May 1915 - At Walker Parish Church, the marriage took place of Dr R.H. Herdman Newton R.N, elder son of Mr Herdman Newton of 3, Eglington Crescent, Edinburgh, and Miss Kathleen Wardroper, youngest daughter of Rev A.S Wardroper and Mrs Wardroper of Walker. The officiating clergy at the service which was fully choral, were the Rev A.S. Wardroper (father of the bride) and the Rev S.T Waugh. The bride was given away by her brother Lieut. A.K Wardroper. She wore a quaint frock of ivory net and chiffon taffetas, the simple net bodice veiling over a corsage of shimmering silver tissue, whilst the short, full net skirt looked sweet, bordered with scallops of the taffetas. The waist was also defined with taffetas scallops. Over the pretty frock fell a Brussels tulle veil, arranged over a coronet of orange blossom, which completed a singularly effective toilette.

Monday 7th June 1915 – 5th Northumberland Fusiliers – wounded. Private Ed. Johnson of 70, Byker Street, Walker 5th N.F has been wounded and action and gassed, and is now in hospital in Sunderland Private R. Davidson, 5th N.F, of Newcastle has been gassed.
6th Northumberland Fusiliers. Mr Jonas Smith of Diamond Row, Walker Colliery, has been informed that his son, Private Jonas W. Smith 6th N.F has been wounded in action and in hospital at Maidstone, Kent.

Tuesday 1st June 1915 – 5th Northumberland Fusiliers – wounded. Mr and Mrs Fairclough, of 114, Byker Street, Walker, have received information that their son, Private George Fairclough, No 2536, 5th N.F, has been wounded and is now in hospital.

Thursday 10th June 1915 - A girl named Mary E. Hill, 11 years of age, of Angus Buildings, Low Walker, was admitted into the Newcastle Infirmary last evening suffering from burns about her body, caused through having come into contact with the live rail on the Riverside branch of the North-Eastern Railway at Low Walker.

In June 1915 the Armstrong Whitworth and Co, Ltd Workmen, Foreman, and time keeper and office staff made their 9th donation to the 'War relief fund' of £110 2s 4d.
Thursday 17th June 1915 – 5th BATALLION NORTHUMBERLAND FUSILIERS. A second appeal. (To the Editor.)
Long Benton Camp, Forest Hall. Newcastle.
Sir – Last autumn I appealed to those interested in this battalion to provide me with comforts – or means to purchase such – for the men under my command, who were then at Gosforth Park undergoing training to fit them for the Front. They left Blyth on 20th April this year for France, and were put practically straight in to the firing line, where they have undergone great hardships and distinguished themselves highly.
I have received letters from both field and company officers detailing deeds of the utmost heroism
And valour on part of the men, both individually and collectively. Through the generosity of my friends and subscribers of last year, I have been able to them comfort in the field. I have sent out nearly 1000 pairs of socks in the past eight weeks, hundreds of shirts and towels, as well as large quantities of soap, tobacco, cigarettes etc; but my stock is diminishing, and I appeal once more to the generosity of the friends of the battalion in Newcastle and Tyneside for further assistance.
Major Luhrs writes:
 "Socks are always acceptable; shirts badly wanted, khaki shirts and handkerchiefs of same colour required by the hundred."

I am sure I need say no more! Parcels and cheques should be addressed to me at the Drill Hall, Walker, Newcastle and the latter made payable to Major Myles.
D.R. MACDONALD Lieut-Colonel.
5th battalion Northumberland Fusiliers.

Thursday 1st July 1915 – Killed – Private Martin Murray, 5th N.F of 150, Byker Street, Walker, was killed in action on June 18.

Saturday 10th July 1915. 5th Northumberland Fusiliers.
Mrs F.Stoddart. 1327 Walker Road, St Anthony's, Newcastle, would be glad to hear and news of her husband Serg.t C. Stobbart No:166. B Company, 5th Northumberland Fusiliers. Missing since 24 May.

In August 1915 the Riveters and Holder-up men from Armstrong Whitworth's Walker shipyard, contributed £10 to the Belgian refugee's fund.

Saturday 7th August 1915 reports the death of Walker barman Michael Fitzpatrick, aged 26.

James O'Brien of 104 Middle Street, Walker said he and Fitzpatrick were both barmen at the Stag Hotel in Walker. On the Saturday night, they had some pork sandwiches to eat and made their way up to Shields Road, and when nearing Albion Row, a woman bumped into Fitzpatrick and using foul language said 'Can't you look where you are going?' Fitzpatrick told her to use better language in the street, he then made a squeak sound in his throat, which was possibly taken as an insult by the woman. A soldier then came over and said to Fitzpatrick that if the lady was with him he ought to teach her better language. The soldier then turned to

Mr Edward Clark said the defendants had absented themselves from their employment without having given proper notice. The claim of 5s per day against each defendant was only nominal. It was necessary at present that as much work as possible should be done in the pits, so that there would be no shortage of coal for war purposes. The manager of the colliery had had notices posted up in the yard. The first one was as follows "Workmen at Walker Colliery; At a general meeting of colliery owners and workmen held at London in London on July 29, the Minister of Munitions asked that every effort should be put forward to increase output of coals. The workmen's representatives promised that this should be done. Are you doing so? During the week ended 7 August, ten hewers worked only 2 days, 32 hewers worked three days, 86 hewers worked four days and 36 hewers worked five days. To which section do you belong?" Other notices were posted up from time to time, drawing the attention of the men to the seriousness of the matter of lost time, but as things did not improve they were bound to bring the men to court.

Friday 10th September 1915 – MISSING. Private M. Hicks Hackett, of the N.F. has been missing since August 11 at the Dardanelles. Any news concerning him will be gladly received by his parents Mr and Mrs Hackett, 1563 Walker Road. Newcastle.

Tuesday 12 October 1915 Mrs McCue of 120, Fisher Street, Walker has received notice that herb son, Private Frank McCue 8th East Yorks, B Company, has been killed in action.

Saturday 12th November 1915 -Elijah Thompson died aged 42, a caulker of 52 North Street, Milburn Place, North Shields, died at Walker Naval Yard (Messrs. Armstrong, Whitworth and Co Ltd) on Wednesday 10th November 1915. Thompson was working on some staging whilst employed in the construction of a ship. To reach the staging he had to cross a plank 11 inches wide and placed 12 feet above the ground. His body was later found immediately under the area where he had been working - face down and with his face in a hole in the ground. When the accident occurred, there was between 6 and 7 feet of water underneath the staging and his body had been submerged until the tide had receded. The jury returned a verdict that Thompson had fallen into the water while suffering an epileptic fit and had drowned.

Thursday 28th October 1916 –TO CLOSE AN ESTATE.
Lot 2 No's 53, 55 and 57, Lamb Street Walker. One house in tenements, comprising ten rooms, occupied by five tenants. Gross annual rental £45 10s. Large yard, wash-house and the usual conveniences. Leasehold, 75 years from 25th March 1874. Annual ground rent £3 10s.
Lot 3 – No's 112, 114, and 116 Byker Street, Walker. One house, in tenements, occupied by four tenants, comprising ten rooms, two yards, wash-house, and the usual conveniences. Gross annual rental £45 10s. Leasehold 75 years from 29th September 1878. Annual ground rent, £3 3s 10d.
Lot 4 – No's 102, 104, 106 Church Street, Walker. Self-contained house of five rooms, bathroom, two attics, scullery, and yard, with usual conveniences. Gross annual rent £67 12s. Leasehold 75 years from 25th March 1850. Annual ground rent £4 6s.
Lot 5 – No's 206, 208, 210 Church Street, Walker. One house, in tenements, occupied by six tenants, comprising ten rooms, large yard, two wash-houses, and conveniences. Gross annual rental £49 8s. Leasehold 64 years from 25th September 1864. Annual ground rent £2 17s.

one of the women who was with him and said "I have only one hand, but I can beat him." Fitzpatrick told the soldier he didn't want any bother. He then received a blow and fell to the ground. The witness could not say whether the soldier used his fist or not. He said he had known Fitzpatrick since his schooldays and that he was not in the habit of taking to drink and was sober on the night in question. The witness did not know the soldier.

David McKenna, a labourer of 19, Denmark Street, Byker said he heard the civilians and the soldier come up. He said Fitzpatrick never attempted to retaliate and the two men with him held his arms back in case he should commence to fight. The soldier struck him on the left side of his face. The soldier then went away. The witness was told that the Fitzpatrick had made a squeak sound in his throat, which may have been construed as an insult by the soldier's wife.

Dr Baumgartner, a police surgeon examined the body later that evening. He said that the blow was not enough to cause death, though there was a bruise on the man's face. His face was blackened as though he had been choked. Some of the partially digested food had been drawn up into his windpipe and he was suffocated. This is likely what had caused the squeak in his throat.

*James Lant of the Northumberland Fusiliers stated to be home from the front owing to wounds, has been charged with manslaughter and will be brought before the magistrates on Monday.

James Carr, a labourer of 182, Albion Row and George Craighill, a hawker of Dalton Street also gave evidence.

P.C James Duffy said he found Fitzpatrick in a state of collapse and Dr Gibson, who was passing, pronounced life extinct. With the assistance of another police constable his body was removed to a nearby livery stable.

Tuesday 10th August 1915. James Lant of 82, Shipley Street, a private in the Northumberland Fusiliers, was charged on remand at Newcastle Police court, yesterday, with having caused the death of Michael Fitzpatrick, a barman, in Shields Road, Byker, on 31st July.

Mr V. B Bateson stated that James O'Brien, a barman, employed at the Stack Hotel, Walker, was in company with Fitzpatrick on the night in question, and they appeared to have an ambulatory sort of meal, which consisted of two port sandwiches, ice-cream, lemonade, pineapple chunks and a bowl of peas. While in the neighbourhood of Albion Row, two women passed them. One collided with Fitzpatrick, and the woman then said "Look where you are going to." Apparently, the soldier (accused) was behind the woman. Fitzpatrick retorted something which was regarded as offensive. The accused who was carrying a child, then said to the woman "Ere, take hold of the child. I have only one arm but I can beat him." A struggle ensued, deceased was knocked to the ground, and was apparently knocked out. There was no direct testimony of any blows having been struck in the struggle. A post-mortem examination had been held and the jury at the inquest had arrived at a verdict of death by misadventure, after hearing the medical evidence and had not considered the question of provocation. That was not sufficient. The man had a full stomach and had vomited in the struggle. A blow from the hand or knee in the abdomen would cause Fitzpatrick to gasp, and probably the vomit had gone down the windpipe and caused suffocation.

Dr Baumgartner, Police surgeon, who had conducted the post-mortem, said he saw the deceased soon after his death. In his opinion, the struggle was not sufficient to cause death, and most probably a blow was struck.

Mr F. E Forster said he did not agree with the deductions of his friend. There would be a complaint as to the amount of provocation.

The accused was remanded till Friday, bail being allowed in his own recognisances.

*Pte James Lant, 1893 – 1950, married Annie Fairley in 1913. Born Byker, Newcastle upon Tyne. James was a'ships marker' out of work on the 1911 census, living at Belvedere Street, Byker, with his parents and three siblings.
Service number 3/8202, James served with the 1st, 12th, 8th, 1/5th, 1st and then 8th Northumberland Fusiliers during the Great War. He received the British War Medal and Victory Medal

The Derby Daily Telegraph, Friday 27th August 1915 ran the following story.
Private James Lant of the Northumberland Fusiliers who had been on remand for a month, charged with the manslaughter of Michael Fitzpatrick, was discharged by the Newcastle magistrates on Thursday. Lant who was on furlough, having been wounded at Hill 60, had taken offence at a remark which he had imagined had been made to Mrs Lant whilst passing in the street and struck Fitzpatrick, who afterwards died.
The evidence at the inquest however, showed that Fitzpatrick's death was due to suffocation, following sickness due to overeating.

24th August 1915 – SALE OF DESIRABLE INVESTMENTS TO CLOSE TWO TRUSTED ESTEATES……. Lot 3 – No's 56 and 58, Foster Street, Walker. Leasehold dwelling House in flats, containing 2 rooms and scullery downstairs, 3 rooms, attic and scullery upstairs, with separate yards and out-offices. Gross annual rent £28 12.s 0d. This property is held on lease for an unexpired term of 57 years at an annual ground rent of £2 1s 6d.

Saturday 4th September 1916 – DEATH OF MR 'TIM' PURVIS – We regret to announce the death of Mr Thomas Purvis, the well-known Tyneside sculler, which took place yesterday morning at the Newcastle Royal Infirmary as the result of an accident. About three months ago the deceased slipped down some stairs at his residence 2, Foster Street, Walker and injured his spine. He was removed to the Infirmary where his death took place as stated yesterday. Though he was only 52 years of age, deceased was popularly known in the local sculling world as 'Old Tim' Purvis. He was a native of Walker and a caulker in the shipbuilding trade. In his teens boat rowing on the Tyne was one of the principal sports of the people......Deceased leaves a widow and a family of five sons and three daughters. The funeral is announced to take place at Walker tomorrow.

Thursday 9th September 1916 – Mr and Mrs Thompson of Eastbourne Avenue, Walker have received news that their son, Seaman Harold Thompson, of the Royal Naval Division, has been wounded at the Dardanelles.

Friday 10th September 1915 _ At Newcastle Police Court, yesterday five men- Luke Craigs of 66 Benson Road; Septimus Walker, 18, Brough Street; William Hall 1678 Walker Road; William Hardy, 44 Fisher Street; Thomas Marshall, 255 Benson Road, employed by the Walker Coal Company - were charged with a breach of contract by having absented themselves from their employment on various dates during August and September. The damages claimed against the men were; Craigs £1 10s; Walker £1 5s; Hall £2; Hardy £1 15s, Marshall £1 - the damages being assessed as 5s per day per man.

Thursday 2nd December 1915. An inquest was held last night in to the death of John Donnelly (38) a plater's helper of 2, St Mary's Place, Walker, who died on Monday as a result of injuries received on November 15th, whilst following his employment at the yard of Messrs William Dobson and Co. Walker.

Robert Thirlway Arkley, yard manager, residing at 54, Station Road, Willington Quay, said that on November 15th he instructed Donnelly, along with other men, to remove three beams from the beam yard to the stem of a ship in the course of construction. The beams, which were about 47 ft. long each weighted 12cwt. The particular derrick which was being used to raise the beams was about 20ft out of the centre of the bogie, which it was stated was 18ft long. The bogie was 20ft. from the derrick, and, as a safeguard, a guide rope was fixed to the load, which consisted of three beams. This rope was wound round a bollard and gradually slackened, after the load was lifted until the rope of the derrick was plumb. Witness afterwards found that the rope, which was practically new, had broken. | Donnelly was usually in charge of the guide rope, but on this occasion a man named Chambers was doing the work.

Michael Chambers, a plater's helper, living at Walker said he was one of the squad engaged on the work. Donnelly told him to put the guide rope once round each head of the bollard, and after about 18in. had been run out, the rope suddenly snapped. Witness admitted that this was the first time he had done such a job, and from a demonstration he gave on a small model of a bollard, it appeared that he had put the rope on in such a manner as to lock it, and this prevent it from slipping freely. Consequently, with heavy pressure at each end of the rope, it was bound to break.

Death was due to a fracture of the skull and laceration of the brain, and the jury returned a verdict of 'accidental death.'

Another estate:

Lot 6 – No's 92-94, 96-98, 100-102, White Street, Low Walker (known as Carlings Buildings.) Three houses in flats, each containing two and three rooms, wash-house yard and the usual conveniences common to the two tenants. Gross annual rental £63 14s. Leasehold 75 years from 29th September 883. Annual ground rent £7 2s 6d.

Thursday 4th November 1915 Councillor J.W and Mrs. Proctor of Church Street, Walker, have received intimation that their son, Private John William Proctor of the 2nd N.F is posted missing. Councillor Proctor would be grateful for any news concerning him.

Saturday 6th November 1915 –WALKER MAN PRISONER. Mrs Stewart, 74, Foster Street, Walker, has received information that her husband, Corporal J.W. Stewart KOSB has been taken prisoner of war and has lost his right arm.

Monday 8th November 1915 John Thomas Terry, son of Mrs. Bradley, Mitchell Street, Walker has died from wounds received at the Dardanelles.

Tuesday 9th November 1915 Mrs. M. Cowe of Church Street, Walker has received an intimation that her nephew, Sergeant T. Reed, 2nd N.F has been wounded, and is at present in Birmingham hospital.

Tuesday 9th November 1915 Mr and Mrs McDaid of 70 Fisher Street, Low Walker, have received information that their son, Private H McDaid, A company, 12th N.F is missing.

Tuesday 14th December 1915 – Killed – Mrs Reynolds of 16, East Terrace, Walker, has received information that her husband, Private John Reynolds, 9th N.F was killed in action on November 20th.

Saturday 1st January 1916 - The landslide at St. Anthony's - On and from Monday, 3rd January, St. Anthony's Station will be temporarily closed. The passenger trains via Riverside Branch, which at present leave for Tynemouth at 38 minutes past the hour, will leave at 48 minutes past the hour.

21 January 1916 - an inquest was held into the death of Daniel McCarthy aged 66 a shipwright of Dibley Street, Byker, who died at Walker accident hospital on Thursday 20th January 1916 following an accident at Messrs. Dobson & Co shipyards. Thomas Rainford, a shipwright of 65, Mitchell Street, Walker, said that at 6.30am on Wednesday, McCarthy along with witness and other men, was working on the bulk head of a ship in the course of construction. It was very dark and the men were using naptha lamps. Fifteen feet from where McCarthy was working there was a hatchway, which was 32 feet long by 18 feet wide. Barring a small section, the hatchway was covered. At around 7am the witness saw the figure of a man disappear through the open section. He went down the ladder into the hold and found McCarthy bleeding from the mouth, lying on top of a tank. He had fallen 24 feet. John Newbury, the foreman, said the hatch had been covered the previous night and it was common place for men to walk over it. The witness was of the opinion that the light at that time was sufficient for the safety of the workmen and a verdict of accidental death was returned.

6th July 1915 - the death of Mr Dixon Cowie of Westbourne Ave, Walker, the general treasurer of the Northumberland Colliery Mechanic's Union - a position he had held since 1897, prior to which he was president. His official connection with the association as committeeman, president and treasurer extended over 30 years. Internment to take place July 7th 1915 at 3.30pm.

Tuesday 1st February 1916 - Mystery of the S.S. APPAM. We learn that amongst the passengers on the Elder-Dempster liner Appam, was Mr Edwin Watson of Walker, who was returning on leave from Nigeria, where he held an appointment under the company. Mr Watson was married about two years ago to the sister of Mr J.W Singlehurst of Wallsend and is well known in Walker and district where much anxiety is manifested as to his safety.

Wounded – News has been received by Mr and Mrs McNally, of 82, Fisher Street, Walker, that their youngest son, Farrier Arthur McNally (No 1327) 5th N.F has been wounded. His elder brother Joseph was wounded in April last year, and is now in action again.

Royal Engineers – died from wounds – Mrs Smith, of 5, Western Glower, Low Walker, has received information that her husband, Corporal A. Smith, Royal Engineers, has died from wounds received in action.

2nd February 1916 an inquest was held into the death of Richard Hobbs, aged about 56 and who was staying at McCoy's lodging house, Walker and was fatally injured when knocked down by a tramcar the previous Sunday night.

John McAndrews, a fellow lodger, said that on the Sunday night Hobbs and he went for a walk and after having five glasses of beer, they returned together. They were crossing the road arm-in-arm when a tramcar struck them, and witness was "knocked stupid." His hearing, he said was at times, not very good, and they were talking at the time.

Andrew Robert Glasgow, of 25 Eastbourne Avenue, said he was proceeding along Church Street at about 8.20pm when he heard two men talking loudly. He then noticed a tramcar going in the direction of Welbeck Road. The motorman repeatedly sounded the gong and then he heard the life-saver drop and the conductor's whistle blow. It was very dark and when the car stopped, the witness found McAndrews lying unconscious. After first-aid treatment, however he came around. The flare from the trolley showed Hobbs to be at the other end of the car. He was removed to Walker Hospital. A verdict of 'accidental death' was recorded and the driver exonerated from blame.

Tuesday 15th February 1916 – Death from wounds – Pte. David Mair 22235 5th N.F, husband of Mrs Olive Mair, of Byker Street, Walker has died from wounds.

Saturday February 19th 1916 – The annual meeting of the Walker Shipyard Ambulance Classes took place in the offices of the company, under the presidency of the captain of the corps. Mr T. Dixon. The honorary secretary (Mr Robert Sloan) read the annual report, which stated that the members attended 150 cases of accident, and two of illness within the yard, showing a decrease of 49 as compared with the previous year. The total cases in which members have rendered qualified first aid since the inception of the corps in 1891 is 4,768. The number of minor cases of accidents and bruises and the removal of foreign matters from the eyes was considerably less than that of the previous year, totalling 5,156. The following members of the corps are serving with the colours:- The Hon. Captain, Colonel D.R MacDonald, the Hon. Surgeon- Instructor, Surgeon Major F.N Grinling; Wm. Bly, David Downie, Sidney Robson, Hugh Russell, R Webster, Arthur Woods and Alex. Fenwick. It was gratifying to know that up to the end of the year no fatalities had occurred amongst them, but Fred Downie R.N.R had been interned in Germany since the fall of Antwerp, and Wm. Bly was invalided home with a broken leg.

4 March 1916 - John Harvey of 296 Church Street was killed in an accident at the Armstrong Whitworth Walker shipyard. Some men from Pearson's Works at Wallsend had been sub-contracted to fit a fan to a ship there. They raised the fan 15 feet on wire ropes which were strong enough to hold 2 tons (as had done with 2 previous fans safely.) When within 3 feet of the fixed position the rope was substituted for an independent rope which then snapped and the fan fell, crushing John Harvey (37) and another man, who were working in the boiler room below. John was injured about the head, back and legs and he succumbed the following day, Thursday 2nd March 1916.

Friday 7th April 1916. WALKER HIGHLANDER WOUNDED. Pte W Higginson, Black Watch, has been wounded.
Saturday 13th May 1916 – Private Joseph Lamb, N.F was killed in action on April 29. His widow resides at 42, Middle Street, Walker. Private Lamb was 34.

Monday 15th May 1916 - on Saturday 13th May an inquest was held in to the death of Andrew Reed (38) a shipyard worker, residing in Walker. Ellen Ann Reed, his widow, said that her husband was given to drinking and at times became very depressed. On the Friday morning, he had gone to work as usual and returned about 2p.m. slightly drunk. She later learned that he had gone out and going after him she saw him in a field at Fisher's Hill. She told her two daughters to watch over him. Soon after they came and told her that he was in a pond at Brick's Hill and two men were trying to pull him out.

Michael Rogers, with the help of another man pulled the body from the pond and applied artificial respiration without success. A verdict of 'suicide while in a depressed state of mind was returned.'

Wednesday 7th June 1916 - The housing committee of the Newcastle Corporation will submit a report to the City Council today with reference to the Walker housing scheme. The committee state that, owing to the inability of the builders to enter into contracts satisfactory to the committee for the erection within the period stipulated by the Ministry of Munitions as a condition of the Exchequer grant-in-aid for the erection of 336 dwellings approved by the council on December 6t, it has not been possible to proceed with the scheme and the Local Government Board therefore propose to cancel the sanctions issued for the borrowing of £63, 229.

Thursday 23rd June 1916 - Mrs Brown, widow of the late Mr John Brown, chemist, died at her residence, Byker Terrace, Walker, after a long illness. Mrs Brown took great interest in the Mother's meetings connected with the Walker Parish Church. She was also one of the founders and an active member of the committee of the Walker Nursing Association. She leaves a grown-up family of two sons and four daughters. The elder son Sergeant-Major R.B Brown is with the R.A.M.C abroad and the younger son W Noel, is in the Navy.

Saturday 22nd July 1916 – Wounded and ill – Private William Joicey, Parade Crescent, Walker, brother of Private J.E Joicey, Walker, who has been killed, is wounded.

Wednesday 2nd August 1916 - By permission of Colonel Dashwood and officers, the 1st Bn. Northumberland Fusiliers Band will give a concert in the Walker Park tonight. Tomorrow night, the Newcastle A.M.U Military Band will play in Elswick Park.

Friday 26th August 1916 - THREE WALKER BROTHERS KILLED. Private William Maughan, Private Archie Maughan Private Andrew Maughan, sons of the late Mr S. Maughan and Mrs Maughan, 23, Mitchell Street, Low Walker, have all been killed in action.

Monday 11th September 1916 ROYAL VICTORIA INFIRMARY _- The House Committee of the Royal Victoria Infirmary, Newcastle, acknowledge with thanks the gift of 3s Miss Sarah Dodd Mein aged 10, 192 Byker Street, Walker, being the proceeds of sale of dolls, and 22s from Mrs G.G. Robson 529, Welbeck Road, Walker & Mrs J. Smith 531, Welbeck Road, Walker being proceeds of the sale of dolls, to buy cigarettes for the wounded soldiers.

Wednesday 12th July 1916 – Private John Maddison, Walker, has been wounded.
Mrs Johnson, 48, Middle Street, Walker has received intimation that her husband, Private S Johnson has been wounded in action, and is now in hospital in London.

Wednesday 27th September 1916 – Private John W. Johnson, 117 Middle Street, Walker, killed on July 7.

Reported on 5 October 1916 - Wm. Blackburn, 86 years of age, who lived at 14, Diamond Row, Walker, was killed yesterday at the colliery level crossing at Low Walker. While passing over the line he was knocked down by a coal waggon and died almost immediately from injuries sustained.

Thursday 19th October 1916, JOHNSON – at 10, Fisher Street, Walker, on 17th inst. Aged 73 years, John Winthorp, beloved husband of the late Jane Johnson, later of Stamfordham; for 23 years with Walker and Wallsend Union Gas Company. Interment on Saturday at Walker Churchyard, cortege leaving at 2.30. All friends kindly accept this intimation. Hexham papers please copy.

Tuesday 12 December 1916 – A WOMAN'S SAD DEATH – Last night at Newcastle Infirmary, Mr Alfred Appleby held an inquiry concerning the death of Jane Ann Charlton (43) of Byker Street, Walker, who died in the institution on Sunday from burns received at her home on the previous Friday. The evidence showed the deceased's brother went to bed, leaving his sister and her daughter in the kitchen, where they slept. A few minutes later he heard his niece screaming, and on-going to the kitchen found his sister's nightdress in flames. She wrapped a sheet around herself, but that also caught fire, and he extinguished the flames with a blanket. Deceased's daughter was also burned in attempting to assist her mother, and was lying in the infirmary. His sister told him she was standing on a table to take a shawl from a window when a lighted candle she had on the table set fire to her nightdress. A verdict of "Death from burns accidentally received" was returned.

Monday 13th November 1916 – Mrs Hopkins 31, East Terrace, Low Walker, has received information that her husband, Private Edward Hopkins, previously reported missing since July 1st, is now reported killed. Previous to joining the army he worked at the Rising Sun Colliery, Wallsend.

Saturday 16th December 1916 – Unobscured lights – The following were fined at the Newcastle Police Court yesterday for not having obscured their lights in accordance with the regulations: - Joseph Adams, plater, 64, Foster Street Walker 20s………

Tuesday 9th January 1917 – GRAY. At 35, Middle Street, Walker on the 6th inst.; aged 43 years, William John, beloved husband of Catherine Gray (ex-Police) and son of the late Thomas and Euphemia Gray, late of Gallowfied, Rothbury. Interment at Heaton Cemetery on Tuesday 3.30. All friends kindly accept this intimation.

Tuesday 23 January 1917 _ Address to Walker workmen _ The series of meetings which it has been decided to hold prior to Mr Austen Chamberlain's visit next Monday, in order to explain and popularise the terms of the new War Loan to the working classes, was inaugurated yesterday, when a meeting was held at Messrs Armstrong, Whitworth and Co. works at Walker. Mr P. Docherty, one of the workmen, presided, and there was a very large attendance.
Mr Mowbray Thompson urged upon the men to put their all into the War Loan. They were living in days of artificial prosperity; wages were high, and there was plenty of money in this part of the country. But the time would come when matters would be different, and only those who had saved

Wednesday 13th June 1917 – Mrs D Bruce, Fisher Street, Low Walker has received information that her husband, Corporal Bruce, has been wounded.

Tuesday 20th March 1917 - Alleged assault - Henry Clark, who I said to be 24 years of age, was charged yesterday at the Newcastle Police Court with having assaulted, on February 21, Kate Bradford aged 19, employed as a polisher at Walker shipyards. (sister of Private JOHN R. BRADFORD 39162, 2nd Bn. Kings Own Yorkshire Light Infantry, who died aged 19 on

13th Apr 1918). Mr Edward Clark prosecuted for Sir W.G Armstrong, Whitworth and Company, and Mr Swinburn G Wilson defended accused on oath denied the charge. He said he had been married about six years and had a wife and three children and his occupation was that of a riveter. The Chairman (Mr Stephen Easton) intimated that defendant would be committed for trial - accused was remanded for the depositions to be completed. Bail was allowed. Anderson was on the corrugated iron gantry attending to the guide ropes. It was a frosty morning and the gantry was slippy. He fell and went through the glass roof. William Renshaw, who was working in the plumber's shop said the man had fallen 20 to 25 feet and was bleeding from the head. A verdict of accidental death was returned.

Monday 9th July 1917.WALKER PRESBYTARIAN CHURCH. A special service was held at the above church yesterday morning for the purpose of unveiling a Roll of Honour of members and adherents of the church. Major Rev. A E. Bray senior N.C. Chaplain. Northern Command, conducted the service. He stated that the Roll of Honour contained the names of 39 of their members and adherents who had answered their country's call; seven had been killed and seven had been wounded. Two of their members had received distinctions, Viz., Lieut Mitchell Miller Brodie M.C. and Richard Robbie M.M. The Roll of Honour was unveiled by Miss Howartson, daughter of the Rev Howartson, pastor of the church. The service concluded with the National Anthem.

Friday 14th September 1917. WALKER MINER'S DEATH. An inquest was held last night at Newcastle by Mr Alfred Appleby, city coroner, on Thomas Costello (31) miner, who lived at Walker, and was employed at Walker Colliery. The evidence was to the effect that some six months ago, while working in the pit, he strained his back lifting a tub.

A fellow workman stated that Costello told him that in addition to the sprain, a piece of stone fell on to his back, but a deputy overman stated that when Costello reported the matter to him he made no mention of the stone. There was no indication at the place that stone had fallen. Costello had not since been able to walk without a stick. He died on Tuesday last.

Professor Stewart McDonald stated that death was due to pulmonary phthisis, of longstanding and the disease was probably present at the time of the accident. In reply to Mr Weir, witness could not say whether the strain accelerated the disease. The jury returned a verdict in accordance with the medical testimony.

Friday 12th October 1917 Deaths – PIKE- At 1, Parade Crescent, Walker, on the 9th inst; Catherine, beloved wife of George Pike. Interment at Walker Churchyard on Saturday at 3. Kindly accept this (the only) intimation.

On Saturday 20th October 1917, the Walker Naval Shipyard Plater's Soldiers Fund Committee entertained about 68 wounded soldiers. They took them to a matinee at the Empire and then for tea at Lockharts' café on Nun Street. A concert followed with Mr J Mitchell presiding. Frank Huntley's 'Optimists' consisted of the following artists - Miss M Swindale, Mr a McClellan, Mr Bernard McNally, Master W Thompson, Mr Tom Mc Evoy, Mr J Thompson, Mr G Newby, Mr Nichol Bewick (ventriloquist) Mr H Thoburn (violinist), Mr Wilson (concertinaist) and Mr Frank Huntley with Miss Dorothy Thoburn as accompanist.

This was the fifteenth occasion that the committee has entertained wounded soldiers.

Walker War Memorials.

The war memorial, in Walker Park, Newcastle upon Tyne, is a commemoration to the 5th Battalion, Northumberland Fusiliers in the Great War. Made from Portland stone, it is made of grey granite, and sits above a three-stepped pillar. 'Memorial to World War One casualties from the 5th Northumberland Fusiliers.'

On Sunday the 24th of May 2015, there was a service held at Walker Parish Church, to dedicate the roll of Honour to the men of the 5th Battalion Northumberland Fusiliers, who gave their lives in The Great War.

During the service, the names of the 46 men who died at the battle of Bellewarde (Second Battle of Ypres) on Whit Sunday the 24th of May 1915, exactly 100 years ago to the day were read out by ex-Padre Cecil Dick. Of the 46 me who were killed that day only 6 have a known grave, the others are remembered on the Menin Gate Memorial, Ypres in Belgium. The roll of honour book was placed in a specially made cabinet, alongside the colours of that Battalion.

On 30th July 1916, the War Memorial to the 5th Battalion was re-dedicated with a new plaque.

Memorial to the 5th Northumberland Fusiliers In Walker Park

Originally unveiled on the 24th of May 1921 by Col. E.P.A. Riddell, C.M.G., D.S.O.; Dedicated by Rev. A. S. Wardroper, vicar of Longhirst

The memorial is dedicated to the 190 officers and 4,000 men who fought in France, of whom 45 officers and 1003 men were killed.

The Memorial is an obelisk, 16' high, standing on a base of fine dressed steps. At the top of the obelisk is a bronze casting of the Northumberland Fusilier's badge of St. George and the Dragon, and on the face of the monument is a bronze plaque. The quotation is carved into one side of the pedestal, using fancy capitals and substituting a 'V' for a 'U'.

The inscription reads -

Fifth Battalion
Northumberland Fusiliers
In memory of the officers and men of
The Battalion who gave their lives for
Their country in the Great War,
1914-1918
Erected by members and friends of
The Battalion
"Quo Fata Vocant"

The inscription on the plinth reads –
Dvlce et decorvm
est
Pro patria mori

The new inscription on the Memorial, which was unveiled at its rededication in 2016 was updated to include the conflicts since WW1.

The colours of the 5th Battalion hang in Walker Parish church.

On Scrogg Road, just outside of the park, there is another memorial – a memorial to all the men from Walker whose life was sacrificed in both World Wars.

Walker War memorial, Scrogg Road.

The angel, who sits atop the monument, faces east looking over Walker Park. She has an outstretched right arm in which originally she held a laurel wreath in her hand. The monument was vandalised and the wreath and hand broken off. The hand was later replaced, but not the wreath. The simple inscription carved in to the stone reads

Erected by public subscription in honoured memory of the gallant men of Walker who sacrificed their lives in the Great War 1914-1918, 1939-1945.

50th Northumbrian Division Memorial

To Commemorate the beginning of the first World War, the Walker Churchyard Memorial group unveiled a display in the church hall at the beginning of August 1914. It was a resounding success and later in the year was on display in St Nicholas Cathedral in Newcastle. In 2015 a Roll of honour was produced and purchased thoruogh donations and now resided inside the Church. In 2016 a rededication of the 5th Batallion Northumberland Fusilers is planned ot coincide with the 100th anniversary of the 1st July 1916 – the first day of the battle of the Somme.

In Belgium, not far from Ypres and near to the Oxford Road cemetery, stands a memorial dedicated 'to the enduring memory of all ranks of the 50th (Northumbrian) Division who fell in the Great War'.

Dedicated to all ranks of the 50th Northumbrian Division who fell in the Great War. An inscription below commemorates 'their comrades of the same Division who gave their lives in the War of 1939-1945 for the liberation of France, Belgium and Holland'.

Sapper Bob Edwards (Pictured front cover, right.)

This memorial book to the men of Walker who played a part in the Great War is also dedicated to my Grandfather Sapper 863 later Private 463062 John Robert 'Bob' Edwards who was born in Benwell, Newcastle upon Tyne, in 1894. He served alongside the Walker boys – as a Sapper with the Royal Engineers. 149th Brigade, 50th Division.

Prior to the outbreak of war Bob had been a linesman with the General Post Office in Newcastle and was living with his parents at 79 Hugh Street, Benwell. Bob attested, aged 18, on the 7 April 1913 to the 50th Northumbrian Division, Royal Engineers (Territorial Force) and was embodied on 5 Aug 1914 when war broke out. He served in France and Belgium from 15 April 1915 until early 1919 when he was demobilised. During that 4 years he only had 2 periods of leave home - on both occasions his mother made him strip off his uniform as soon as he walked through the door and put it in the oven so that the heat would kill the lice, hidden in the seams and linings.

Bob survived the war with only a 'slight' wound which he received on 9 Mar 1918 at the Chemin des Dames, France.

In February 1919, he had his photograph taken standing with hundreds of other allied troops in front of the Arc De Triomphe in Paris.

Bob came home to 34, Clara Street, Benwell, and returned to his position with the G.P.O. After marrying Gertrude Brewis in 1923 and having two children, the family lived on Branxton Crescent, Walker, for a number of years.

During the WWII bombing raids over the city, Bob refused to go into the shelter, stating he had been through much worse in the trenches. Even at night he would stay in bed whilst everyone else retired to the relative safety of the Anderson shelter in the garden. He did though suffer from nightmares right up until the end of his life, waking up sweating, wrapped up in the bed sheets, crying out in his sleep and fighting off imaginary advancing German's. My Nana insisted he suffered from undiagnosed neurasthenia – he very likely did.

As a small child, I would ask him about the war and all he would ever say is "It was terrible, terrible…" Then change the subject. Bob worked right up until he was in his eighties – riding his bicycle to work every day. His final job was in the offices at Swan Hunter's shipyards at Walker. He was forced to retire so as to allow a younger man to take the job. Bob died on 30 Dec 1984, aged 90.

Printed in Great Britain
by Amazon